JOURNALISM
The Evolving Perspective

strengthen antimonopoly laws in the first decade of this century.

Finally, let's include Edward R. Murrow, whose World War II broadcasts from London were a key factor in establishing CBS leadership in the radio news field and who later brought the news documentary to television with his See It Now series.

Thousands of additional names could be added to this list. Although the four we mentioned may not be entirely typical, we can have little doubt that all of them would be identified as journalists; all are likely to be mentioned in any contemporary history-of-journalism book. They also remind us that journalists are not limited by sex, race, or the type of medium for which they work. But what, if anything, do they have in common?

JOURNALISTS ARE COMMUNICATORS

One identifying mark of journalists is that they are participants in the process of human communication. Since at least two parties always play a part in the process of human communication—one who transmits stimuli and another in whom a response to that stimuli is evoked, often referred to as senders and receivers or, even more simply, as writers and readers or speakers and listeners—it is important to note which of these parties the journalists most characteristically are. Journalists do an enormous amount of reading and listening.

That work as receivers of communication is, in fact, along with observation, among the chief means by which they gather the knowledge that they formulate into messages. But those who *only* do this are not recognized as journalists. Greeley, Douglass, Tarbell, Murrow, and all the others we identify as journalists are most noted for originating the messages that are part of the communication process.

Journalists are those who are responsible for the *content* of what is sent out, transmitted, and conveyed to others. Greeley began his career as a typesetter and printer, but that was not the work of a journalist, for he was not then responsible for selecting or creating the messages that he set into type and then duplicated.

Pressmen, studio technicians, laboratory workers, delivery people, and many others may greatly assist the process of journalism, but their work is not the work of journalism. Journalists have control over what is said; the others may be responsible for the reproduction or circulation of what the journalists produce.

The signs that journalists use to convey their messages are most often verbal and probably more often written than oral. Graphic signs such as pictures, graphs, and drawings also play a part in both the print and oral media. Most of the messages that we will consider will be those that are expressed by written words, but unless stated otherwise, the comments will refer also to the other means of communication.

OTHERS ARE COMMUNICATORS, ALSO

Journalists, however, are not the only ones who create messages. Poets, novelists, playwrights, and others are also responsible for the content of pieces of communication. How do they differ from journalists?

Journalists send out messages that purport to be literally and at least preponderantly true or factual. Such words as "true" and "factual," of course, almost cry out for definition and explication will be given their due. For now, it will suffice to restate this characteristic in negative terms.

Journalistic messages, let us say, do not purport to be false, erroneous, made up, invented, imagined, or fictional. They may, of course, actually be false or invented, but the journalists do not introduce them that way. Journalists are responsible for messages about things that they claim have really happened, are really happening, or are really intended, planned, or likely to happen.

The media in which pieces of journalism appear, it is true, are rarely occupied only by journalistic communications. Commercial television gives most of its time to pieces of fiction. Some may be *based* on fact, a circumstance that, can cause

Preface

With new technology and practices, story telling has never been so complicated and at the same time so filled with potential for readers, viewers, and users to fully understands the context of any journalistic story. This printed instructor's manual combined with a version of it on a website and, of course, the textbook itself, offers instructors and their students an opportunity to more fully explore the potential to tell stories in unique and more interactive and integrated ways.

Visual journalism, a term that expands the professions of photojournalism, reporting, writing, and graphic design, is a challenge to teach and a challenge to perform. Combining words in the form of text and audio, images in the form of still and moving messages, informational graphics, and graphic design for print and interactive multimedia presentations for the World Wide Web is a great challenge. It is a challenge for anyone to learn well all the tasks necessary for new media design and production within specific courses of study and even throughout the career of a mass communicator.

It is hoped that by the introduction of this manual, the website, and the textbook it will help advance the field of visual journalism. Consequently, the skills necessary for its production will be made easier and second nature for its practitioners. Within this manual are sections that should help the task of learning this new field. The first section contains three syllabi that are useful in teaching visual journalism: a visual journalism design and production course, a photojournalism course with emphasis on visual journalism production, and a World Wide Web design and production syllabus.

Included with each syllabus are assignments, exams, and other materials to help ease the transition from traditional journalism courses to visual journalism courses. Feel free to adjust the assignments and deadline requirements as you see fit. For example, it is probably necessary to teach the elements of visual journalism production over several semesters, rather than in only one.

Use the syllabi as a guide for your thinking about teaching this new field. Additional sections include writings by the authors concerning visual communication, photojournalism, and the World Wide Web. These essays and articles can be used as additional readings for your students. At the end is a collection of websites that may be of interest for additional information. The website for this textbook will contain the websites and other materials in an interactive format.

Chapter 1

Introduction

To begin our exploration of what journalism is, we might consider that common usage suggests it is something that people *do*. Just as doctors practice medicine and architects work at architecture, so journalists perform journalism.

But does saying that really accomplish more than pushing us around in a circle? After all, if journalism is what is done by journalists, we can then swing around to the question: And who are journalists? They, of course, are people who do journalism.

Whatever that is. We seem to have chased the question to the point where its mouth bites its tail. But that is not quite true. First of all, we will later see that many streams flow from this source: Journalism is an *activity*.

For now, however, let's focus on the other point. The statement that journalism is what is done by *journalists*, although it seems to dance us in a loop, may be just the means by which we break out of the circle and actually discover what journalism is.

Some twenty-three centuries ago, Plato faced a problem similar to ours. In the *Meno*, Socrates and Meno are attempting to answer the question: What is virtue? Any attempt to find the answer seems either unnecessary or impossible. That is, if one can talk about virtue, one must already know what it is; or, if one doesn't already know what it is, one cannot talk about it in order to explain what it is.

Mortimer Adler, who was also struggling with a definitional problem in his book *The Idea of Freedom*, restated the Platonic paradox this way:

How can men look for a definition of virtue if they have no definition of it to start with, for without a definition how can they identify the subject of their inquiry? On the other hand, if they can begin by identifying the subject of their inquiry, they appear to define it also, and so they have no need to look further for a definition.

BREAKING OUT OF THE CIRCLE

The solution to the problem, Adler suggested, lies in making a careful distinction between an identification and a definition. An identification points at and is a relatively vague designation of the subject under discussion; a definition, on the other hand, provides precise knowledge of that subject. One way to make an identification is to give examples of what one wishes to define.

For instance, Adler says, one could identify "democracy" by indicating that it is represented by the present governments of the United States, Great Britain, Switzerland, France, and the Scandinavian countries. With this start, one can then examine the governmental form in the examples, see what they have in common, and proceed to structure a definition.

Why not use the same process in our endeavor to determine what journalism is? Let's identify some journalists, see what they do in common, and, proceeding from there, begin to bring journalism forth for further examination.

Horace Greeley seems to be a safe person to head our list. This nineteenthcentury founder and editor of the *New York Tribune* was described by Willard G. Bleyer as the person whose influence "has never been exceeded by that of any other American journalist". We can next add Frederick Douglass. This contemporary of Greeley wrote for many papers, but is probably best known for his antislavery publication *The North Star*, a weekly with circulation in Europe and the West Indies as well as in the United States.

The journalistic muckraker Ida Tarbell deserves mention, especially for her exposé of the Standard Oil Company in a nineteen-part series for *McClure's* magazine that helped serious confusion, but usually the viewers are provided with sufficient clues to enable them to distinguish the journalistic fact from the fiction. Radio devotes much of its time to music, a nonverbal form of communication.

The periodical media that rely heavily on the written word are the forms most strongly devoted to journalism, but they also are likely to contain at least some material that is not to be read as though it were literally true.

Historically, newspapers are the media most frequently associated with journalism, but newspaper work and the work of journalism are not identical.

Not all newspapermen or -women are journalists. In general, therefore, journalism is a function that should not be identified with any of the media, although it does rely on some of them.

NOR ARE JOURNALISTS THE ONLY NONFICTION COMMUNICATORS

Journalists, however, are not alone as originators of what they purport to be nonfiction communications. Philosophers, economists, sociologists, physicists, and many others also devise messages that they intend their readers to accept as literally true. Among them, the group that seems most akin to journalists are the historians.

Journalism, in fact, is sometimes referred to as contemporary or current history. But a careful examination of the differences between historians (as well as philosophers, economists, and similar communicators) and journalists will reveal a crucial characteristic of journalism.

Does the difference consist of this: historians write about the past whereas journalists write about the present? Not at all. Although historians commonly say such things as "the task of the historian" is "to order and interpret the events of the past", the time factor is not critical. What is the present? It is but a moving edge between the past and the future.

Most journalistic messages, just like historical writings, deal with what has happened, not with what is happening or will happen. The historian's past is often more remote than that in which the journalist is interested, but that is only a matter of degree, not of essence.

What, then, is the essence of history? That is a difficult question and historians themselves disagree on the answer. Erich Kahler insists that "history is to be understood as the happening itself, not the description or investigation of this happening." Edward H. Carr does not think so. History, he says, "is a continuous process of interaction between the historian and his facts, an unending dialogue between the present and the past." R. G. Collingwood says, "Every historian would agree, I think, that history is a kind of research or inquiry... generically it belongs to what we call the sciences: that is, the forms of thought whereby we ask questions and try to answer them."

Collingwood has surely overstated the degree of agreement, yet his does seem to be the preponderant view. Arnold Toynbee, for instance, has a similar opinion: "I do not think that history... is a succession of facts, nor history-writing the narration of these facts. Historians, like all human observers, have to make reality comprehensible, and this involves them in continuous judgments about what is true and what is significant."

THE DIFFERENCE BETWEEN HISTORY AND JOURNALISM

Even if one accepts the dominant view about the nature of history, what, if anything, does it say that will help us distinguish history from journalism? First, we must be careful not to be misled by one obvious but not unimportant difference. Journalism is a type of communication. History is not that. If one accepts Kahler, it is what has been going on.

If one accepts Collingwood and most other historians, it is knowledge, organized knowledge, of what has been going on. Thus the parallel with journalism is not history itself but rather the *communication* of history. But this is not the crucial point. Both journalism and history deal with knowledge. Journalism is the communication of a type of knowledge that has been acquired.

History is the acquisition of a type of knowledge that will be communicated. Both are concerned with the communication of knowledge. But the important factor is neither when the knowledge is acquired nor *when* it is communicated. Rather, what requires our attention is the *type* of knowledge that is acquired and communicated.

Traditionally, two broad categories of knowledge have been recognized. One is knowledge that is acquired for the sake of knowledge. It is knowledge for its own sake. It is knowledge for the sheer pleasure of knowing. This is called theoretical knowledge. The other is acquired to procure by some kind of activity the good of people. It is knowledge that is put to use. This is called practical knowledge. In *How to Read a Book,* Mortimer Adler and Charles Van Doren explain the difference this way:

Some books and some teachers are interested only in the knowledge itself that they have to communicate. This does not mean that they deny its utility, or that they insist that knowledge is good *only* for its own sake. They simply limit themselves to one kind of communication or teaching, and leave the other kind to other men. These others have an interest beyond knowledge for its own sake. They are concerned with the problems of human life that knowledge can help to solve. They communicate knowledge, too, but always with a view to and an emphasis upon its application.

Historians are interested in this first kind of knowledge. If one asks why historians do what they do, Toynbee answers that there can be several reasons; "the strongest and most estimable of these" is simply to satisfy curiosity. "In the field of human affairs," he says, "curiosity prompts us to seek a panoramic view in order to gain a vision of reality that will make it as intelligible as possible for a human mind." When historians communicate their historical knowledge they do so, dominantly and most properly, simply to help people understand what has happened.

But journalists, to the extent that they are practicing journalism, have a practical goal in mind. They acquire and communicate knowledge for the sake of providing people with what they need to know to make good decisions about what should be done or what should be avoided concerning the issues currently facing them.

If one wants to distinguish historians from journalists, one can say that the former are concerned not only with the past but with the past primarily as merely something to be known. In one sense, this type of knowledge might be viewed as useful, but it is useful for increasing understanding, not for determining future actions. Journalists, on the other hand, are ultimately concerned with helping people decide what would be good things to do or to avoid doing.

BOTH CAN BE MISDIRECTED AND MISUSED

As events discussed by historians creep closer to the present, a temptation tags along to apply historical knowledge to the solution of contemporary problems. If historians give way to this temptation, however, they edge into the domain of the journalists. But journalists also face their own temptation. They may fall short of the practical goal that is their reason for being.

Perceiving, achieving, and maintaining the distinction between the theoretical and the practical are enormously difficult, for they require the concurrence of message senders and message receivers. History and journalism both can be misdirected and misused.

For example, a historian examining the letters of Thomas Jefferson finds they set forth some radical changes in his attitudes toward newspapers. Before he became president, Jefferson esteemed the press highly, writing that, if he had to make a choice, he would prefer newspapers without government rather than government without newspapers. But after he was president, Jefferson criticized the press mightily, claiming it was so filled with lies that a man who never reads a newspaper is better informed than one who does.

Now the historian's proper task is to discover what, in many contexts, Jefferson's letters mean and to find, if he can, the reasons for the changing attitudes reflected in them. But instead of communicating to us this knowledge, he might discard the historian's garb and, using these letters as evidence, try to convince us that we should not trust the campaign words of presidential candidates when they laud the press, for even the best of them is bound to have a change of mind once elected.

Sometimes we can spot what pseudohistorians are doing, especially if they are blatant in their misuse of documents or relics of the past. We might even charge that, no longer historians, they have become propagandists. By that we probably mean that they are trying to mislead us, trying to incline us toward what we believe to be some inappropriate course of action. We are less likely to spot the sacrifice of history if the writers are proposing something with which we agree. Yet whether we agree or not, propaganda is not good history.

Even when a piece of writing *is* historical writing, some readers might misuse it by attempting to turn it to some practical purpose.

Just as Pablo Pi- casso's great painting *Guernica* might be cut in half and hung sideways merely to cover a long crack in the wall, so one might try to turn Thucydides' *History of the Peloponnesian War* into a guidebook for fighting a twentieth-century battle.

In a more recent example, General Albert Wedemeyer book *Wedemeyer Reports!* was intended to help us understand the major battles of World War II, but it could have been misused as a handbook for conducting the war in Vietnam. Journalism, too, can be misdirected or misused. But for now and throughout the succeeding pages, we must keep in mind one dominant characteristic of journalism: properly done, it deals with useful, practical knowledge. If we lose touch with this core, the effort to discover journalism will fail.

OTHERS ALSO COMMUNICATE PRACTICAL KNOWLEDGE

Journalists, however, are not the only ones who communicate useful knowledge. Parents, profiting from their own experience, advise their children on how to make the first car purchase or diaper the first grandchild. A dietician informs a heart patient of the foods that will lower fat and cholesterol. A psychiatrist tells an overworked employer how to reduce stress. All of these tend to work on a one-to-one, face-to-face basis. Perhaps more instructive for our purposes would be the comparison between journalists and trial lawyers, since lawyers, in addition to their one-on-one dialogues with judges and witnesses, often have a group of people—a jury—with whom to communicate.

In addition to their mutual interest in the recent past, trial lawyers, like journalists, have practical goals in mind. Their ultimate goal in criminal trials is ostensibly to help assure that the guilty are punished and the innocent set free and exonerated. Both journalists and lawyers engage in communications to help others determine what ought to be done or avoided. But how do they differ?

Once again, some of the most obvious differences may not be the most important. Whereas journalists communicate about a wide range of topics, lawyers travel within the relatively narrower compass of the law. More significant, however, is the extent of the communications, and the number and type of persons reached by the communicators.

Lawyers who communicate in the process of a jury trial attempt to reach several people, thus exceeding the one-to-one communications previously mentioned, but they are not engaged in what is usually called "mass communications." Journalists, however, whenever they are functioning as journalists, are always participants in mass communications. But how does communicating with several or even many persons differ from communicating with a mass of people?

THE MEANINGS OF MASS COMMUNICATIONS

The term "mass communications" means different things to different writers and speakers. Another excellent scholar, Charles R. Wright, a contemporary of Schramm, presented a somewhat clearer explanation—clear enough, at least, to show what modifications must be made if we are to see the relationship between journalism and mass communications.

Wright makes quite clear that he is writing about "modern mass communications", but he does not identify or describe any mass communications before the modern period. At least he does not do so explicitly. One can look at what he has to say about modern mass communications, subtract the modern and qualify a few other items, and then set forth the characteristics of basic mass communications.

But why go to all this trouble? Why not simply accept Wright's formulation as he expressed it? Well, even if one extends the modern period back to the middle of the last century, limiting mass communications to that time forces a dilemma: either journalism did not exist before approximately 1850 or journalism, if it did exist before that time, must not be a type of mass communications.

The first choice would ignore the hundreds of books on the history of journalism that set earlier dates for those working in this field, including one of our prototype journalists, Horace Greeley, who was already an experienced journalist when he founded his *New York Tribune* in 1841. The second removes an effective means by which we can distinguish journalism from other practical communications, such as law.

Another, perhaps stronger, reason for removing the "modern" qualification is that the notion of "modern mass communications" is no longer apt. Wright distinguishes modern mass communications from earlier individual communications in this way:

Mass communications is organized communication. Unlike the lone artist or writer, the "communicator" in mass media works through a complex organization embodying an extensive division of labour and an accompanying degree of expense.

To be sure, in the 1950s when Wright was preparing his book, mass communications seemed to be moving in the direction of complexity, expensiveness, and a division of labour that resulted in more workers per communication enterprise but fewer and fewer independently controlled media institutions. What Morris L. Ernst had ironically called the "sweep of progress" had continued, seemingly unabated, a decade later. The tide apparently was moving toward bigger but fewer media institutions. Both print and broadcast outlets were getting larger, but their number, and the competition between the members, was decreasing.

This movement, especially among daily newspapers, had flowed along steadily since the second decade of this century. A new type of mass communications, therefore, seemed to be acquiring characteristics that were the inevitable flooding from the past. Thus it could have seemed quite reasonable to Wright to ignore the fact that the communications operations of a century or two earlier were *not* complex and expensive, for the flow of history seemed to show that those days were gone forever.

But technology outwitted the course of history. The machines that had been growing larger, requiring more people to operate and vastly more money to acquire, suddenly began to move in the opposite direction. Computers that had occupied enormous air-cooled rooms shrank until they fit on the lap of a businessman jetting from Chicago to Los Angeles. Minicams plus public access channels brought the possibility of television journalism within the financial range of even the lower middle class.

Desktop publishing moved the production of periodicals into small offices, even into homes. Computer bulletin boards opened a vast range of new ways of distributing messages. In other words, technology opened doors back into the mass media environment that had existed at the beginning of the nineteenth century: once again, a single person with only a modest investment could convey messages to large numbers of persons in a very short period of time.

If those processes that possess the characteristics of mass communications, except that they involve simple and inexpensive production, are not included in the category of mass communications, then we would have to create another category to accommodate them. But what are we to call the broadsheets introduced by the missionaries in Nigeria a century before that country's independence? They were examples of mass communications, but they were not produced through complex or expensive facilities.

The handwritten newsletters circulated among the refusniks in the USSR; the wall posters that appeared in China during the Cultural Revolution; the mimeographed sheets of church agencies, universities, and justice and peace groups in South and Central America; the *Drudge Report* that appears on the web pages of the Internet: these and many other relatively contemporary communication activities have all the characteristics of early nineteenth-century mass communications. It seems unnecessary to invent another name for the category that merely lacks the complex organization, the division of labour, and the great expense mentioned by Wright.

Many others of Wright's points about mass communications, however, help clarify this confusing term. He says, for instance, that the audience of mass communications is relatively large and that so many people are exposed to the message in a short period of time and are of such numbers "that the communicator could not interact with its members on a face-to-face basis". He also says that the audience is anonymous so that its members "generally remain personally unknown to the communicator".

Moreover, mass communications are public; because the messages "are addressed to no one in particular, their content is open for public surveillance." Also, "They are rapid because the messages are meant to reach large audiences within a relatively short time, or even simultaneously." And, "They are transient because they are usually intended to be consumed immediately".

Even so brief an account tells us enough to help us distinguish journalistic communications from lawyer-courtroom communications. When lawyers address juries, they are addressing several people, but not so many that the lawyers are unable to be aware of them as individuals.

Jurors cannot normally respond verbally to the words of the lawyers, but they have available many nonverbal means of communicating. If one jury member's facial expression indicates skepticism at what the lawyer is saying, the latter can modify his or her communication to take that into consideration.

If another juror shows surprise, the lawyer may realise that an opportunity for pressing a point now exists. If still another juror is falling asleep, that may tell the lawyer it is time to request a recess.

Thus interpersonal communication can exist even when a number of people are involved. How large can that number be? There is no magic figure. Normally, the limit is the number of people to whom the communicator can react as individuals when they provide verbal or nonverbal responses to what the communicator is saying. Consider, for example, the politician who is addressing a thousand people at a political rally. They may cheer or they may boo at what the politician has to say.

The speaker may modify what he had intended to say as a result, but the reaction is to the audience as a collectivity, not to them as individuals. The speaker is engaging in mass communications. But let's say that one person leaps up and begins to engage the speaker in a debate. If the speaker responds, what had been only mass communications then becomes a mixture of mass and interpersonal communications.

When a young couple sends out a thousand wedding invitations to friends and relatives, the process is interpersonal communications in spite of the large number of persons to whom the message is sent. Each person to whom that message is sent can--and is probably expected to--respond individually. Some will attend. Some will send regrets. A few might ask whether they may bring a friend. But when the commander of a thousand troops orders them to attack at dawn, no individual responses are expected and none is likely to take place.

Then the process is solely mass communications. Thus, although in mass communications one or a relatively few people send a message to relatively many people, the exact size of that receiving group is not important.

More important is what Wright refers to as the anonymity of the audience. The audience may be known as a certain category of persons, as when the army commander knows he is addressing infantrymen rather than pilots or when the publisher of a religious newspaper knows the readers are Lutherans rather than Methodists. But these people are not individually spoken to or even precisely thought of as individuals.

Likewise, when a magazine publisher goes to a list broker to buy a thousand names and addresses of people who the publisher hopes will become subscribers, the subscription offers will go out to individually named persons, but they are persons unknown to the publisher. They are as anonymous as "occupant."

The last example reveals a slight modification of Wright's statement that mass communications messages "are addressed to no one in particular" and that the messages are "open for public surveillance." What Wright says is very often true, especially when broadcast mass communications are involved.

But it is less true when the mass communications medium is a periodical sent to a list of subscribers. Large circulation magazines are usually open for public scrutiny at newsstands and libraries, of course, but there are many hundreds of highly practical and specialized publications--for example, trade journals such as Implement and Tractor, China Glass and Tableware, and Western Outfitter-that are not. They are rarely available for inspection by anyone other than subscribers.

Wright's point concerning the transience of mass communications also needs qualification. Mass produced novels, poems, and other works of fiction may endure for centuries, and so also may theoretical nonfiction works such as books of philosophy or natural science.

Such works as Charles Dickens A Tale of Two Cities and Albert Einstein The Meaning of Relativity possess all the qualities Wright attributes to mass communications except transience.

Interestingly, however, the mass communications that are transient are likely to be the journalistic ones, for once they have served their practical purpose, once the decisions have been made from the knowledge that journalism supplies, then the messages cease to be useful, cease to be journalism, and become, like treaties, diaries, and other artifacts, the raw materials of history.

BASIC MASS COMMUNICATIONS

Thus there is a type of mass communications that not only exists in the modern period but also has existed for many earlier centuries.

In this basic mass communications, one person or a relatively few people (relatively few in comparison to the number of people who receive the message) convey one or more messages to a relatively large number of persons.

Often the receivers perceive the messages simultaneously; if not simultaneously, at least they perceive them more quickly than they would if the message had to be originated for each individual. Even if the messages are individually addressed, the receivers are not thought of as individuals; they are thought of as groups or types or masses of people; for all practical purposes, the receivers are anonymous.

Each of those who receive the message does not prepare and deliver an equivalent response to those who send the message. They may, however, respond as a group (as when Pontius Pilate asked the people what he should do with Jesus and they all replied, "Let Him be crucified!"). Sometimes the group reply will be through action rather than through words (as when soldiers, in response to the commander's order "Charge!" go dashing into the field of battle). Thus, although mass communications seem to be one-way, they are not totally so; the sender may well get a response, but not an equivalent response, from each one who receives the message.

A few situations require special attention. Although not all the receivers will give an equivalent response, some of them might do so. For example, a newspaper reader might respond to an editorial with an equivalent letter to the editor.

If this letter is delivered to the editorial writer, that person may or may not provide a personal reply.

If the editorial writer does so, then there has been a transition from a mass communication to an interpersonal communication between the letter writer and the editorial writer. Or the editor may decide to publish the letter in the newspaper; if so, a new phase of mass communications takes place, one in which the letter writer is the sender and the other readers of the paper are the receivers.

Quite clearly, not everyone who is involved in a mass communication process is a mass communicator. That name is reserved for those who have control over the content of messages and intend to deliver their messages to masses of people. The readers of newspapers, although participants in the mass communications process, are not normally mass communicators.

Nor are the printers, delivery people, newsstand salespersons, and others who lack the authority to originate or modify the content of the messages. Writers, speakers, editors, photographers, cartoonists, and the like, however, can be mass communicators, if they intend their messages to go out to the masses.

To clarify this latter point, let us consider for a moment the call-in programs often heard on radio, often late at night. The subjects discussed are sometimes quite personal: the sex life or economic problems of the callers, for example.

The host of the show is clearly a mass communicator. He or she wants the program's messages to be heard by as many people as possible. The host's popularity and income depend upon a wide, anonymous, unrestricted audience.

The host, in other words, is not communicating only with the person who calls in; the host would like to think that he or she is communicating with "the world." But what about the person who calls in? That person is also involved in a mass communications process and originates a portion of the messages that are sent out. But is that person also, like the host, a mass communicator? Perhaps not. Although the caller participates voluntarily in a mass communications process, he or she does not, in many instances, really desire to do so. To obtain free advice, the caller tolerates one type of communication, mass communication, but would probably prefer another type, interpersonal communication.

If the caller happens to be an exhibitionist or propagandist, however, then the caller does become, like the host, a mass communicator.

But because we cannot always establish the truth of intentions, it will sometimes be difficult or impossible to know whether or not a certain person is a mass communicator. Yet in most instances, the evidence and circumstances are so clear that we have no doubts. To those who participate in the mass communications process regularly and for a living, it is particularly easy to grant the title of mass communicator.

Two additional glosses on Wright's mention of anonymity as a characteristic of mass communications are relevant. First, not only do mass communicators not know the recipients of their communications as individuals, but those recipients usually do not know one another as individuals.

They often think of themselves as existing in isolation. Second, partly because of the anonymity of the audience, mass communicators must guess at the level of background knowledge, literacy, and sophistication of the message recipients. The messages are often directed at a level somewhat below the median, to the distress of those who exist at the extremes.

LAWYERS AND JOURNALISTS RECONSIDERED

With all this in mind, we can perhaps better understand how journalists differ from lawyers, even when both groups employ the communication of literally true, practical knowledge.

The former are mass communicators; the latter are not. Courtroom lawyers may direct their messages to a number of people—the judge, jurors, witnesses, the other lawyers—but they are people with whom it is possible for the lawyers to interact as individuals. Although there are prominent exceptions, most lawyers in the courtroom are not interested in addressing the nebulous, anonymous public at large.

The lawyers defending civil-rights activists in the 1960s and 1970s may have been extending their remarks to an audience far outside the courtroom. They may have wanted their words to be political statements to the entire nation about racial injustice.

If so, to that extent they were assuming the role of mass communicators. But, usually, trial lawyers direct their messages to the limited group of persons at hand in the courtroom.

Their aim, like that of journalists, is a practical one, but their audience is the relatively few people who are able to determine the outcome of legal proceedings. In most instances, lawyers control their messages so that they impact on that select group.

In addition, this is an immediate group, one whom lawyers, simply by a turn of the head, can address face-to-face. Any overt reactions by members of this group can be readily known and dealt with by the lawyers. Thus, not only in their private relations with clients in their offices but also in the public arena of the courtroom, lawyers are normally interpersonal communicators. Journalists, on the other hand, are mass communicators.

THE GENERIC MEANING OF JOURNALISM

We have reached the point where we are ready to set forth the basic definition of journalism. Many refinements will be added in the succeeding pages, but the following seems to sum up the comments we have made so far.

Journalism is a type of mass communications:

- That provides useful and practical (rather than theoretical) knowledge;
- That actually is or at least purports to be literally true, rather than invented or fictional;
- That is provided by persons who have at least some control over the content of the messages that are communicated;

- And that aids the recipients of the knowledge in making decisions on issues presently facing them.

Journalism is the type of activity that has all of the attributes just described. Journalists are the persons who engage in that type of activity.

Journalism does not exist aside from the persons who practice it. It is not like a tree or a frying pan or a light bulb; it cannot grow by itself, nor, once made, can it exist by itself. The *products* of journalism—news stories, editorials, video tapes, photographs—can have an independent existence, but journalism itself cannot.

Journalists, however, do exist independently of their journalism. A sleeping Horace Greeley, Frederick Douglass, Ida Tarbell, or Edward R. Murrow would have been identified as a journalist even though, while sleeping, he or she was not practicing journalism.

All of this seems quite clear. What may not be so clear is the correlative point: just as those readily identified as journalists often continue to be called journalists even when they are not practicing journalism, so also those who are not ordinarily identified as journalists ought to be called journalists as soon as they begin to practice journalism.

Journalism is not a custom-made dress or suit available to only a few select people. It is a cloak which almost anybody can throw on.

Journalism is an activity that can be employed by everyone except those who have not yet acquired or who have lost their communicative faculties. Whenever plumbers or clerks or architects or musicians become participants in the activities identified earlier, *they become journalists.*

This point, sometimes ignored, becomes especially important when questions concerning the legal protection of journalists arise.

Such protection belongs to all of us. It is also important when we consider our national educational system, for it means that all citizens should be prepared to practice the arts of journalism, should they ever desire to do so. Thus one of the dangers of attempting to define journalism, now becomes less worrisome. There is no need to license journalists as a restricted class of people when nearly everyone is or legitimately can be a journalist.

SOME OF THE SPECIES OF JOURNALISM

Some people would grant the title of "journalist" only to those for whom the work is a full-time job. But such a viewpoint not only carries with it some of the dangers already mentioned but would be analogous to denying T. S. Eliot the title of poet because he made his living working at Lloyd's Bank or saying William Carlos Williams should not be called a poet because all his life he was a practicing physician.

Thus it seems much better to recognize that, although for some their regular, full-time job is doing the work of journalism, there are many more who practice journalism only occasionally. *New York Tribune* editor Horace Greeley belongs to the first group; Robert Dale Owen, a Democratic congressman from Indiana, who wrote a letter published in the *Tribune* on October 23, 1862, appealing for a Proclamation of Emancipation, belongs to the second.

The first are often called professional journalists in the sense that the principal source of their livelihood is the practice of journalism. For the second, we have no well-accepted designation. Perhaps it is adequate simply to call them amateur or occasional journalists.

Although professional journalists are sometimes given privileges not available to occasional journalists, access to a press box at a baseball game, for example, or access to the press gallery in the U. S. Senate chambers, the legal rights of both the amateurs and the professionals are the same, and whenever they are doing the work described earlier they deserve to be called journalists.

Another set of species is quite obvious, for it is based on the medium employed by journalists to convey their messages to the public. Thus there are newspaper, magazine, radio, television, film, book, and other types of journalists, even though no journalist is inextricably tied to a single medium. Many, in fact, move from one to another, as did William L.

Shirer, who switched from the *Chicago Tribune* to radio, television, and books.

Others use several media at the same time, as did David Gergen, who was an editor of *U.S. News and World Report* at the same time that he was a news analyst on public television. But most professional journalists are usually identified with the medium to which they devote most of their time and from which they derive the greater part of their income.

PUBLIC AFFAIRS AND PERSONAL AFFAIRS JOURNALISM

One of the most important, yet also one of the most ignored, divisions of journalism is that into public affairs journalism and personal affairs journalism.

It is easy to understand why it receives so little attention: although both journalists and the public have a quiet awareness that the distinction exists, they seldom discuss it explicitly. But it is so essential to an understanding of journalism that explicit discussion is essential, briefly here and more extensively later on.

The brief description of the generic meaning of journalism is that it provides useful, practical knowledge. But useful for what purpose? Useful to help those who are consumers of journalism decide what should be done or what should be avoided concerning the issues currently facing them. Journalism exists to help all of us decide what is good to do and what is good not to do.

The concept of good, of course, has a multitude of meanings. Here we think of it in relation to those for whom something can be considered good. We can say that something is good for me or we can say that something is good for us.

That is, we can make a choice in order to improve, profit, delight, enhance, benefit our individual selves or to do one or all of these things for the improvement and benefit of the community, group, organization, or society of which we individuals are members.

For example, let's consider a fictitious Hiram. Hiram never married and is now retired from his job as a clothing salesman. He lives in a small apartment, is in good health, likes spectator sports, has a satisfactory income from Social Security and a few investments, pays taxes, and is, in general, a rather average person.

Every day, Hiram has to make thousands of decisions. Some are so personal—shall I sleep another five minutes or should I get out of bed right now?—that no other person can be of much help to him in deciding what is the good thing to do. But hundreds of his decisions can be more or less well made depending on the knowledge that is communicated to him from the outside world.

He likes to watch the local baseball team. Is the team playing today? Is the weather likely to be good for baseball? Are the normal means of transportation in operation? Is the admission price the same as last time he went to a game? What time of the day will the game be played? Will it also be shown on television?

How well has the team been doing? Has any starter been injured and thus is unavailable to play? He can probably find the answers to these and to numerous other questions affecting his personal welfare by consulting his daily newspaper or listening to the news reports on radio or television.

The knowledge he receives will help him decide whether or not it would be good for him to attend the baseball game. Learning that the game will be shown on television, Hiram may decide to watch it at home rather than go out to the ballpark. Many others, receiving the same information, may decide just the opposite. Hiram's decision is a personal decision in the sense that he decides what is good for himself. Other baseball fans can make similar or different personal decisions. It is not necessary that there be just one decision.

Now let's say that while reading the newspaper Hiram learns that next Tuesday the city will hold a referendum to determine whether or not money will be borrowed to build a new high school. In this situation, the decision to be made is not what is good for Hiram but rather what is good for the city, not "for me" but "for us." Whatever the decision is, it will be one decision. It will be assumed that even those who might have preferred a different decision will go along with the one that is made.

If the voters decide to approve of the borrowing, that decision will be against Hiram's personal welfare: his taxes will probably increase, and he has no children who will benefit from the new school.

But if the new school is truly needed, the public welfare might well require that money be borrowed to build it. In fact, Hiram himself, recognizing the dominant character of the public welfare, of the common good, might put aside consideration of his own personal good to vote in favour of the referendum.

What, then, is the difference between personal affairs journalism and public affairs journalism? The first type provides the knowledge people can use to make good decisions about their personal, current welfare. Each person decides what is good for him or her, independent of the decisions being made by others. Much of the journalism dealing with sports, business, and entertainment (just to name a few possibilities) is of that type.

The second type of journalism provides the knowledge people need for decisions concerning the current welfare of some community, group, organization, or society of which they are a part. Here a decision will be made (perhaps by all the members, perhaps by one or a few) concerning what will be good for that community or group. It will be a decision concerning the welfare of the whole collectivity, and the members will be expected to go along with it even if they would have preferred some other decision.

Most of the activities of federal, state, and local governments are the business of public affairs journalism, but the latter can also extend to private groups: fraternities or businesses, for instance.

The welfare of these, too, requires decisions concerning the good of the whole, and public affairs journalism contributes to the goodness of those decisions. If one company is considering a merger with another, this decision concerns the welfare of both companies and is a decision in which the managements, stockholders, and employees have a stake.

All need knowledge so that the decision can be well made, and most of the knowledge that is needed comes through the work of public affairs journalism. One might ask: Why should members of a public pay attention to issues-such as a proposal to raise tax rates—which seem beyond the public's powers of determination? Some answers will be found in our later discussions of public opinion and electoral processes.

For now, it may be sufficient to recollect that mass communications always extend messages to more people than have a direct need for them. Can we also say that the communications tasks associated with public relations and with advertising ought to be viewed as additional types or species of journalism? That question has been the source of many heated disagreements.

One of the most vigorous of these disagreements took place in the 1950s when Sigma Delta Chi, the Society of Professional Journalists (SPJ), debated the problem of membership eligibility. Having already excluded advertising people from the organization, the members now decided that, in the future, public relations practitioners would also be excluded because neither group was composed of true journalists.

Some public relations practitioners do spend their time analyzing situations and providing interpersonal consultation to their clients. Similarly, some advertising people spend time in market and media research and in similar interpersonal communications.

Thus, to the extent they are not engaged in mass communications, they would not fit the definition of journalists.

But the activities of most people in both fields culminate in their preparing messages for the mass media. To the extent that those messages convey useful knowledge that at least purports to be true, the work they do fits the concept of journalism.

Why, then, did SPJ claim they were *not* journalists? For years, the society had differentiated between those acceptable persons who prepared and disseminated information in the "public interest" and those nonacceptable persons who did so in what the members called the "private interest." They concluded that all advertising people were in the latter category; but in 1952, they admitted, at least for a few years, that this was not true of all public relations practitioners.

Those who wrote for civic organizations, social agencies, benevolent foundations, educational institutions, and governmental departments (with the interesting exception of the military) and who had an "acceptable background of experience in news work for newspapers, magazines or in broadcasting" could be considered to be working in the public interest and thus be eligible for membership.

But in the summer of 1958, a select panel had second thoughts about even these exceptions and submitted a report proposing, among other things, that there be no initiation of public relations men in the future. A heated and extensive debate ensued, much of it carried out in the pages of *Quill*, the society's journal, concluding with a vote at the 1958 national convention that endorsed the report.

One of the more interesting contributions to the debate came from a group of distinguished public relations persons themselves. Although they were grandfathered into the society, they said they recognized differences between their work and that of many other members:

We accept your tighter definition of journalism. Although we prepare and disseminate news stories, we admit we do so, at least in part, in the interest of our clients and employers. Newsmen, on the other hand, generally work without obligation to any special interest. Both activities may well be in the public interest, but there is a fundamental difference which is important to Sigma Delta Chi.

Several years later, David Berkman seemed to express a similar thought. In discussing whether public relations courses have a place within journalism programs, he wrote, "If we accept—and how can we not do so?—that the purpose of the journalist is to discover and report truth, while that of those in public relations is to serve the interests of their clients or employers, then the answer is clearly 'no'".

Even though public relations practitioners serve the interests of clients or employers, it does not necessarily follow that such a type of service precludes the discovering and reporting of truth.

Journalists, no matter whether they are newswriters, public relations practitioners, or advertising personnel, can have a variety of motives when they do their work. They can be working for their own welfare, for the welfare of a cause in which they are interested, for the welfare of their employers, for the welfare of the public, or for many other possible objectives.

To say that only one of these goals is good and all the rest are suspect is to assume an arbitrary and unreasonable moral standard. Any or all of them can be good, and no one of them need necessarily exclude the others. Any moralistic approach to the definition of journalism depends in part on the precarious possibility of detecting the intentions of message senders.

Although some journalists are morally good and some morally deficient, it is not the case that all newspeople are in the first category and all public relations and advertising people in the second.

It did not seem, for instance, that former *Wall Street Journal* reporter R. Foster Winans had been acting as a very ethical journalist when he was convicted in 1985 of using his "Heard on the Street" stock market column to further an insider trading scheme that netted him $31,000.

Unfortunately, deceptions on various levels have not been infrequent among newspeople during the history of journalism.

During the first months of 1998, Stephen Glass of the *New Republic,* Patricia Smith of the *Boston Globe,* and April Oliver of CNN lost their jobs for concocting material that turned out not to be factual. But they certainly are not typical of all reporters, columnists, and television producers.

Likewise, some advertising and public relations practitioners lack the integrity we ought to expect of people who work in those fields even though most of them adhere to the goals of their professions. The Public Relations Society of America*Code of Professional Standards* says, "A member shall conduct his or her professional life in accord with the public interest."

Also, advertising personnel aim at stimulating business competition, resulting in improved products and more economical ways to produce and distribute them; thus in the end "the consumer benefits by the availability of new and better products".

To increase the likelihood of such good performance is one reason for incorporating advertising and public relations instruction in journalism programs.

The journalism/advertising identification is further complicated because some advertising, like newspaper, magazine, and broadcast editorials, argues for or against public issues.

The Mobil Oil Company produces this type of editorial advertising frequently. The American Federation of Teachers buys space in the *New York Times* on the first Sunday of each month so that its president can discuss matters of public policy.

Similarly, political public relations contribute to the public discussion of public affairs. The public relations writer, of course, advances the position of the person or party who is paying the bill, but print and broadcast editorial writers also advance the positions of the editors, publishers, or station managers who employ them.

Ideological, ethnic, religious, and other special interest newspapers, magazines, and cable systems are as much devoted to advancing private agendas as are public relations and advertising practitioners.

And at least since the period of the penny press in the 1830s, a strong feeling has existed that some members of the information media function more to sell copies and enrich their owners than to serve the public. The contemporary members of this trend might be the tabloids conveniently placed along the supermarket checkout lanes.

ADVERTISING AND PUBLIC RELATIONS ARE SPECIES OF JOURNALISM

Thus it seems that as long as advertising and public relations people use the mass media to convey purportedly true knowledge that can help people make good decisions about what to do and what to avoid in regard to issues currently facing them, advertising and public relations people ought to be considered journalists as much as anyone else who does that type of work.

They are, in particular, much like print and broadcast editorial writers, columnists, and commentators. Like them, advertising and public relations practitioners are persuaders. It is true that they advance products or causes in which they or their employers are interested, but so also did Greeley, Douglass, Tarbell, and Murrow—and nearly all of those whom we are proud to identify as journalists.

It is also true that, unlike some other journalists, advertising journalists buy space or time in media that they do not own. This makes them different from those who own or those who are employed by those who own their media. But every type of journalist is different from other types: photojournalists differ from word journalists, broadcast journalists from print journalists, public affairs journalists from personal affairs journalists.

The fact that a person is this type of journalist rather than another *type* of journalist need not deprive that person of identification as *a journalist*. Many public relations practitioners produce their own media: newsletters, company newspapers, brochures, slide presentations, annual reports, and video- tapes.

Many of the others supply, at no cost, informational, analytical, and persuasive material to the general mass media. Some studies indicate that more than half of the nonwire, nonsyndicated editorial content of newspapers comes from releases or memos generated by public relations sources. Some press agents have misused their abilities, it is true, but the same can be said of those in any field of endeavor. Nothing in the nature of the work they do requires either the lying or fictionizing that would exclude them from journalism.

JOURNALISM AND THE NEWS

As we continue to examine the nature and functions of journalism in greater detail, we see immediately that another term is so closely associated with journalists that it is sometimes used as a synonym.

During the prolonged Society of Professional Journalists-Sigma Delta Chi debate on the meaning of journalism, for example, Edward Lindsay, editor of the Lindsay-Schaub newspapers in Decatur, Illinois, sometimes substituted "fraternity of newsmen" for "society of professional journalists".

Indeed, in the mind of many persons, news reporters and newswriters seem to occupy the centermost chambers in the house of journalism. Therefore, although journalism consists of much more than the acquisition and presentation of news, it is appropriate that we now turn our attention to that important but highly ambiguous term.

Chapter 2

The Evolution of Journalism

Looking into the future, we can forecast with total certainty that the nature of journalism and the stories that it tells will change. Journalism always has been changing. Today's norms about what is news are far from absolutes. Contemporary discussions about blurring the line between news and entertainment usually are interpreted as meaning that this behaviour is a violation of the standards of journalism.

A viable alternative interpretation is that this behaviour is simply a major contemporary feature in the ongoing, albeit not always salubrious and straight-line, evolution of journalism. It is possible to identify many of the prominent characteristics of this evolution over recent decades and even over past centuries. However, we cannot with any certainty predict the course of this evolution and identify precisely which characteristics of journalism will be paramount in future decades.

We can with certainty predict two things: The change will be neither orderly nor even, and some changes will be thoughtful and deliberate, whereas others will be reactions to immediate drastic circumstances. At least for the short term, Sept. 11 swept mainstream journalism's years of preoccupation with the scandalous, salacious and sensational off the agenda and turned its attention to more significant topics at home and abroad.

Was this a temporary aberration, or a significant, long-term shift in the focus of journalism? Even if the effects of Sept. 11 were temporary, no one can predict with any certainty what other events or trends might reshape journalism in the future.

From one perspective, this indeterminacy is fortunate because a major goal of this book is to foster discussion and debate—perhaps even have some influence—on the course of this evolution in the new media setting.

Although no one knows exactly what will emerge in the next decade or two, individuals can have some influence on what does emerge because the creative and entrepreneurial spirit of journalists, singly and in various combinations, has been a potent force in the evolution of American journalism during the past two centuries.

An important point to keep in mind is that the shifting nature of journalism over the 19th and 20th centuries and now in the opening decade of the 21st century basically has been evolutionary rather than characterized by abrupt shifts at specific historical junctures.

This is the case because the changes in journalism—and, more broadly, the changes in mass communication—over these centuries result from the confluence of three major factors:

- New developments in technology.
- Changes in the undergirding social conditions.
- And creative and entrepreneurial impulses.

In the 1830s, when mass communication began with the penny press, the convergence of influences producing this phenomenon was the new technology of steam-driven printing presses capable of producing large numbers of copies of newspapers; widespread literacy as the supporting social condition; and a key entrepreneur, Benjamin Day, who launched the *New York Sun.* But Day alone did not create the style and the norms for this new journalism.

Those were the product of numerous editors and working journalists, a few well known to us, such as James Gordon Bennett and Horace Greeley, but most anonymous.

THIRTY-YEAR VANTAGE POINTS

Any activity such as journalism that results from the

creative and intellectual efforts of hundreds of different organizations geographically scattered across many cities will be characterized largely by evolution. It is difficult, if not impossible, to perceive distinct changes from day to day or even from month to month.

But as these shifts and changes accumulate over time, they do become apparent. An optimum strategy for observing the evolution of American journalism from the days of the penny press to the present is to dip into this historical stream at intervals of 30 years.

Not only is three decades a sufficiently broad interval of time to make changes in the nature of journalism readily apparent, an interval of three decades also means that a new generation has come onto the scene and made its mark. Those persons who would have been novices at one point in time will have become, 30 years later, the cadre of experienced journalists and editors occupying most of the key positions in news organizations.

Today's 22-year-old graduating with a bachelor's degree in journalism may well be, by age 52, the managing editor or even editor of a daily newspaper—or occupying a similar high level position in other news media. No generation is a perfect clone of its predecessor. Each generation brings change and by the time that 30 years have passed, each new generation is likely to have made its mark on the practice of journalism.

This situation is not unique to journalism. Arthur M. Schlesinger Jr. noted the utility that the concept of generation has generally for historical analysis and explanations of change: In traditional societies, where change was imperceptible and each generation lives as its parents and grandparents had lived before it, the passage of generations made little difference. But, with the acceleration in the velocity of history, new generations began to undergo novel experiences and thereby to achieve distinctive outlooks.

He also noted the influence of Auguste Comte—in Schlesinger's view, the first person to recognize the historical significance of generations—on John Stuart Mill who asserted that historical change should be measured by "intervals of one generation, during which a new set of human beings have been educated, have grown up from childhood, and taken possession of society."

Although both Jose Ortega y Gasset and Karl Mannheim identified a generation's lifetime as 30 years—an interval also used by Schlesinger to analyse the 20th century political history of the United States as alternating cycles in the dominance of public purpose and private interest—Ortega y Gasset urged caution: There is no arithmetical inevitability in the generational sequence. A generation is a rough, not an exact, unit; almost a metaphor.

This idea of generations, in particular generational replacement, also has been used to explain fundamental changes in public opinion over time. Few people radically shift their opinions about the issues of the times, but over time, one generation of opinion holders is replaced by a new generation with new perspectives and opinions on the issues of the day.

Journalist Samuel Lubell attributed the long-running success of the Democratic Party in the 1930s and 1940s to the generations of voters that came of age during the Great Depression. Later generations shifted the tide to the Republican Party.

As an international example, the strongest support for social welfare policies in both the United States and western Europe is found among the generations that attained adulthood after these programs were already in place in the societies in which they grew up. There are many other examples of differences between generations and their differing approach to the times.

Without delving too deeply into the historical details, think about a historical timeline of American journalism from the 1830s to the present. Thirty years after the appearance of the penny press is the time of the Civil War with news stories frequently constructed in inverted pyramids and modeled on the principle of objectivity.

Thirty years later is the end of the 19th century and a time when the yellow journalism of William Randolph Hearst and Joseph Pulitzer epitomized much of mainstream journalism.

Next are the 1920s and the perceived need in the complex aftermath of World War I to offer news analysis as well as spot news about the events of the day. By the mid-20th century, television news was a major part of mass communication and a continuing influence on the style of journalism.

The final decades of the 20th century are the ones that define for many journalists, including us as the authors of this book, significant portions of their professional careers. Contemporary journalism is delivered through far more channels than it was when we were college undergraduates in journalism.

Daily newspapers and both network and local television still command significant, though shrinking, audiences. Now these media share the public arena with a multitude of cable news channels, online newspapers and a variety of other news sources.

CHANGING STYLES OF NEWS

Much more has changed than the variety of media that deliver the news. The style of that news also has changed significantly.

A succinct portrait of this evolutionary pattern in contemporary journalism during the final decades of the 20th century is found in Thomas Patterson's *"Out of Order"* an analysis of how the news media covered our presidential elections from 1960 to 1992. Again, an interval of approximately 30 years proves a useful vantage point for sketching these changes.

In 1960, an interpretative framework—rather than the more traditional descriptive framework used to report the presidential election—was found in only a small fraction of the news stories on the front page of the *New York Times*.

By 1972, there was parity between the two styles of election reporting; in the 1988 and 1992 elections, interpretative stories dominated the front page of the *New*

York Times by a ratio of 4-to-l. Over a period of approximately 30 years, the preferred style for reporting the presidential election had turned upside down.

By 1960 there already was an emphasis on politics as a game in which reporting a candidate's strategy for winning and conjuring with such things as "who won the day" and "who is ahead by how much" were key elements.

That is, the thrust of the reportage was on the campaign as a contest between parties and politicians rather than on the election as a method for the public to make a decision about its future.

In that 1960 election, the split between reporting on the game and reporting on the issues was close to 50-50. This already was very different from elections in earlier periods, but that 50-50 split was just the baseline for major changes appearing in the 1972 and 1976 elections.

By 1972, reporting on the game prevailed by about 2-to-l. By 1976, the ratio of game coverage to issue coverage had reached a new plateau of about 4-to-l.

Among the most powerful influences driving the startling shift to a 4-1 ratio of strategic, insider reporting over issues reporting was Theodore H. White.

Starting in 1960, White, a veteran reporter, produced a best-selling series of quadrennial books, "*The Making of the President.* " Remarkable in their detailed reporting from inside the presidential campaigns, the books set a new standard for depth and insight into the strategic and human calculations that elected presidents.

White was writing history, but the seemingly authenticating details that his books contained proved irresistible to the political press; never mind that they were reported months after the votes were cast.

The Associated Press, for instance, messaged its political reporters, "When Teddy White's book comes out, there shouldn't be a single story in that book that we haven't reported ourselves.

" And A. M. Rosenthal, managing editor of the *New York Times*, instructed his staff, "We aren't going to wait until a year after the election to read in Teddy White's book what we should have reported ourselves. "

The impact of such commands was to drive political reporting further and further inside the campaigns and away from issue coverage. The narrative illusion was if you can report what's in the candidate's stomach, that is, if you know what he had for breakfast, then you surely must also know what's in his head and heart.

What journalists failed to recognize was that White's books were not helpful to the public in terms of picking a leader, for the rich details they contained were published months after the votes were cast. They were conceived and executed as history, not contemporary journalism. Nevertheless, the hunger for glimpses into the inner circles and thoughts of the campaigns moved political reporting ever further from anything that could be useful, or even very interesting, to average voters.

Even White himself came to regret his reportorial invention. "It's appalling what we've done, " White said during the 1972 campaign, the fourth of the five he chronicled. "All of us are observing him (the candidate), taking notes like mad, getting all the little details. Which I think I invented as a method of reporting and which I now sincerely regret. If you write about this, say that I sincerely regret it. Who gives a ... if the guy had milk and Total for breakfast?"

Not surprisingly, as shifts occurred among the aspects of the campaign that were emphasized in news reports, the journalist's voice also became more prominent in setting the tone of election reports. Back in 1960, the candidates themselves and partisan participants in the election set the tone in two-thirds of the stories. Praise for a candidate came from his supporters, attacks and criticism from his opponent and the opponent's supporters. By the 1972 presidential election, journalists were setting the tone of most articles.

Looking more closely at the nature of that tone reveals another pattern that turned upside down across those nine elections from 1960 to 1992; good news versus bad news. Back in 1960, the ratio of good news to bad news was about 3-to-1.

This ratio seesawed up and down over the next four elections but in 1980 moved to a new plateau where the ratio of good news to bad news was 2-to-3, another 30-year reversal in the prevailing style of political reporting.

This 30-year trend is graphically illustrated by the titles on *Time* magazine's cover stories. In 1960, they were simply "Candidate Kennedy" and "Candidate Nixon.

" In 1992, they included "Nobody's Perfect: The Doubts About Ross Perot" and "Waiting for Perot: He's Leading in the Polls, But Can He Lead the Nation?. " Bush's cover story was "The Fight of His Life" and Clinton's cover stories included "Why Voters Don't Trust Clinton" and "Is Bill Clinton for Real?. "

In sum, the pattern of presidential election coverage that evolved bit by bit from 1960 to 1992 resulted in a fundamentally different election journalism. In 1960, journalists described the campaign, issue coverage was priority, partisans set the tone of the coverage, and good news prevailed over bad news. Thirty years later, journalists interpreted the campaign, game coverage was the priority, the tone of the coverage was set by journalists, and bad news prevailed over good news.

The sequence of these steps in the evolution of a new style of political reporting is where the Xs mark elections with significant increases over past journalistic practice. This stair-step pattern is a succinct portrait of shifting professional perspectives, the evolution of a new set of "cookie cutters" that shape contemporary political journalism.

Beyond political journalism and presidential elections, there are numerous other cookie cutters used to shape the daily news, many with long histories of use. Noting the repetition of master narratives—even rather specific stories—over and over through the years, even centuries, Robert Darnton metaphorically summarized his time as a journalist:

We simply drew on the traditional repertory of genres. It was like making cookies from an antique cookie cutter.

Among the most ancient sets of journalistic cookie cutters are political, financial and sexual scandals, cookie cutters extensively employed in the final decade of the 20th century whose historical origins are in the broadside ballads, news books and French canards of the 16th and 17th century.

In reporting the news of the moment, journalists depend for the most part on a set of standard conventions about how a news story should be written. Some of these are very ancient, some very recent.

The mix of cookie cutters in common use is constantly evolving, and an interval of 30 years is a useful vantage point for observing what has changed and what has remained constant in reporting the news.

Journalism changed in the closing decades of the 20th century, in particular adding a strong interpretive element to the reporting of public affairs in general, not just political campaigns.

Undoubtedly, journalism will change again during the opening decades of this century. Part of the change will result from the tremendous changes in communication technology and its diffusion among the public.

In *"Mediamorphosis: Understanding New Media"* Roger Fidler cited Paul Saffo, a director at the Institute for the Future in Menlo Park, Calif., who "posits that the amount of time required for new ideas to fully seep into a culture has consistently averaged about three decades for at least the past five centuries. He calls this the 30-year rule. "

EVOLUTION OF JOURNALISM

Our purpose here is not to present a history of journalism using intervals of 30 years or any other vantage point. That is a massive undertaking for another book. Rather, our purpose is to make the point that the nature of journalism constantly evolves in response to the social, technological and creative environment in which people work.

Furthermore, the defining characteristics of this evolution need to be made explicit and the subject of intense scrutiny and debate, especially in this time when a rapidly changing technological environment arguably offers more options than at any time in the past.

Not all of these options—or even the current emphases of news, however long they last—are beneficial ones for society or for journalism. It is especially important to note "wrong turns" along the way or the failure to shed some bad habits.

And there is the need to more explicitly guide this evolutionary pattern of the new journalism, not a new style of newspaper journalism or broadcast journalism, but rather a journalism resulting from the convergence of many media on the contemporary stage.

Chapter 3

The Cultural Space of Journalism

Many journalists today feel that the boundaries between news and entertainment are blurring, particularly in the television medium. In this book, I examine these boundary concepts and attempt to answer a few complicated questions, such as: Why and how are journalism's boundaries socially constructed? How are they negotiated by different groups of people with interests in mass communications? And—perhaps most importantly—how do journalists breach these boundaries and then respond to the breaches through boundary-maintenance exercises? I hope to recover some of the messiness of the boundaries through this inquiry.

The impetus for this study are the numerous observations and arguments that network television news and tabloid television entertainment programs are converging in style and content into a new genre called "reality-based programming."

This study will examine some of these arguments, looking for how this phenomenon is described, the explanations given for it, as well as the ex planations for why it has become an issue. As analyst, I will not be in a position to reach a definitive conclusion about the boundaries of these categories. Rather, I will describe how interested players draw the boundaries. It is important to note that boundary work is committed within the day-to-day work of journalism as well as in the latter representations and reconstructions of journalism content and practice.

To accomplish these goals, I will examine three case studies—specific instances of boundary construction, negotiation, and maintenance in journalism. Most of the emphasis will be on how these boundaries affect television journalism, but other journalism media are also examined. According to Justin Lewis, television is arguably the greatest culture-producing machinery on earth. For that reason, and because many conceive of television as primarily an entertainment medium, most of the attention in this study will be focused on television journalism boundaries.

SIGNIFICANCE OF THE PROJECT

As Peter Dahlgren says (perhaps understatedly), "Journalism's centrality in politics and culture, as well as its vested economic and occupational interests, make questions regarding its boundaries, uses and contingencies of more than idle concern".

Some of the questions along this vein that demand our attention include: How have journalists been able to demarcate their area of mass communication from other types of mass communication? What do they gain from such work? Do journalists maintain control over the production and evaluation of news? How are journalists able to maintain the public perception that they are authoritative or credible? How do journalists convert cultural authority into other opportunities, such as jobs, political influence, and prestige? How do journalists respond to threats or challenges to their cultural authority? Admittedly, this study is just a start in this line of research.

Journalists assert that they have the authority to perform an important function in our democratic society: to truthfully report the news and to inform the public. This authority depends on the trust of the publics that the news media serve. American journalists say the defining characteristics of their work are that it is true, accurate, and in the interest of the audience—yet these are irrelevant unless audiences believe in the truthfulness and accuracy of journalistic accounts. If the public believes in the accuracy of journalism, then journalists gain authority—the authority to tell the news.

Other culture-producing mass media institutions, such as the advertising, public relations, and entertainment industries, also communicate to the masses. When these institutions and industries produce messages that appear similar to journalism, journalists interpret these events as threats to the boundaries and authority of journalism. The cultural authority of the institution of journalism depends on the ability of people to distinguish between it and other kinds of mass communication.

It is useful for us to examine what sociologists of science call *boundary-work rhetoric*: the rhetorical strategy of one group wishing to distinguish itself from another. For example, medical doctors draw a boundary—within their discourse and routine practices—between what they do and what faith healers do. Likewise, journalists who consider themselves mainstream draw boundaries between what they do and what other mass communicators do. As I will show, these other communicators include people such as entertainment talk show hosts and tabloid journalists.

When the public does not notice the difference between a faith healer and a doctor, either the doctor, the faith healer, or both will engage in boundary-work rhetoric; socially constructing a boundary in order to protect the authority to do their work. Likewise, journalists engage in boundary-work rhetoric because they want the public to be aware of the differences between news work and entertainment work.

RESEARCH QUESTIONS

The main questions I examine in this study are: How and why have television journalists and others defined "television news" and the goals, norms, and ideologies of television journalism as they have? How have the boundaries between entertainment and news been constructed and negotiated as they have; and what rhetorical moves do journalists and others make to distinguish between the two? What are the differences in the uses of distinguishing characteristics between those within the journalism profession and those outside the profession?

In effect: Who does boundary work, and how do different groups do it differently? And finally, how do the interests and strategies of boundary-work rhetoric along the news/ entertainment boundary compare to the interests and strategies of rhetoric uncovered along other boundaries, such as science/non-science; and what is it about the news/ entertainment boundary that makes these strategies different—or similar?

To understand the significance of these questions, we must first examine some of the concepts that seem to be at stake here, such as authority, jurisdiction, and autonomy.

THE AUTHORITY AND SELF-DEFINITION OF JOURNALISM

The institution of American journalism has earned a mantle of authority in American society. The mere fact that many historians rely on newspaper and magazine accounts as primary source material indicates in a small way how journalism and the work of journalists become authoritative. As purveyors of facts and interpretation, journalists use this authority to describe events and everyday life to the public.

Gieryn and Figert describe this kind of authority as social power: "'Cognitive authority' is the legitimate power (in designated contexts) to define, describe or explain bounded realms of reality". The public entrusts journalists with this cognitive authority to the extent that they believe in journalists and their work. When the authority is threatened, journalists respond to consolidate their power.

Paul Starr, in his studies of the medical profession, calls this power *cultural authority*. He says "cultural authority entails the construction of reality through definitions of fact and value". Starr distinguishes cultural authority from social authority, which he says "involves the control of action through the giving of commands."

Cultural authority, on the other hand, is derived from performing a service and from the ability to determine the *needs* of clients. If journalists perform the service of informing public debates, then they determine which cultural conversations people need to be aware of and engaged in. The cultural authority of journalists, therefore... is based on the dependence of the public on the ability of journalists to present important information in a coherent and reliable fashion, or at least make it seem that way. This authority is reproduced in and through the everyday practices of journalists as well as later through boundary work rhetoric.

Starr says the cultural authority of medical doctors rests on three aspects of legitimacy: collegial, cognitive, and moral. For journalistic cultural authority, these same aspects of legitimacy are appropriate:

- The collegial legitimacy of the journalist—the acceptance by others in their profession;
- The cognitive legitimacy of the journalistic product—it is perceived to be based on rational, objective methods; and
- The moral legitimacy of the journalist—journalists' judgments are expected to be oriented toward altruism and public service.

Threats to cultural authority of an institution or profession do not always come from outside the institution or profession. A well-publicized case of fraud or fakery is perhaps the prime example of an internal threat to the cultural authority of a social institution or profession. Such turmoil is publicly discussed and thereby constructed as an issue or problem. The discussion of the issue occurs as discourse within journalistic media by journalists who control the content and topics of the medium.

For example, in 1980, *Washington* Post reporter Janet Cooke fabricated a news story about an imaginary eight-year-old heroin addict and was on the verge of accepting a Pulitzer Prize for it when the deception was revealed. The *Post*'s subsequent analysis of the deception argued that the problem was not organizational, the problem was that Cooke was an aberration—a compulsive liar.

As Dahlgren notes, one of the distinctive aspects of turmoil within the institution of journalism is that those within the institution "strive to maintain discursive control over such turmoil. Among other things, this helps to consolidate and legitimate professional practices and identity (by)... retain(ing) definitional control of the field, its problems and potential solutions".

Definitional control of the boundaries of journalism is also accomplished by journalists when they do things like formulate definitions of news and news work. It is also accomplished through the selection of news topics.

Defining news is not a simple task. A 1965 textbook for journalists admits, "To recognize news is easier than to define it". Yet the primary role of journalists is to determine what is newsworthy, that is, to define news. In defining news, journalists also define what it is they do. This study shows how journalists often define journalism in relation to its neighboring professions.

SOME BACKGROUND ABOUT "THE PROBLEM"

Many journalism critics have recently argued that American journalism is undergoing a profound change because it now regularly mixes entertainment with the news. Critics typically argue that this entertainment is in the form of sensationalistic celebrity-scandal.

In fact, there is a long history of sensationalism in American journalism, a fact documented by several journalism historians.

But the main point of contemporary critics is that sensationalism and tabloid-style techniques, which were always present on the fringes of journalism, are now becoming the norm in American journalism, and are being adopted by so-called "mainstream" media as part of economic survival strategies in the cutthroat business climate of American mass media.

These contemporary critics typically argue that there should be a rigid boundary between mainstream journalism and other kinds of mass communication such as tabloid journalism.

The critics imply that one kind of communication is more legitimate in certain contexts than the other, and even that tabloid journalism is not journalism at all but is instead entertainment.

As noted above, one of the claims made by mass media critics is that journalism just recently got worse. But this may be a perennial complaint.

A quick review of journalism criticism reveals that the argument that journalism used to be better but just recently got worse is common throughout the history of journalism. The critiques usually say that journalism used to make bold distinctions between news and entertainment but now combines the two. These critiques construct the logical conclusion that journalism has steadily decreased in quality over many years.

Taken together, the criticisms add up to the conclusions that the people who used to do journalism were better and had higher standards than those of today and that the distinctions between news and entertainment used to be greater. Examples of this critique can be found in even the earliest discussions of American journalism.

For instance, critics panned Benjamin Day New York Sun of the early 1830s because it often contained humour and sensational news of suicides. Similarly, some critics hated James Gordon Bennett New York Herald of the mid- to late-1830s because it contained entertaining, satirically written police court reports, as well as in-depth crime stories. Bennett pioneered the "human-interest story" or feature story, when he wrote in vivid detail in 1836 about the grisly murder of the prostitute Helen Jewett, quoting her madam and describing Jewett's apartment in minute detail.

Bennett's day-by-day narrative of the ensuing sensational trial reminds us of how journalism and entertaining literature have been combined for many years to make newsworthy stories "more palatable for consumption." Bennett was soundly criticized by his competitors and others for blurring the boundary between journalism and entertainment.

His detractors, many of them his competitors, waged what they called a "Moral War" in the late 1830s against Bennett and his enjoyable but sensationalistic newspaper. They maintained that Bennett was a "deviant" journalist because he blurred the boundaries of journalism by making his newspaper entertaining and popular. Those running the "Moral War" against Bennett were unsuccessful at running him out of the journalism business, but they did seriously wound his business.

In the 1920s, many journalists were labeled "yellow journalists" because they sensationalized and twisted the news by appealing to prurient interests and base instincts. In 1962, philosopher Jürgen Habermas argued that the boundaries between news and entertainment are blurring because people prefer "entertaining" news and its immediate rewards: Public affairs, social problems, economic matters, education and health... 'delayed reward news'—are not only pushed into the background by 'immediate reward news' (comics, corruption, accidents, disasters, sports, recreation, social events, and human interest) but, as the characteristic label already indicates, are already read less and more rarely.

In the end the news generally assumes some sort of guise and is made to resemble a narrative from its form down to stylistic detail (news stories); the rigorous distinction between fact and fiction is ever more frequently abandoned.

News and reports and even editorial opinions are dressed up with all the accouterments of entertainment literature, whereas on the other hand the belletrist contributions aim for the strictly 'realistic' reduplication of reality "as it is" on the level of clichès and thus, in turn, erase the line between fiction and report.

The integration of the once separate domains of journalism and literature... brings about a peculiar shifting of reality—even a conflation of different levels of reality. Under the common denominator of so-called human interest emerges the mixtum compositum of a pleasant and at the same time convenient subject for entertainment that, instead of doing justice to reality, has a tendency to present a substitute more palatable for consumption and more likely to give rise to an impersonal indulgence in stimulating relaxation than to a public use by reason.

Habermas, in making the observation that literature and news were "once separate domains," is doing, in 1962, journalism/entertainment boundary work. An example of a similar critique of journalism boundary-degradation—but attributed to a different root cause—is the melodramatic opening paragraphs of Ron Powers' 1977 book *The Newscasters,* which says the sea-change in journalism happened in the 1970s: The biggest heist of the 1970s never made it on the five o'clock news.

The biggest heist of the 1970s *was* the five o'clock news. The salesmen took it. They took it away from the journalists, slowly, patiently, gradually, and with such finesse that nobody noticed until it was too late.

By the 1970s, an extravagant proportion of television news—local news in particular—answered less to the description of "journalism" than to that of "show business." This transformation, carried out by the sales-oriented station managers in an unbounded quest for profits, bore the profoundest implications in the way Americans were to receive information and perceive political choices. Many local newscasts ceased serving the public (at best, they served the public only incidentally) and bequeathed their primary allegiance to the advertisers.

Powers blames the quest for profits, instead of journalistic values, for the swing toward show business techniques and content.

Similarly, Edwin Diamond, in 1975, notes that the potential for profits associated with high ratings points for news programs led to the downfall of journalistic control in local television newsrooms around the country.

The responsibility of controlling the news process was relinquished to news consultants who had no knowledge of journalism but who were well-versed in audience survey techniques and behavioral psychology. In other words, they knew how to design a local news programme that would attract a mass audience but not one that would inform it: Up until a few years ago, television news was in the hands of professional news directors and producers, traditionally trained in newspaper or magazine work or broadcast journalism.

It still is at the networks. But local station management has not had the same professional approach, especially since the local stations began discovering that their news times could be highly salable, often cheaper to run than straight entertainment shows, and attractive to many advertisers. Not only has television news become longer... [it] has become too important to be left to the newspeople. Audience research has been perceived as the key to ratings success.

For Diamond, "professionals" are those trained in journalism, especially in newspaper and magazine journalism, areas where audience research has not been pursued as thoroughly as in television.

In taking control away from the professionals, journalism has taken a back seat to superficiality, and news judgments are now made by managers skilled in audience research.

Powers' and Diamond's critiques of television journalism are quite similar to the critiques that were raised throughout the early history of the television medium.

They seem to argue for a monopolization of authority and protection of autonomy for journalists. In other words, Powers and Diamond would like to see journalists maintain control over all aspects of journalism and keep others from controlling any aspects of it.

Recently, Steven Stark, a commentator on popular culture for National Public Radio, wrote that the root cause of increased sensationalism in radio and television news is the advent of all-news channels in the 1980s, such as CNN. He says the increased demand for news around the clock has caused journalists to become irresponsible:

Unlike the old days, when there were, at most, two news cycles a day, there is now a 24-hour demand for information. That means the network news and newspapers have to provide a different product than they once did, because they assume people get their headlines elsewhere.

The result has been a considerable broadening of what is considered reportable news and analysis—much of it far less objectively verifiable than in the past. We now have fields of news that didn't exist 15 years ago, such as entertainment reporting. News from the tabloids is considered fair game. Call-in shows can put forward any "expert" they can drum up, while encouraging callers to speculate and gossip. Some TV commentary itself is close to staged: Crossfire and The McLaughlin Group are to James Reston and Edward R. Murrow what pro wrestling is to sports.

Because of the incessant demand, news is also presented more quickly to the public, with the inevitable result that there's a far thinner line between fact and rumor—one reason why personal details about celebrities get reported more quickly, if not falsely—than before.... This is all part of a far larger cultural pattern—the babble of a postmodern age that has seen feeling gain pre-eminence over thought, while elites collapse.

Stark's theory that journalists responded to the increased frequency of news "cycles" and an increased demand for news by lowering their standards for newsworthiness implies that journalists are not doing their jobs, and are, in fact, remiss in their responsibility to decide what counts as news. This is not a new critique, though the root cause selected by Stark may be a new idea.

Many other examples could be cited of journalists and others arguing that journalism is changing, moving toward more entertainment and less information. The critique is indeed perennial. As shown above, examples of it can be shown from the very beginnings of American journalism right up to the present. Journalism professor and historian Mitchell Stephens puts this kind of criticism in context:

Some of the criticism television journalism inspires is... shortsighted.... News and entertainment [did not] meet and mate for the first time on often giggly, often frivolous, local television newscasts in the United States; their affair dates back at least as far as criers and minstrels. Television news, in other words, did not inject a foreign substance—playfulness—into the news; news has been enjoyed for as long as it has been exchanged.

Like the penny papers of the 1830s, the yellow journals of the 1880s and 1890s and the tabloids of the 1920s, television has succeeded in attracting a new audience to the news. Once television sets became affordable, news became available to audiences of many millions, including even those lacking the energy, skill or maturity to read a newspaper or concentrate on a radio narrative.

If the critique is perennial, then there must be a reason for it being so persistent. Perhaps these critiques serve an important purpose. Instead of evaluating the legitimacy of these claims and critiques, the constructivist approach to this debate focuses on how self-interested stakeholders (relevant actors) construct a conception of journalism that makes sense to them and that helps to consolidate their power and prestige.

These stakeholders believe that the cultural authority of their institution depends on distinct boundaries, which, in turn, rest on concepts such as the perceived credibility and objectivity of their work. This constructivist approach to the issue helps us understand how the boundaries of journalism are constructed, negotiated, and maintained, giving us insights into what journalism means to people. To say that these boundaries are *constructed* implies that they have no firm, absolute contours. Instead, they are contextually contingent, local, and episodic, with the *potential* to become stable and widespread.

To give a brief example of boundary-work analysis, let us examine the words of the authors cited earlier in their arguments about the blurring of the news/entertainment boundary. They all imply that "real" journalism is something different from what we have now. The characteristics of "real" journalism that the various authors mentioned earlier in this section cite include distinctions such as: News is meant to inform, not entertain; it presents facts, not fiction; it does not include speculation or gossip; and it is controlled by professionals who serve the public, not by advertisers who seek only profits.

These are demarcation criteria that help journalists "construct" their role in society—and help them understand the shape and contours of the *cultural space* in which journalism resides. Looking at the claims more closely, it appears that the authors mentioned earlier in this section cite the *functional* differences between news and entertainment: One informs, the other entertains. They also note *epistemological* differences: One is a factual kind of knowledge, the other contains fiction.

They also cite *methodological* and *organizational* differences: One uses gossip and speculation, the other does not; and one is controlled by professionals who serve the public, the other serves less-altruistic goals. Instead, I look at how others solve them. In particular, I examine the apparent goals of boundary debates; how interested parties pick out the essential elements of the boundaries; and whether and how their work achieves any results.

The goal is to analyse how the boundaries between news and entertainment are "constructed" by relevant actors. To accomplish that goal, I look at several examples of constructions of monopoly, deviance, and autonomy as "social issues" with stakeholders in journalism. The constructivist approach to questions about what is journalism and what is not replaces the answer with the question as the thing to be studied.

In other words, I do not try to find a definitive-necessarily essentialist—answer to the question "What are the boundaries of journalism?" Instead, I analyse and examine how journalists and others have attempted to answer this perplexing question, particularly when they claim that certain acts and practices are not journalism but are entertainment. In these kinds of claims, we gain valuable in sight into the ways journalists make sense of what they do, and about the role of journalism in society.

Journalism, like all social institutions, is socially constructed. Questions about where journalism ends and entertainment begins are a viable field of study that up to this point, has been largely ignored. This project should begin to remedy this situation by examining what many call journalism ethics issues from a constructivist point of view. The way journalists make distinctions about acceptable behaviors, intentions, and content says a lot about culture production and how society creates and defines itself.

Throughout this study, cartographic metaphors—mapping images-are used as a way of thinking about the relationships between different institutions in American culture.

Journalists map out the cultural space of journalism by specifying where the boundaries are located. As Gieryn notes, cartographic metaphors are useful when discussing the idea of a cultural space—territorial markers that people use to make sense of the world around them.

He says, "cartographic metaphors offer a robust language for thinking about relations among cultural phenomena," particularly the relations between adjacent phenomena. In the cultural space of mass media, news and entertainment appear to be adjacent phenomena.

Gieryn suggests thatwe consider using cartographic terms such as "contours, landmarks, scale, orientation, coordinates, points of interest, and legend". These terms compel us to examine how this cultural space was slowly carved out of the cultural landscape rather than privilege journalism-as-it-is as the only logical outcome.

Some of the boundaries of journalism may be moving and flexible or perhaps blurry and indistinct. In other places they may be uncontested and easy to see.

In any case, it is the players on either side of the alleged boundary (or in the middle of it) who are the primary stakeholders in constitutive rhetoric that attempts to delineate borders. That is why the primary site of this study is in the rhetoric of journalists: They have the most to gain or lose by such rhetoric about the boundaries of journalism.

This chapter is an ethnographic analysis of the process whereby anomalous journalists who are perceived to be a threat to the institution are ritually "relocated" to the outer edges of the boundaries of journalism. It is an examination of a case of journalistic misconduct that was discussed in great detail within the institution of journalism. Dateline NBC, a network news division-produced weekly newsmagazine, broadcast a story in 1992 about General Motors pickup trucks; it contained a fiery simulated crash scene, which was staged by the program's producers.

This staging was not disclosed to the audience. Michael Gartner, then president of NBC News, was held responsible for the misconduct, which was labeled an act of journalistic fraud. The rhetoric by journalists that followed this example of journalistic deviance resembles what Harold Garfinkel calls a successful status degradation ceremony, whereby deviant members are expelled from an institution (in this case, the institution of journalism) in order to minimize harm to the institution as a whole.

Garfinkel has had a profound impact on sociological theory. As the founder of the ethnomethodology movement, his social constructivist emphasis on the way members of a group "make sense of, find their way about in, and act on the circumstances in which they find themselves" has opened up a vast new territory within sociology.

This chapter utilizes Garfinkel's theory and methods to examine one way in which journalists demarcate the realm of journalism within the cultural landscape.

This rhetorical analysis scrutinizes the naturally occurring discourse among journalists following the *Dateline* broadcast, focusing attention on the elements of status degradation ceremonies described by Garfinkel.

This is an examination of the rhetorical strategies of journalists reacting to accusations that the NBC News division used fraudulent methods in presenting the news and that Michael Gartner failed his profession by allowing it to happen.

Deviance in American journalism is defined and confronted by the official agents and apologists of the institution of journalism--namely, other journalists who discuss the practices of journalism as an interpretive community.

This chapter is an examination of how members of a public institution produce cultural meaning and reproduce social structures by engaging in rhetorical discourse designed to map out the cultural space of a social institution.

The "universe" sample for this chapter included all the articles listed in the NEXIS database containing the words "Dateline NBC" and "General Motors" appearing in major American newspapers, magazines, and wire services between November 1, 1992, and June 30, 1993 (some 521 articles). Also examined: a videotape of a conference of journalists who examined the Dateline scandal; a lawyer's report commissioned by NBC and released March 21, 1993; as well as some earlier articles about Gartner and NBC News that were examined for historical context.

SOME BACKGROUND ON THE DATELINE NBC/GM "EVENT"

Dateline NBC was a weekly network newsmagazine programme that began in April 1992. On November 17, 1992, Dateline NBC broadcast a report entitled, "Waiting to Explode?," which criticized the design of General Motors full-size pickup trucks built between 1973 and 1987, alleging that they were more susceptible to dangerous explosions when involved in side-impact vehicle collisions. The news report included a powerful visual demonstration of the problem: footage described as an "unscientific crash demonstration," which included a fiery explosion.

General Motors Corporation investigated the charges made in the story and then filed a defamation lawsuit against NBC. GM took the unprecedented step of announcing their lawsuit via a two-hour globally televised press conference on February 8, 1993. During the press conference, GM lawyers alleged that Dateline's producers allowed "incendiary" or "sparking devices" (model rocket engines) to be attached to the underside of the trucks to ensure that any gasoline spilled during the simulated accident would ignite--and that Dateline then failed to publicly disclose this fact in the programme.

NBC responded with an on-the-air apology the next night, read by Dateline anchors Jane Pauley and Stone Phillips. GM dropped its lawsuit shortly after the apology. Michael Gartner resigned on March 2, 1993. Three producers responsible for the GM pickup story segment were forced to resign on March 19, 1993. NBC President and CEO Robert Wright publicly apologized to viewers and to GM on March 22, 1993.

The news media covered the story of NBC's fraud in detail, and many journalism critics discussed it in various newspapers, magazines, professional journals, and on television programs. The Poynter Institute for Media Studies in St. Petersburg, Florida, sponsored a conference entitled "When Good Journalists Do Bad Things: Truthtelling and the Public Trust." The conference included a twohour discussion of the Dateline scandal by professional journalists and journalism professors, which was televised live on C-SPAN on April 15, 1993, recordings of which Poynter now sells on videocassette.

RESPONDING TO DEVIANCE

The very public outcry by journalists and journalism critics in this case--people who believed they were part of the "mainstream" American journalism institution--was a signal that a boundary line was crossed by Dateline NBC. The line was described as an epistemological boundary between different kinds of knowledge (truth and fiction), as a functional boundary between news and entertainment, and as a methodological boundary between disinterestedness and agency. The Dateline story was portrayed as a violation of professional norms that threatened the distinction between mainstream and tabloid journalism, or between news and entertainment.

This public discourse served several purposes:

- To distance the methodology, content, and apparent function of the Dateline episode from commonly accepted journalism standards and to signal that this kind of behaviour is deviant.
- To reassure the public that professional journalists are able to police their ranks.
- To maintain the social boundaries between journalism and entertainment (or between mainstream and tabloid television news) by showing that deviant

behaviour that results in products that resemble these other genres of communication will not go unpunished.

To demonstrate the contours of the boundaries of journalism, Gartner and his associates were labeled as deviant journalists. There are both costs and benefits to revealing deviant behaviour: "the basic dilemma of social control: to publicize or not to publicize deviant behaviour". Such publicity is negative and can serve to undermine public confidence in the institution--especially in the short term. A pattern of unpunished violations of norms, however, could be more damaging to the perceived integrity of the profession in the long run.

Durkheim says the public sanction of deviance is a healthy exercise for a group or institution because it helps to show group members how to recognize the area between acceptable and unacceptable behaviour. In his study on the sociology of deviance among the Puritan settlers of America, Kai Erickson notes that "the interactions which do the most effective job of locating and publicizing the group's outer edges would seem to be those which take place between deviant persons on the one side and official agents of the community on the other".

The official agents of the journalistic community are fellow journalists, who operate together as an interpretive community, "united through their collective interpretations of key public events. The shared discourse that they produce is thus a marker of how they see themselves as journalists". One of the distinctive aspects of turmoil within the institution of journalism (probably much like turmoil in other institutions) is that those within the institution "strive to maintain discursive control over such turmoil. Among other things, this helps to consolidate and legitimate professional practices and identity (by)... retain(ing) definitional control of the field, its problems and potential solutions".

The site of this chapter is in the symbolic actions of journalists-their communicative acts--as they respond to threats to the cultural authority and boundaries of the institution of journalism in America. These rhetorical actions are interpreted and evaluated as components of a successful status degradation ceremony. Such a ceremony consists of "communicative work directed to transforming an individual's total identity into an identity lower in the group's scheme of social types".

The individual in this case is Michael Gartner, former president of NBC News. The other three Dateline workers who were fired over the controversy--executive producer Jeff Diamond, senior producer David Rummel, and field segment producer Robert Read--were also denigrated somewhat by their peers, but Gartner received the major blame for the controversy because he was ultimately responsible as head of the NBC news division.

Because he served as a lightning rod for criticism, most of the attention here will be given to Gartner and the rhetoric directed at him. It is clear that--to his detractors--Gartner symbolized everything that was wrong with NBC News and everything that was wrong with American television journalism.

Throughout the 1980s and 1990s, Michael Gartner was one of the most well-known and outspoken personalities in the journalism profession. Gartner--with his trademark bow tie--was an icon for First Amendment absolutism. A third generation journalist, his father and grandfather both worked at newspapers in Iowa. Some of his previous accomplishments include: page one editor, Wall Street Journal; editor and co-owner, Ames Iowa, Daily Tribune; general news executive, Gannett Co.; president, Des Moines Register and Tribune Co.; editor, Louisville Courier-Journal and Louisville Times; member, Pulitzer Prize board; and president, American Society of Newspaper Editors.

A New York University Law School graduate, Gartner is known as a strict interpreter of First Amendment press rights. For instance, Gartner once argued that "there is no right to privacy--except from the government". This stance led to some controversial decisions, such as NBC's decision to identify the alleged rape victim in the William Kennedy Smith trial.

Gartner is also known among journalists for his strict stand on the use of anonymous sources.

He says it is wrong for reporters to use anonymous sources "in all but the most delicate of stories," because it damages the credibility of all journalism. Gartner is also known for his business and financial expertise. In 1984, he managed to get the Gannett Co. into a bidding war for control of The Des Moines Register, and reportedly pocketed more than $3 million from the deal.

THE STATUS DEGRADATION CEREMONY

Garfinkel theorized that there are eight sequential stages of a successful status degradation ceremony, consisting of specific "effects that the communicative tactics of the denouncer must be designed to accomplish". These eight types of arguments must be put forward by people within a community or institution that wants to banish deviants and at the same time, minimize harm to the institution itself.

The eight stages of this rhetorical ceremony are:

- Both the event and the perpetrators are made to look unusual.
- The perpetrators are compared to bad stereotypes—implying that they are not just accidentally bad.
- The denouncers show that they belong to the community and that they are speaking for the community or institution, not just as private individuals.
- The denouncers show that the values of the community are salient, and that they are correct and justified.
- The denouncers show that they speak for these values.
- The denouncers show that they have support from the community.
- The deviants are banished.
- The deviants are ritually separated from the community so that the community may go on as before.

Next is a detailed examination of each of the steps in the status degradation ceremony. Journalists made arguments before, during, and after the *Dateline* fiasco that seem to resemble each of the stages described by Garfinkel 40 years ago. The charges against NBC first came to light when GM staged its global press conference to announce its lawsuit. Harry Pearce, executive vice president and general counsel of General Motors Corp., said: "We now face a poisoned environment spawned by the cheap, dishonest, sensationalism of NBC's programme 'Waiting to Explode?' and its aftermath." GM's attack was quickly reported by journalists who seemed shocked that NBC had apparently used "other than standard" newsgathering techniques.

Journalists argued that *Dateline* used methods journalists don't normally use—they hired a biased subcontractor who staged a news story. NBC had hired The Institute for Safety Analysis (TISA) as a subcontractor to conduct the "unscientific crash demonstration." TISA is commonly hired to provide evidence for plaintiffs in personal injury lawsuits.

GM argued that the Institute had an agenda to promote, and *Dateline* did not disclose this fact, nor did it attempt to balance TISA's views with those of disinterested sources. It appeared that *Dateline* had crossed an epistemological and methodological boundary into the realm of agency, fiction, and entertainment. The information was gathered using entertainment-style methods, so it was fictional—designed to shock or entertain.

NBC was also charged with stonewalling—for not quickly admitting guilt but instead trying to rationalize its methods and its story. Stonewalling is one thing journalists particularly despise—but love to publicize. Eventually, Gartner realized that he should come clean: "I realized that we were just plain wrong.... We were stonewalling them, using all kinds of excuses and rationalizations. What we had done was just plain dumb, and wrong. And I was raised to admit you're wrong when you're wrong". Gartner did not come to this realization, however, until after GM initiated its multimillion dollar lawsuit.

Michael Gartner, *Dateline NBC*, and NBC News were made to appear strange, and their offenses were made to look like elementary violations of common sense.

Howard Rosenberg of the *Los Angeles Times* delivered a potent insult: "A high school journalism student knows that staging or faking or fabricating or falsifying news is, under any circumstances, absolutely forbidden. The big lie, the ultimate corruption.

Sweep that ethic under the rug, and a news organization becomes morally barren". Rosenberg's rhetoric implies that *Dateline*'s producers were not journalists at all because they apparently did not receive (and do not reproduce) the methodological training common to all journalists (even high school journalists); they were made to seem unusual.

Even before the *Dateline NBC*/GM event, critics charged that NBC was unable to launch a successful newsmagazine or other types of news programming, implying that NBC had an inferior network news division.

NBC News was also criticized for inadequate checks on accuracy and journalistic standards. Peter Herford, a 26-year veteran broadcast journalist from CBS, said the *Dateline NBC*/ GM event would have never happened at ABC, where someone is in charge of standards. Herford, who now heads the broadcasting programme at Columbia University Graduate School of Journalism, said,

At ABC, they had a full-time person, a vice president for news standards, who had a staff, who did nothing but review every investigative piece that went on the air, every major magazine piece that went on the air. He read all the scripts, etc., etc., etc.... At ABC, that ['Dateline'] piece never would have gotten past him. Thus, the NBC News division was portrayed as an unusually inferior organization, with no one doing the normal task of enforcing journalistic standards.

In some of the rhetoric following the event, Gartner was portrayed as an outsider to broadcast journalism. For instance, Jonathan Alter noted that a few years before he went to work in broadcast journalism Gartner once told some ABC News producers that he thought

TV News is nothing more than a "shallow comic book"... a superficial medium incapable of complex ideas. Today Gartner is in danger of being fired as president of NBC News, in essence for living down to his low expectations for the medium in which he works.... Ultimately he looked down his nose a bit at what he did for a living—and it showed. That both loosened his own standards and left him without allies below him.

Alter thus argues that Gartner's outsider attitude toward television journalism carried on during his tenure at NBC News and could be one of the causes for this scandal. Alter also criticized Gartner for being more of a money manager than a journalist. This is a familiar charge among journalists who bristle at the thought of money managers— "bean counters"—invading their ranks (penetrating their jurisdictional boundaries) and controlling journalistic output. It is an attempt by journalists to equate the journalist/manager organizational boundary with a "good" journalism/"bad" journalism boundary.

In the rhetoric examined here, Gartner, NBC News, and *Dateline*, were all made to seem unusual—as deviants who lacked knowledge of basic journalistic standards and thus operated outside the realm—the boundaries—of journalism.

One of the ways journalists made sense of the *Dateline NBC*/GM event was to stereotype it as similar to other well-publicized instances of journalistic deviance. The 1980 Janet Cooke/*Washington Post* scandal and the 1989 scandal following ABC News's re-enactment of the Felix Bloch suspected spy case were mentioned by several journalists as examples of similar lapses in journalistic standards.

In the infamous Janet Cooke case, a *Washington Post* reporter fabricated a story about an eight-year-old heroin addict and then passed the fiction off as reality. In the Felix Bloch case, ABC's World News Tonight showed a tape that it identified as suspected spy Felix Bloch, passing a briefcase of secrets to a Soviet spy. The people in the video were actually actors hired by ABC, and the video was doctored to make it look like a surveillance tape.

By stereotyping the practices of *Dateline NBC* as similar to those of other well-known journalistic scandals, journalists were able to quickly make sense of the event, understand its significance, and formulate responses to it. Four authors mentioned the Cooke scandal and one mentioned the Bloch scandal as stereotypical examples of the same kind of fraud.

Another author implies that the *Dateline NBC*/GM event is stereotypical of news values used in other countries where simulations, staging, and nondisclosure are not taboo in journalism:

If NBC is looking for some consolation, it can find plenty of company in Japan. Staging the news is so commonplace that the Japanese have a word for it: *yarase.*

"In America, it's the exception rather than the rule," says *Newsweek*'s Tokyo Bureau Chief Bill Powell. "Here, it's just standard operating procedure. There is much greater latitude given to producers to set things up if it doesn't work out." Adds Dorian Benkoil, an Associated Press editor who researched Japanese media on a Fulbright journalism fellowship: "In the U. S. the lines between entertainment and news are blurring recently. In Japan they never developed."

The implication of this rhetorical claim is that the way *Dateline NBC* operates is completely foreign (literally and figuratively) to American journalists.

Another of the rhetorical claims made by journalists following the *Dateline NBC*/GM event was that the "unscientific crash demonstration" was methodologically similar to things done on tabloid television programs, and that there were organizational similarities between *Dateline* and the tabloids. Others noted that some of the people who worked on the *Dateline NBC* programme had previously worked at the tabloids.

Ironically, tabloid producers used the *Dateline NBC* event as an opportunity to argue that their standards were higher—if anything-than NBC's network news standards. John Terenzio, executive producer of A Current Affair, was quoted in a *New York Times* article: "We would not have re-enacted a car crash using little rockets to blow up the car.... We would have felt that was not correct, and our legal department would not have allowed it". Terenzio thus delivers the fatal rhetorical blow to *Dateline NBC*: Its standards are even lower than those of tabloid television programs. Rosenberg makes a similar point about NBC News's standards when he notes that none of the tabloid shows identified the alleged rape victim of William Kennedy Smith, though NBC's Nightly News did.

Stereotyped as anomalous, Gartner, NBC News, and *Dateline NBC* are rhetorically "moved" outside the realm of journalism to the cultural space where tabloid television, "reality-based programming," and entertainment television programs reside.

Journalists demonstrated that judgment on Gartner and the *Dateline* scandal was only to be passed by fellow journalists—who understood the nuances of journalism—and who alone had the jurisdiction to police their ranks and control the boundaries of their profession. The Poynter Institute conference in which the actions of NBC in the GM truck incident were debated was filled almost exclusively with members of the journalism community—reporters, editors, producers, and journalism professors.

Lawyers were notably absent from the field of invited participants. Lawyers did get involved when NBC hired "outside" counsel, Robert Warren of Gibson, Dunn & Crutcher in Los Angeles, and Lewis Kaden of Davis, Polk & Wardwell in New York, to conduct an investigation of how the exploding truck story came to be broadcast. This concerned some journalists who felt threatened by the fact that people from outside the institution of journalism were going to judge the performance of journalists:

Some NBC News staffers have questioned why the network hired lawyers to investigate the case rather than... asking a respected journalist to conduct an internal inquiry. NBC's [spokeswoman Peggy] Hubble said that management felt outsiders would provide the most impartial investigation. [But]... one source speculated that hiring attorneys may be in part to protect lawyer-client confidentiality and to protect the network [from] lawsuits.

In the final analysis, journalists quickly assumed the role of jury in this case, undercutting any attempts by General Motors to have the trial go to a real court.

Later, at the Poynter conference, Michael Gartner said that he wanted to settle the case quickly and get it behind them, and this is why the on-air apology was broadcast the day after GM filed its lawsuit. He also said that he had complete authority on the wording of the apology, and whether to accept the conditions of it or not.

Chapter 4

Objectivity to Interpretive Sufficiency

The contemporary version of the press traces its beginning to the 1890s. The media developed into an industrial structure, and the first forays into journalism education appeared. The press took shape as a complex and diversified social institution, with journalists an expert class pursuing specialized tasks.

The North American press began understanding itself during this decade not as a political forum or socializing force, but as a corporate economic structure marketing a commodity for consumers.

Structural patterns of authority and accountability were utilitarian in form, and utilitarianism characterized the press's organizational culture, which in turn was rooted in industrial production and market distribution.

The industrialization and commercialization of the media displaced an earlier news culture that had used partisan advantage as its main standard. With the industrialization of the press, media occupations, especially journalism, began to redefine themselves as middle-class professions and sought a place within the rising university system.

A university education for journalists was first seriously attempted late in the 19th century. By 1910 when Flexner had written his monumental Report to the Carnegie Foundation for the Advancement of Teaching on professional training in a university context, journalism education had adopted a functional model for itself compatible with the utility theory that dominated the first debates about the commercial press' character and role.

The key impetus behind the creation of these early university programs in journalism was the need for the press to enhance its respectability in the face of heated public criticism. In the early and mid-19th century, journalism was a low-prestige occupation in a highly competitive market. Because journalists were perceived to have very little power, the public was not impressed by the typical newspaper or reporter, but was not especially alarmed either.

However, circumstances began to change dramatically as the 19th century neared its end. The press expanded rapidly in all the urban centers of Britain, with major national newspapers coming into existence and playing a prominent role in British journalism for most of the following century. While multiple ownership of weekly newspapers started early in the 18th century, press chains created by the press barons in the late 19th and early 20th centuries began gaining a dominant market position.

Newspapers in the United States grew in circulation, industrialized their production, and introduced economies of scale through modern distribution and through reliance on advertising that led to increasing monopolization of local markets in the later 19th and early 20th centuries. The rising power of the press made lapses that earlier had been colorful now seem to be dangerous. Newspaper owners, like railroad magnates, were seen by many as robber barons and anti-democrats. This popular perception of corruption had a significant amount of truth to it. In response, respectable elements of the press sought to develop a more polished public image.

Major new communication technologies between 1837 (telegraph) and World War I gave birth to the modern international communication system. These technologies spawned some of the first transnational companies: Marconi (operating in several countries with the parent company in the United Kingdom); Siemens and Slaby-Arco in Germany; Thomson in France; Western Union, AT&T, and United

Wireless in the United States; Philips in the Netherlands. The first submarine cable was laid across the straits of Dover in 1851, and the first transatlantic cable was laid in 1866. Britain completed its first direct cable to Bombay in 1870 and to Australia in 1872.

With the development of the submarine telegraph, the turn of the century marked the zenith of the monopolistic power of the great cable companies, to be overturned themselves by Marconi.

Monopoly became a crucial issue for international communication henceforth, with regulation entangled by domestic and imperial interests. "The period up to World War I was one of rising nationalism, creation and consolidation of empires, and intense commercial rivalry. The tendency was to equate national interests with those of a country's major industrial concerns".

As long distance technologies established new centralizations of power, cooperation was necessary for technical reasons. However, in these early years of the transnational communication system, "it was nation against nation, company versus company, suspicion opposing suspicion ... [in the] competition to control the means of communication and to establish commercial hegemonies and information monopolies".

OBJECTIVITY AS NORM

Concerns about media ethics followed the same trajectory. Journalistic conduct has been criticized and debated since the oldest known newspaper published in Germany in 1609. However, abuses of the press were not explicitly linked to ethical principles until the end of the 19th century. During the 1890s a transition occurred from everyday commentary in newspaper articles to a more reflective period related to ethical precepts. A commonsense utilitarianism emerged as the overall framework. Sensationalism had been a staple of the entire century, but it took serious institutional form in the late 1890s from the Hearst and Pulitzer circulation battles during the Spanish-American War.

As electronic communication systems were established, privacy became an urgent issue as sensitive diplomatic, military, and commercial information crossed multiple borders, especially in Europe. Freebies and junkets, scourged by media critics since 1870, were treated more systematically in the context of individual accountability. A platform was laid for the free press-fair trial debate, although with virtually no progress beyond insisting on the press's rights. The initial work of the 1890s, though rudimentary in ethics, evolved into a serious effort during the 1920s as journalism education was established within the liberal arts. Four important textbooks in journalism ethics emerged from America's heartland during this period: Crawford's *Ethics of Journalism*, Flint's The *Conscience of the Newspaper*, Gibbons's *Newspaper Ethics*, and Henning's *Ethics and Practices of Journalism*.

None recognized the others in quotation or argument, yet they were similar in the topics they considered central: reporters and sources, economic temptations and conflicts of interest, national security, free press-fair trial, deception, fairness, accuracy, sensationalism, and protection of privacy.

This arousal of ethical inquiry followed a period of intense media criticism. Muckrakers such as Sinclair exposed the corruption of the money power in the wire services and in daily newspapers that were increasingly monopolis tic. Thinkers such as Lippmann perceived the fundamental irrationality of public opinion and the failure of journalism to inform it properly. Some professional leaders themselves recognized the perils.

Writing in 1924, Lord Reith of the BBC, for example, articulated a strong ethos of public service: "I think it will be admitted by all that to have exploited so great a scientific invention [radio] for the purpose and pursuit of entertainment alone would have been a prostitution of its powers and an insult to the character and intelligence of the people".

Moreover, the experience of propaganda in World War I and the rise of the motion picture in the 1900s and 1910s produced a palpable feeling of cultural peril among both reformers and traditional opinion leaders.

However, the flurry of activity in the 1920s, the growth of professional societies with codes of ethics, the expansion of curricula into the liberal arts— none of these could prevent the demise of ethics in the face of an antithetical worldview, scientific naturalism.

Scientific naturalism aggressively ordered the structure of knowing during this period—naturalism in the sense that genuine knowledge can be identified only in the natural laws of the hard sciences. For Quine, philosophical inquiry was natural science reflecting on itself, and all meaningful knowledge was continuous with the paradigmatic disciplines—physics, chemistry, and biology.

Advances in the physical sciences became the applauded ideal as academicians —including those in communication— promoted its methods and principles. One pacesetting educator, Murphy, concluded in 1924: "Journalism ... is emerging from an imaginative type of writing into one governed by scientifically sound principles.

We now recognize that the scientific attitude toward news materials is the only safeguard we have against journalism graduates being capricious and emotional". Centered on human rationality and armed with the scientific method, the facts in news were said to mirror reality.

Universities institutionalized the conventions of objective reporting in journalism curricula. The period from the 1930s is typically described as the social scientific phase of communications study, and objectivity was a quasi-scientific method appropriate to it. Carey correctly attributed the emergence of objectivity in journalism to the struggle within the press for a legitimate place to stand within the complexities of rapid industrialization:

With the end of partisan journalism, journalists were deprived of a point of view from which to describe the world they inhabited.

That world was less and less governed by political parties, and journalists were set free of those parties in any event, so journal ists, capitalizing on the growing prestige of science, positioned themselves outside the system of politics, as observers stationed on an Archimedean point above the fray of social life.

Originally this form of journalism—beginning most prominently with the wire services—was rooted "in a purely commercial motive: the need of the mass newspaper to serve politically heterogeneous audiences without alienating a significant segment" of them. Subsequently this strategy of reporting "was rationalized into a canon of professional competence and ideology of professional responsibility. " Journalists became "a relatively passive link in a communication chain that records the passing scene for audiences".

Stretched across the fact-value dichotomy of scientific naturalism, journalistic morality became equivalent to unbiased reporting of neutral data. The seeds of this ethic of independence existed already in Henning, though duty to the public realm dominated. Presenting unvarnished facts was heralded as the standard of good performance, with readers and viewers presumably deciding for themselves what the facts meant.

Objective reporting was not merely a technique, but a moral imperative. Reporters considered it virtuous to bracket value judgments from the transmission of information. In C. P. Scott's famous declaration in the *Manchester Guardian*: A newspaper's "primary office is the gathering of news ... The unclouded face of trust [must not] suffer wrong. Comment is free, but facts are sacred". Patterson, for example, made an impassioned plea in his Don R. Mellet Memorial Lecture that reporters demonstrate moral leadership in improving democratic life, and the cornerstone of their responsibility he considered "objective reporting and unslanted facts. " News corresponds to context-free neutral algorithms, and ethics is equated with impartiality.

Concern for ethics during the 30s through 60s occurred only on isolated occasions. The Report of the Commission on Freedom of the Press in 1947 was the most famous counterstatement of this period. Occasionally there were pockets of resistance in journalism's intellectual and vocational life, but the professional statistical model prevailed nonetheless. The scientific worldview was the ruling paradigm. A preoccupation with that value-centered enterprise called ethics seemed out of place in an academic and professional environment committed to facticity.

Attacks on the objectivist worldview have multiplied through hermeneutics, critical theory in the Frankfurt School, American pragmatism, Wittgenstein's linguistic philosophy, Gramsci, and, in their own way, Lyotard's denial of master narratives and Derrida's sliding signifiers.

The antifoundationalism of our own day indicates a crisis in maintaining an incontrovertible domain separate from human consciousness.

Institutional structures and policies remain neutrality-driven, but in principle the tide has turned at present toward restricting objectivism to the territory of mathematics, physics, and the natural sciences. Objectivity has become increasingly controversial as the working press's professional standard, though it remains entrenched in various forms in our ordinary practices of news production and dissemination. In Carey's more dramatic terms:

The conventions of objective reporting were developed as part of an essentially utilitariancapitalist-scientific orientation toward events.... Yet despite their obsolescence, we continue to live with these conventions as if a silent conspiracy had been undertaken between government, the reporter, and the audience to keep the house locked up tight even though all the windows have been blown out.

INTERPRETIVE SUFFICIENCY

This mainstream view of news as objective information is too narrow for today's social and political complexities. A more sophisticated concept is truth in journalism as authentic disclosure. The notable Hutchins Commission Report called for this alternative in 1947. It advocated a deeper definition of the press's mission as a "truthful, comprehensive and intelligent account of the day's events in a context which gives them meaning".

Bonhoeffer's Ethics contends correctly that a truthful account takes hold of the context, motives, and presuppositions involved. In his terms, telling the truth depends on the quality of discernment so that penultimates do not gain ultimacy. Truth means, in other words, to strike gold, to get at "the core, the essence, the nub, the heart of the matter".

QUALITATIVE METHODS

Once knowledge is released from epistemological objectivism, guidelines must be sought somewhere. For their orientation and specificity, media that enhance public life turn to interpretive studies or what is often called qualitative research. Forsaking the quest for precision journalism does not mean imprecision, but precision in disclosure and authenticity. To replace news gathering rooted in the methods of the natural sciences, rigorous qualitative procedures must be followed instead.

Fiction and fabrication are not acceptable substitutes for fact and accuracy. Reporters aiming for critical consciousness among the public will seek what might be called interpretive sufficiency. They will polish their research and writing skills in terms of qualitative strategies. Explicit appeal to the interpretive approach will enhance the news story's completeness, rather than crudely tailoring events into a cosmetic cohesion.

While interpretive suffi ciency, in some form, has long served as a trademark of distinguished journalism, it is an everyday imperative for citizen-based reporting. In effect, with interpretive sufficiency we raise the ante, weaving it into our expectation of ordinary press performance.

Interpretive studies are an alternative view of human knowing. In this perspective, investigations must be grounded historically and biographically, so that they represent complex cultures adequately. The concepts of social science are not derived from a free-floating and abstruse mathematics, but resonate with the attitudes, definitions, and language of the people actually being studied. Journalists trained in qualitative research identify with social meanings in their role as participants and as observers formulate seminal conclusions about these meanings.

Through disciplined abstractions (Lofland), ethnomethodology, contextualization, thick description (Geertz), coherent frames of reference (Schutz), case studies, naturalistic observation, and other research practices, news workers can stake out a claim to interpretive sufficiency and assume responsibility for their efforts.

Through an understanding of interpretive methodologies, reporters come to grips with the complex ways ethnographers insert themselves into the research process. A rich literature has been developed on constructing the life histories of ordinary people.

In a fundamental sense, qualitative approaches are a temperament of mind— "the sociological imagination," Mills called it—rather than merely a series of techniques for handling the telephone, minicam, or interview pad. However, while the creative process always remains central, tough-minded standards and valid procedures can be taught and learned.

VALIDITY

It is widely understood and accepted that research in the objectivist tradition must be externally and internally valid. Interpretive approaches need to meet these criteria as well, though in terms consistent with their own assumptions. Interpretive studies enforce the maxim that research imprisoned within itself, and therefore self-validating, is unacceptable. The principle of external validity compels naturalistic observers to be circumspect in generalizing to other situations.

The cases and illustrations that have been selected must be representative of the class, social unit, tribe, or organization to which they properly belong. Interpretation arises in natural settings, not contrived ones; therefore, the more densely textured the specifics, the more external validity is maintained. This concern is particularly apropos in preparing case studies, a favourite qualitative tool because it allows in-depth and holistic probing. The goal is identifying representative cases for examination rather than spectacular ones that are anecdotal and idiosyncratic.

Regarding internal validity, interpretive accounts must reflect genuine features of the situation under study and not represent the aberrations or hurried conclusions of observer opinion. There must be sympathetic immersion in the material until the researcher or journalist establishes, in Blumer's phrase, "poetic resonance" with it. Does the investigator know enough to identify the principal aspects of the event being studied and to distinguish these main features from digressions and parentheses?

Using the body as an analogy, the blood and brain must be separated from fingers and skin, all of which are parts of the whole organism but of differing significance. If true inferiority has occurred—that is, if the details accurately reflect the natural circumstances —then the data are valid and reliable even though not based upon randomization, repeated and controlled observation, measurement, and statistical inference.

Interpretive sufficiency seeks to open up public life in all its dynamic dimensions. It means taking seriously lives that are loaded with multiple interpretations and grounded in cultural complexity. Ethnographic accounts have the "depth, detail, emotionality, nuance, and coherence" that permit a "critical consciousness to be formed" by readers and viewers. The thick notion of sufficiency supplants the thinness of the technical, exterior, and statistically precise received view. Rather than reducing social issues to the financial and administrative problems defined by politicians, the news media enable people to come to terms with their everyday experience themselves.

TRIANGULATION

Effective use of triangulation is one way to describe interpretive sufficiency. The goal is to build up a fully rounded analysis of some phenomenon by combining all lines of attack, each probe revealing certain dimensions of the human world being investigated. The point is not to advocate eclecticism as such, but to avoid the personal bias and superficiality that stem from using only one kind of examination. Triangulation takes seriously the way humans attach meanings to social reality.

The process of disentangling from within is complicated by the fact that reporters are interpreting a world that has been interpreted already. "Objective reality can never be captured. We can know a thing only through its representations". The assumption is that the different lines of interpretation each reveal different aspects of reality, "much as a kaleidoscope ... will reveal different colors and configurations of the object to its viewer".

Triangulation occurs in several forms. It may refer, for example, to method— that is, combining document analysis with unstructured interviewing with unob trusive observation, and combining this mixture in order to improve perspective. One can also take a social problem, prisons and incarceration, for instance, and triangulate it by viewing it historically (how does the contemporary situation differ from previous time periods), synchronically (what are the relevant facts about the problem today, using a variety of data sources), and theoretically (what ethical or anthropological system is relevant in gaining perspective on it).

Theoretical triangulation is an obvious possibility, too, focusing several conceptual outlooks on a single object to see which one explains more. In investigator triangulation different evaluators, researchers, and experts are used. Beyond these approaches is a kind of multiple triangulation in which all the various facets and insights generated are placed in interaction and cross-fertilization until the structural features of a setting or event are illuminated.

Comprehension of actual context only accumulates gradually, so the search is always an ongoing one until we finally reveal the exact contours of the details unearthed. "The facts never 'speak for themselves. ' They must be selected, marshaled, linked together, and given a voice". In this sense, the crystal is a better image of interpretive design than the fixed, two-dimensional triangle. Crystals:

Combine symmetry and substance with an infinite variety of shapes, substances, transmutations, multidimensionalities, and angles of approach. Crystals grow, change, and alter, but are not amorphous. Crystals are prisms that reflect externalities *and* refract within themselves ... casting off in different directions.

Also in Denzin's application of the crystalline metaphor: "Triangulation is the display of multiple, refracted realities simultaneously". The aim is always multiple insights. The emphasis in interpretation is on discovery rather than applying routinized procedures. What we see when we view a crystal depends on how we hold it up to the light.

GENERAL MORALITY

The deficiencies in the epistemology of objective social science have become transparent. The enlightenment model placing facts and values in two separate domains has been discredited.

A positivistic epistemology that insists on neutrality regarding definitions of the good and puts human freedom at odds with the moral order is now seen as fundamentally flawed. Objectivity as a unidimensional framework of rational and moral validation accounts for some of the good ends we seek, such as minimal harm, but those issues outside the objectivity calculus are excluded from the decision-making process.

The way power and ideology influence social and political institutions, including the press, is largely ignored. Under a rhetorical patina of rational choice for autonomous actors, a means-ends system operates in fundamentally its own terms.

Even more unsettling has been the recognition that neutrality is not pluralistic but imperialistic. Reflecting on our past experience with it, disinterested investigation under presumed conditions of value freedom is increasingly seen as de facto reinscribing the agenda in its own terms. In the social sciences, quantitative analysis is procedurally committed to equal reckoning, regardless of how research subjects may constitute the substantive ends of life.

However, experimentalism is not a neutral ground for all ideas; rather, it is a "fighting creed" that imposes its own ideas on others while uncritically assuming the "very superiority that powers this imposition". In Foucault's more decisive terms, social science is a regime of power that helps maintain social order by normalizing subjects into categories designed by political authorities. A commitment to objectivity is not neutral but represents only one range of ideals, and is itself incompatible with other good ends.

This noncontextual model that assumes "a morally neutral, objective observer will get the facts right" ignores "the situatedness of power relations associated with gender, sexual orientation, class, ethnicity, race, and nationality. "It is hierarchical (scientist-subject) and biased toward patriarchy. "It glosses the ways in which the observer-ethnographer is implicated and embedded in the 'ruling apparatus' of the society and the culture.

"Scientists "carry the mantle" of university-based authority as they venture out into "local communities to do research". There is no sustained questioning of expertise itself in democratic societies that belong in principle to citizens who do not share this specialized knowledge.

Such historians of reporting as Carey lament an escalating professionalism that wrenches journalism from its civic moorings and recasts it as a scientistic-technocratic estate remote from everyday life. "The practices of writing and reporting the journalist thinks of as constituting objectivity" actually cast the citizen into the disempowered "role of student to be educated by the press rather than a participant in the process of self-government."

Under the procedures of objective reporting, "journalists are reduced to brokers in the communication process ... allied structurally if not sympathetically with the persons and institutions they report". The genius of qualitative approaches is to confront that sequestering and insider mentality head-on; it enables us to work the backyards and sidewalks, but with *savoir faire* and competence.

INTERPRETIVE SOCIAL SCIENCE AND PUBLIC JOURNALISM

Interpretive approaches do not incline us to construct an apparatus of professional ethics. They work instead within the general morality.

Rather than developing rules for experts, their preoccupation is the moral dimension of everyday life. Professionals committed to qualitative standards do not establish codes of ethics for themselves, but reflect the same social and moral space as the citizens they report. How the moral order works itself out in community formation is the issue, not, first of all, what media practitioners by their own standards consider virtuous.

The moral domain is understood to be intrinsic to human beings, not a system of rules, norms, and ideals external to society and culture. Lincoln clarified the issues in these terms: Interpretive social science brings about the collapse of the distinctions between standards, rigor, and quality criteria and the formerly separate consideration of research ethics.

In effect, many of the proposed and emerging standards for quality in interpretive social science are also standards for ethics.... This dissolution of the hard boundaries between rigor and ethics in turn signals that the new research is a relational research—research grounded in the recognition and valuing of connectedness between researcher and researched, and between knowledge elites and the societies and communities in which they live and labour.

Investigators are not constituted as ethical selves antecedently, but moral discernment unfolds dialectically between reporter and citizen. The dualism of means and ends is rejected, with the ends of interpretive sufficiency reconciled with the means for achieving them. "Methods vie among themselves not for experimental robustness, but for vitality and rigor in illuminating ... how we can create human flourishing".

INTERPRETIVE JOURNALISM AND PUBLIC LIFE

Rather than searching for neutral principles to which all parties can appeal, professional guidelines rooted in the general morality rest on a complex view of moral judgments. They are seen as a composite that integrates everyday experience, beliefs about the good, and feelings of approval and shame into an organic whole. This is a philosophical approach that situates the moral domain within the general purposes of life that people share contextually in their personal and social relations. Ideally, it engenders a new normative core for responsible reporting.

In an interpretive perspective, social entities are considered moral orders and not merely lingual structures. Societies are not formed by language alone. There are no selves-in-relation without moral commitments to nurture them. Our widely shared moral intuitions—respect for the dignity of others, for in stance—are developed through discourse within a community.

A self exists within "webs of interlocution, "and all interpretation implicitly or explicitly" acknowledges the necessarily social origin of any and all of our conceptions of the good. "Moral frameworks are as fundamental for orienting us in social space as the need "to establish our bearings in physical space". Consequently, as journalism deals with the moral dimension in news, editorials, features, and investigative reporting, it is not in alien territory.

In fact, according to Taylor, "Developing, maintaining and articulating" our moral intuitions and reactions are as natural for humans as learning up and down, right and left. The sinews that hold citizens together are moral. Our communal web is not primarily political interests or economic interdependence or information technology but a commitment of conscience that preconditions the ethos of external apparatuses.

This bondedness entails an ethics situated in creatureliness. Rather than privileging an individualistic, transcendental rationalism, moral commitments are inscribed in our worldviews through which we share a view of reality and perspectives on the common good. This ontological model is actually closer to the way the moral imagination operates in everyday life and refuses to separate moral agents from all that makes them unique. Instead of constructing a purely conceptual foundation for morality, the moral order is positioned fundamentally in the creaturely and corporeal. "In this way ... being ethical is a primordial movement in the beckoning force of life itself".

From this perspective, public life cannot be facilitated in functional language only, but journalists ought to speak of moral issues in appropriately moral discourse. And when they critique events that are vacuous or unjust, they must do so in terms of common values that have wide acceptance in the community as a whole. In this sense media professionals participate in their readers and viewers' ongoing process of moral articulation.

In fact, culture's continued existence depends on identifying and defending its normative base. Therefore, public texts must enable us "to discover truths about ourselves"; reporting ought to "bring a moral compass into readers' lives" by accounting for things that matter to them. Communities are woven together by narratives that invigorate their common understanding of good and evil, happiness and reward, and the meaning of life and death.

Recovering and refashioning moral discourse help to orient our citizenship. News is not the transmission of specialized data, but, in style and content, a catalyst for moral agency. Taylor emphasized that moral judgments are capable of rational elucidation. Our moral intuitions often seem to be purely instinctual, like taste reactions to food. However, human beings are capable of explaining what merits their obligations and they typically do so in terms of their beliefs about the nature of humanness.

Agreements and disputes about values can be articulated and sifted. In fact, moral commitments cannot be intuitive only; they must be nurtured through discourse derived from and shared by a community. Agreements and disputes about values can be articulated and sifted. In these terms, qualitative researchers or journalists act morally when their accounts enable those studied to specify the character and identity of their moral instincts and to work them out in the public arena.

MORAL LITERACY

If our public life is not merely functional, but knit together by an admixture of social values, then moral literacy ought to be privileged in the media's mission. If societies are moral orders, and not merely lingual structures, in other words, communication in the public arena ought to stimulate the moral imagination. We have heard this language in a sanitized sense. "Do these programs have any redeeming social value?" For an interpretation to be sufficient, it ought to enable us to traverse the moral landscape. At that epiphanal moment when the principial contours of the taken-for-granted world are illuminated, news enhances the moral dimension of social dialogue.

Our understanding of the self and public life increasingly exists in media texts. Therefore, in mass-mediated cultures oriented toward normlessness and illusive textuality, reporters find their appropriate role in opening windows on the moral landscape. As Glasser observed, "The hard-hitting stories, the investigative stories, lack a morally sensitive vocabulary".

Journalism instead ought to appeal to listeners and readers about ordering human values. They further a community's ongoing process of moral evaluation by penetrating through the political and economic surface to the moral dynamics underneath. Rather than merely providing readers and audiences with information, the press's aim is morally literate citizens.

Wherever one observes reenactments of purposeful history and justice, there one sees the results of moral literacy. News can be considered redemptive when it serves as an instrument not of accommodation but of critique and social change. Documentaries, commentators, and public broadcasting often resonate with a redemptive accent, stir the human conscience, and liberate their viewers from the dominant text. We all know stations and reporters who have refused infotainment and sought to awaken the civic conscience.

Major league awards are still won by professionals in journalism who distinguish themselves for public service. Editorials have raised our consciousness of anti-Semitism, and heightened our moral awareness of racism and gender discrimination. Over time and across the media, one observes a redemptive glow on occasion in which the news media have facilitated moral discernment by their insight into humankind as a distinctive species and by their affirmation of purposeful history.

In his classic study, *The Moral Foundations of Professional Ethics,* Goldman argued that the general morality is the ultimate framework for understanding professional norms. For him, "the most fundamental question for professional ethics is whether those in professional roles require special norms and principles to guide their well-intentioned conduct".

For professionals in medicine, law, business, journalism, government, and so forth, we typically assume that their roles require unique principles or specially weighted norms. In fact, the standard approach is to define ethical codes as sharply as possible according to the peculiar demands each field entails—aggressively defending clients in law, for instance, the physician's responsibility to clients, journalists' obligation to sources, and the commitment of business executives to stockholders.

Obviously, "special institutional obligations exist when their recognition has better moral consequences than would refusing to recognize them". Yet Goldman concluded: "The central problem in professional ethics as actually practiced is not that professionals often fail to live up to their unique official codes and professional principles; nor that they lack the will to enforce them. It is rather that they often assume without question that they ought to live up to them". The ultimate standard for professionals is not role-specific ethical principles, but the general morality.

Journalism is an institution of power. Decisions and policies can be self-serving, and practitioners defensive when criticized. Competition and careerism often cloud the application of professional codes or ethical guidelines. Journalists may have an understanding with sources that all information will be treated confidentially, for example, and then change their mind when they come to believe the public has a right to know this privileged material. Whereas we agree in the general morality that we ought to keep our promises, in this case canons of professional practice allow self-defined exceptions for the journalist as expert.

A preoccupation with privilege and authority cuts journalism loose from the very public it is meant to serve. Objectivity rooted in the prestige of science has fueled the status of specialized expertise in the mainstream press. On the other hand, interpretive efficiency presumes that facts and values are intermixed rather than dichotomous.

Given the moral dimension intrinsic to the social order, interpreting its various configurations sufficiently means elaborating the moral component. In addition, to resonate intelligently with peoples' values means that journalists know the general morality, which they share with the public at large. Rather than refining professional codes of ethics, the challenge for journalists is the moral life as a whole—no harm to innocents, truth telling, reparations for wrong actions, beneficence, gratitude, honour contracts, human dignity. For taking journalism to the streets, interpretive standards understand moral behaviour in interactive terms—with reporters operating in the same arena as citizens themselves.

Chapter 5

Textual Analysis in Journalism

Textual analysis is sometimes called careful reading, and it is as important to a journalist as good listening. Textual analysis is a method that communication researchers use to describe, interpret, and evaluate the characteristics of a recorded message. This type of qualitative research and analysis focuses on a particular text to determine its characteristics and place it in a category shared by other similar texts for comparison and contrast purposes.

Qualitative textual analysis can lead to quantitative research methods such as content analysis or Q methodology, which can be used to analyse publications or opinions about texts. For example, researchers might categorize the types of message strategies that politicians use in public campaign speeches as fear-appeals and reward-appeals by studying individual texts, and then conduct a quantitative study.

This research project might study how the *New York Times* and the Los *Angeles Times* covered campaign speeches over the period of a year by focusing on the textual attributes of each paper's campaign coverage. Reporters who write the news stories also use some level of textual analysis to compare and contrast oral and written language. Reporters at the *Washington Post* use personal computers to search for key words in bills and legislation that indicate stakeholders—winners and losers—in the documents.

Mass media textual analysis is closely related to literary criticism, which, broadly used today, encompasses any discourse on any literature, including three distinguishable but overlapping areas: history, theory, and evaluation. Many scholars view literature as part of an historical process, a phenomenon that can be described by internal principles such as types, techniques, and functions, or as objects to be studied, analysed, and judged. Several methods and approaches to criticism fiercely compete for attention in the field. Wellek commented on this new age of criticism:

The variety of voices today is so great that the situation has been compared to the Tower of Babel, with its mutually incompatible languages.

Never before has there been such a ferment in criticism, and critics have never before attracted so much attention and fervent loyalty ... Indeed some scholars argue that this is the age of criticism, since literary critics now often function not only as specialists in literature, but also as general critics of society and civilization.

This chapter focuses on only the most common terms of textual analysis that are used by journalists. It addresses how journalists read, analyse, categorize, describe, and evaluate their own writing as well as the writing and oral language of others.

PURPOSES AND TYPES OF TEXTUAL ANALYSIS

There are two basic uses of textual analysis for practicing journalists. The first is to study the language of their sources for specific stories; the second is to study the language of journalism to refine their art of writing. This broad approach to criticism is relatively new; it has been advanced in recent decades by critiques of English composition and rhetorical analyses of speech communication. In their 1991 book, Investigating Communication, Frey and colleagues explained that textual analysis stems from a systematic attempt to understand how meaning moves from author to audience and how the text is related to other variables that precede it.

Ultimately, textual analysis is a scientific attempt to evaluate a text based on a set of established standards or criteria. Several organizations and publications have begun criticizing the content of the news media on a regular basis for the general public.

They include *News Watch, MediaChannel, Brill's Content, Fairness & Accuracy in Reporting, CounterSpin, Medianews,* and *Media Watch.*

Textual analysis can be applied to any communications medium because photos, illustrations, graphics, and video images can be reduced to textual summaries before analysis. Some language theorists claim that history in general consists of texts to be analysed.

Scripts of radio and television news and entertainment are more readily available than ever, and they often can be secured over the Internet for textual analysis.

Five types of media criticism use textual analysis: Aristotelian, genre, historical, dramatic, and fantasy theme. The first is a return to Aristotle's judicial, logical, and formal analysis centered on the work itself rather than its historical, moral or religious context.

Genre critics group texts that are similar in function, purpose, and form, and then evaluate each text based on the established attributes of the genre. An example of genre criticism is Cawelti's *Adventure, Mystery, and Romance: Formula Stories as Art and Popular Culture,* published by the University of Chicago Press in 1976. Historical criticism consists of oral histories, case studies, bibliographical studies and social movement studies.

The historical critic attempts to evaluate the influence of events on the creation of the text. Dramatic critics study principles drawn from theater—act, purpose, agent, agency, and scene—to evaluate texts. Finally, fantasy theme critics focus on stories with characters that symbolize cultural moral principles or philosophies. Examples of this type of criticism include Chance's *The Lord of the Rings: The Mythology of Power,* published by Twayne Publishers of New York in 1992.

Each of these critical approaches used to study journalism and media share a common list of textual attributes that can be identified and then described, analysed, and evaluated by a community of readers.

Careful and comparative reading and analysis by knowledgeable critics help to create a richer understanding of the function and value of any single text, and such case studies contribute to the general knowledge in the field.

While some media criticism attempts to measure the influence of the mass media on society, in general, textual analysis attempts to categorize, analyse, and evaluate one particular text. Visual forms such as the inverted pyramid are tools of textual analysis that critics use to classify one piece of writing as a report, another as a story, and still another as an essay. Careless use of these forms contribute to confusion and imprecision in the profession.

Thus, textual analysis is an activity that reporters, editors, publishers, news directors, producers, media critics, and researchers use on a daily basis.

For example, a reporter writes a 25-inch news story on Afghanistan, but how good is it.? How can working journalists evaluate the quality of the texts they receive and create on a daily basis? Textual analysis can help.

Attributes of nonfiction prose, including journalism, can be used to categorize, analyse, and evaluate any news report or feature story.

Many of these textual attributes can be applied to texts of sources, too, but some other specialization, including terminology from a field other than journalism, may be required for such an analysis.

TEXTUAL ANALYSIS OF NEWS WRITING

Evan Mahoney, a reporter for the Fund for Investigative Reporting and a professor at University of North Carolina at Asheville, uses the following terms when teaching, analyzing, and evaluating news writing: abstraction, attribution, connotation, denotation, contrast, lead, nut graph, narration, exposition, form, induction, deduction, tone, voice, mood, style, thesis, quotation, and metaphor.

Consistently careful use of such attributes of language can enrich the experience of reading in addition to simply informing the public. For example, smell and fragrance have the same denotative (literal) meaning, but one has a positive connotative (suggestive) meaning while the other is negative.

A quick reading, without textual analysis, can miss connotations. Exposition is logical explanation, and form is the overall structure of an article.

Induction is reasoning that moves from specific details to a generalization, while deduction moves from a generalization to specifics. Tone and mood refer to word choices that indicate seriousness, humour, glee or depression, to name only a few emotions.

Paying careful attention to these attributes of language can lead to an enriched understanding of a text. Mahoney urged writers to check for these attributes when revising their texts to enrich their writing and make it more engaging.

Diana Fishlock, diversity reporter for the Harrison (Penn.) Patriot-News, considered brainstorming, ambiguity, cliches, character, close-ups (concrete, sensory details), and editorializing when evaluating her own writing and the writing of others.

Brainstorming is a method for analyzing topics or ideas for a news story. It ranges from making simple lists of ideas and ranking them in importance to semantic webbing, in which the writer begins with a key word and diagrammatically connects it to another word, whatever comes to mind, and so on, through lines and circles. New connections are made in this playful act of discovery, and the process helps the writer see new possibilities for the article.

Fishlock explains: Brainstorming often is extremely useful. Brainstorming and simply having time to let a concept percolate in my mind help me to explore more facets of the idea. Is there a historical context? What about religion? Given the time (or brainstorming input from other people) the story becomes much more complete ... Often character makes or breaks a story. If the character is compelling and the writer is able to show that, I'll read about someone doing almost anything-even something I may have no interest in.

Media criticism is growing as a classroom and newsroom practice, so news writers must become more sophisticated about their use of language. Textual analysis is a qualitative method that can be used to create, defend, and improve writing skills. "Making meaning clear does not mean making the copy tedious," Peter Jacobi explained during the Association for Education in Journalism and Mass Communication's Gannett Teaching Fellows Workshop at Indiana University. "Exposition [information delivery] must go beyond a dictionary definition and be as bright and intriguing as narration [story telling]."

TEXTUAL ANALYSIS OF CIVIC JOURNALISM

Reporters conducted textual analysis of community conversations that were conducted with a wide range of citizens in Columbia, Missouri. The project began with University of Missouri School of Journalism Professor Edmund Lambeth who studied and taught civic journalism, a movement debated in research and trade journals throughout the 1990s.

Lambeth established the Civic Journalism Interest Group of the Association for Education in Journalism and Mass Communication and guided the university's Columbia *Missourian* newspaper staff through a civic journalism project that became known as "Faith in Our Community". Lambeth said public journalism could be viewed as a form of journalism that seeks to:

- Listen systematically to the stories and ideas of citizens even while protecting its freedom to choose what to cover.
- Examine alternative ways to frame stories on important community issues.
- Choose frames that stand the best chance to stimulate citizen deliberation and build public understanding of issues.
- Take the initiative to report on major public problems in a way that advances public knowledge of possible solutions and the values served by alternative courses of action.
- Pay continuing and systematic attention to how well and how credibly it is communicating with the public.

To test the effects of one of civic journalism's reporting tools, community conversations, a group of radio, TV, and newspaper journalists worked together to conduct a civic journalism project and publish a series of news stories during the week of May 26, 1996. With the support of their editors and station managers, the group planned a week-long collaborative strategy that included all three media because Lambeth's earlier research indicated that citizens learn more from multimedia presentations.

Missourian Managing Editor George Kennedy said the media managers selected the topic during a discussion session. They settled on religion because it had high relevance to the community and inadequate coverage. He said the goal was to raise the level of public awareness concerning the relationship between religion and public life.

Research began in Fall 1995 when five resource panels were conducted. Each resource panel consisted of about five experts who were knowledgeable in some aspect of religion and public life. Media managers moderated the panels, and the audience consisted of reporters and editors. These panels were used for background information only.

Eight community conversations were planned. These, too, were used only for background information. Participants were told in advance that they would not be quoted in the newspaper or recorded for radio or TV, although minutes of the meetings were recorded and reported to project members. Confidentiality enabled participants to speak more openly and freely, said a reporter who conducted the public policy conversation.

Otherwise, the citizen-participants might have been reluctant to be honest and forthright about controversial issues, he said, adding that the conversations were good for generating sources and story ideas. One reservation was expressed by a reporter who said the time and effort required to organize, conduct, and analyse community conversations could be costly in day-to-day reporting.

The advantage of using them on a collaborative project, he said, was that several reporters could attend and benefit from one community conversation. Throughout the civic journalism project previously described, Lambeth met with graduate journalism students to study and analyse the significance of these practices to working journalists. One of his classes discussed a list of characteristics of civic journalism, which could be used to identify the Language of civic journalism.

These characteristic attributes of civic journalism were identified as coverage of citizen viewpoints, invitations to action in news stories, reporter-reader interaction, identification of personal and social values, identification of consequences associated with the events-issues covered, and identification of the stakeholders involved in the coverage.

This list of attributes complemented the attributes of traditional news stories that researchers have previously identified as characteristics of news: impact, proximity, timeliness, prominence, novelty, and conflict.

Two hypotheses emerged from this exercise:

- Textual analysis of a civic journalism news story should produce attributes significantly different from those of a traditional news story;
- At least most of the attributes of civic journalism identified by Lambeth and his students should be found in civic journalism texts. The original list was modified according to suggestions in a memo from newspaper editor Davis Merritt, one of the founders of the public journalism movement:

The objective isn't to quantify things and make a judgment about whether or how much a newspaper is succeeding, though that might be a small side effect. Rather, the objective is to provide a list of traits that we think constitute public journalism and examples to illustrate those traits—and how they differ from traditional practice —as a step toward a working definition that journalists can understand.

A sample of readers was asked to rate these news criteria from low to high on a 7-point scale after reading several blocks of news coverage that resulted from the civic journalism project titled "Faith in Our Community" and samples of more traditional news coverage from the same period and newspaper.

Some blocks contained traditional news coverage, some civic journalism style reporting, and some were mixed. The following are the textual attributes and their definitions that were rated in this pilot study.

- *Citizen viewpoints*: Citizens are identified as contributors in solving a public issue.
- *Impact*: Many citizens are likely to be significantly affected by this news.
- *Invitations to action*: This news coverage presents ways readers can actively respond.
- *Proximity*: This takes place close to readers' homes.
- *Reporter-reader interaction*: This indicates reporters have communicated with citizens.
- *Timeliness*: This news is based on recent events.
- *Values*: The values (moral—ethical principles) underlying courses of action are explained.
- *Prominence*: This news includes well-known personalities or celebrities.
- *Consequences*: Consequences (the outcome or end results) of actual or possible decisions are explained.
- *Novelty*: This news is based on the odd or unusual.
- *Stakeholders*: Who (individuals or groups) stands to gain and who stands to lose are clearly identified (in the news story).
- *Conflict*: This news emphasizes opposing sides.

A procedure was designed to test two hypotheses about the characteristics of the news coverage.

The researcher wanted to learn:

- Whether readers would identify civic journalism stories,
- Whether readers would rate civic journalism stories differently from traditional news stories.

The readers for this pilot study consisted of 12, specifically selected journalism students who had completed a basic news writing course and were in a media history course. This sample was used because the members possessed a basic knowledge of the elements of journalism.

Each subject was asked to read five to six blocks of news and rate each block, which represented part of a newspaper page and contained some of the "Faith in our Community" project. The block included headlines, teasers, photos, captions, and other news devices. The blocks were rated according to the 12 textual attributes previously listed.

At least two readers rated each block, and scores for each of the criteria were averaged for each copy block. The scores were grouped into a public journalism (PJ) index (statements 1, 3, 5, 7, 9, and 11 previously mentioned) and a traditional journalism (TJ) index (2, 4, 6, 8, 10, and 12). Each block received PJ index and TJ index scores. Scoring on a 7-point scale, the readers gave the public journalism blocks an average of 4.62 for public journalism and only 3.62 for traditional journalism; they gave the traditional journalism blocks a 4.16 for traditional journalism and a 3.67 for public journalism.

The public journalism index score was a full point above the traditional journalism index score for the blocks that contained the public journalism news. This shows that the readers correctly identified which news blocks contained more public journalism language attributes. They had identified public journalism by its textual attributes.

Textual analysis can be useful to reporters, editors, news directors, and researchers, who use it to explain how mass media affect our everyday lives. Mahoney and Fishlock used textual analysis to help strengthen individual journalists' writing skills by offering models to identify, describe, and evaluate vari ous types of news writing. Miller and Dewar used textual analysis of complex government documents to uncover important issues clouded by legalese.

Finally, textual analysis offers benefits through identifying, describing, and evaluating various genres of journalism as shown by the civic journalism project in Missouri. That textual analysis revealed that a purposive sample of journalism students could identify public journalism texts by language attributes.

Manzella frames the civic journalism debate of the 1990s as a battle between the news of record, inverted-pyramid journalists versus the narrative, storytelling journalists. Before deciding which is the one best style tor journalism, media critics, editors, and news writers must carefully identify, describe, and evaluate the various genres of news writing. After seeing valid alternatives, the questions to ask, as Merritt suggested, involve the characteristics of various forms of journalism, and the set of circumstances that call for the use of each form.

The questions that can be addressed through textual analysis are qualitative. As researchers analyse a text, they ask the overarching question, "What are the qualities of this particular text, and how does this text compare and contrast to other texts?" Under this umbrella, they may ask other questions such as, "Can readers distinguish a public journalism text from a traditional journalism text?" or "What's the difference between a story and a report?" or "How does interactivity affect the language of journalism?" Textual analysis takes more time than routine reading, and it may require some computer hardware and software, but it is an effective method for understanding and evaluating news writing, complex documents and journalism genres.

Chapter 6

News Gatherers Versus Broadcasters

A clash of cultures between two generations of TV journalists splits the Washington TV press corps into competing camps. One camp, idealistic and traditional, mourns the passage of an alleged golden age when TV networks covered the globe and the nation with a mobile corps of fact-oriented news gatherers.

They decry the increased influence of the business side of broadcasting in determining the scope of good journalism. Moreover, they are pessimistic over the deterioration of quality reporting and the diminished presence of what they define as hard news on network evening newscasts.

Another side, pragmatic and reconciled to the so-called new realities imposed by competition for audiences, is skilled in the latest arts of video packaging. Persuaded that a new style of evening newscast is needed in the growing competition for television audiences, these professionals pride themselves on what they consider to be their broadcasting abilities as well as their aptitude for spotting and interpreting news trends.

Over and above gathering the news, these practitioners see themselves as able to accentuate the principal theme of a news story in terse prose while projecting the message with warmth and sincerity.

Yet a third force, the marketeers, dominates network headquarters in New York, imposing budget cuts and seeking to make news divisions—once viewed as a public responsibility as well as a necessary concession to Washington regulators—into profit centers in their own right.

Although New York producers have always called the tune on what is reported from Washington, the current crop of absentee editors is judged by some old Washington hands to be especially sensitive to corporate managers in the quest to hold dwindling network audiences, sometimes sacrificing news standards to a combination of straight facts with material calculated to appeal to mass viewers-infotainment.

Different schools of thought on the consequences of this trend are represented by two Washington correspondents who have spent their careers with the same network.

THE TRADITIONALIST REPORTER

There are still twenty or thirty million households looking at network news to find out what is going on. In our own operations at NBC we still put out a sixteen-ounce package but it only contains four ounces of journalism.

The *Nightly News* is a fraud in its present format. You have to spend a little money to get news. If Boeing built airplanes the way we do the news, they would be out of business.

When the viewer is taken out in the country to experience something for himself, something television does superbly, it costs thousands of dollars each time. We used to do seven or eight stories a night. Now we do four. The pictures illustrate stories already decided upon. New York calls and tells them what pictures they want. The reporting function has been dropped for packages masquerading as reporting.

THE PRAGMATIST BROADCASTER

Good producers make good money, in the six figures. I get more because I am a good communicator. Television news has a lot more to do with the presenter than the material being presented. We all have about the same material. The facts and the quotes we work with are about the same. The good communicator will get on the air more. As long as I can do strong journalism and get on the air, I'm happy. If they start breaking my journalistic standards, then I would have to think again. But that's not happening.

There are two realistic facts of life around here: one, the money crunch, and two, some local reporters are nearly as good as network reporters and network pieces are only a little better because they are produced better. Doing a network story is like pulling a lot of string together and presenting it effectively. That's what we are good at. I can go to Little Rock and the local reporter will know more about the story than I do. But I can do it better and faster. That's why they pay me so well.

These two categories tell us more about respective attitudes than about the abilities of those who fall chiefly in one camp or the other. The traditionalist reporters are also fully capable of cutting tape when a real need arises; the communicators have usually done their stint in digging for hard news in a hurry. The difference is the seriousness with which present-day Washington correspondents view the accommodations made by the evening news programs for which they work to what is construed as the demands of a changing marketplace.

Morale in the Washington bureaus of all three major networks is generally poor. People are scared of losing their jobs and fearful of the future of network television news in both its past and its present incarnations. The average Washington TV correspondent and producer are not sure what is in store for the kind of work they now perform or whether they would enjoy prospective alternatives.

Some of this anxiety is the result of what is regarded as corporate insensitivity in cutting budgets and downsizing the staff. Some results from a surprising level of hostility from the Washington corps toward the news values and practices of the executive producers in New York, particularly at NBC and CBS—matched by New York's suspicion that Washington staff has an inflated idea of its own importance.

There has also been a swing away from evening news programs as the chief revenue-producers for network news divisions and an increasing emphasis on prime-time newsmagazine programs, which are cheaper to produce than standard entertainment fare. More attuned to supposed popular tastes than to coverage of hard news, these long-form programs are less interested in daily news out of Washington and as a rule recruit their talent from sources other than network correspondents. When they do employ network correspondents, they look for storytellers, that is, reporters who tell the news best in terms of its attention-grabbing dimensions.

ABC has been the last of the three major networks to take serious hits in its Washington bureau, where the staff's feelings of pride in being "number one in news" have been dampened by personnel cuts. These include the unexpected transfer to New York in 1993 of most of the Washington producers working for 20/20, the successful prime-time magazine programme, and the virtual elimination of the Washington staff of Good Morning America. The network was surprised by the number of employees in Washington who chose an offer of buy-outs during the 1992-93 season rather than risk their prospects over the long term.

Critical to the clash between professional journalistic standards and marketing forces seeking to shape network news programs is the fact that the Federal Communications Commission--charged with overseeing broadcasters to protect the "public interest, convenience and necessity"--no longer exercises much influence, direct or indirect, on the networks' obligation to supply news and public-affairs information to justify their commercial use of public air waves.

In the years since the deregulation of broadcasting, which began under President Carter and accelerated during the Reagan-Bush era, the FCC has rarely served as a bully pulpit to alert the public to the chief transgressions of commercial broadcasting. There has been less insistence on a record of adequate coverage of public affairs when station licenses come up for renewal. Since FCC commissioners can serve out individual and staggered fixed terms, it will take the Clinton administration, if it is so disposed, some time to affect FCC policies.

It took ten months in office for the administration to name a new FCC chairman, Reed C. Hundt, a Washington lawyer. Preliminary indications were that it was not likely that the FCC would concentrate on promoting better coverage of public affairs so much as it would try to decide between competing interests seeking to exploit the capabilities of new technology in bringing expanded forms of information to every American home.

Time was when news departments were viewed by the networks as a necessary gesture to justify the large profits reaped by local TV stations and themselves. The talk now is how the FCC can help preserve "free TV" against the competitive assault of cable television and liberate the networks from restrictions on producing and syndicating the entertainment shows that they had heretofore been required to buy from independent producers.

Some Washington broadcast correspondents feel that their access to government information has been deteriorating at the same time that the executives in charge of network news shows at broadcast centers in New York have been less interested in, if not actually hostile toward stories from the capital. Although the arrival of the Clinton Administration provoked a spate of new interest from New York toward Washington, the suspicion is that there was less a renewed interest in substance than in reflecting a perhaps temporary fascination in the viewer marketplace for a fresh face at the White House. Indeed, the ups and downs of Clinton's first days in office made for the kind of political journalism that television likes best.

Unfortunately, the temporarily reawakened interest in Washington news coincided with a reduced ability, thanks to network downsizing, to cover the daily flow of news. The ranks of general assignment reporters have been thinned. Beats such as the environment and individual federal agencies have been eliminated. Supreme Court and State Department coverage has been downgraded. The number of correspondents covering Congress has been sharply reduced. The emphasis on "productivity"--the number of on-air appearances logged by individual reporters, especially on the evening news programs--has discouraged reporters from digging deeper into the stories behind government handouts.

The cutbacks in domestic and foreign bureaus make it more difficult for Washington-based correspondents to broaden the perspective of their findings. Although great lip service is paid to the idea of getting beyond the Beltway to cover issues raised in Congress and government agencies, the fact is that to reduce costs many of these stories consist of interpretive sound tracks by Washington correspondents over videotapes shot for local network affiliates.

These are some of the conclusions I reached after about seventy-five one-onone interviews with Washington correspondents and producers who work for the three major TV networks. Many are former students at the Graduate School of Journalism at Columbia University, where I taught for twenty-seven years. I conducted these interviews originally as a Guest Scholar at the Media Studies Project of the Woodrow Wilson International Centre for Scholars in 1991-92, and followed up with more interviews after the inauguration of President Clinton in 1993.

In the course of this research I also visited the newsrooms of all three network bureaus, observing the daily assignment and selection of Washington stories to be carried on the network evening news. I interviewed bureau executives at ABC and CBS. (NBC was less cooperative.) I personally observed the activities of the broadcast press corps as well as interviewing them individually at the White House, the Congressional press galleries, the Pentagon, and the State Department.

In that process I attended a number of press conferences held by the president, cabinet officers, and members of Congress, as well as press briefings by government public affairs staff. I also monitored the evening network newscasts on a daily basis in order to match their coverage against the day's events in Washington. In gathering interviews I made use of a structured questionnaire to enhance comparability of data.

The impressions gained during these firsthand experiences are the basis of this book. I found at the outset that the only practical way to gather testimony from these sources was on a not-for-attribution basis. Under present corporate management of the networks, there have been severe penalties imposed on those journalists perceived by management not to be team players.

The participants for this study were in some cases torn by two pulls:

- Real anxiety if they should be identified as the source of comments critical of the present state of their network (some network contracts specifically forbid such criticism in public),
- A passionate desire to get the word out concerning their professional misgivings over the trends in the network news.

Verbatim quotes gathered in this survey are included in this book; an entire section is based on testimony from correspondents and producers on major Washington beats: the White House, Congress, the Pentagon, the State Department, the Supreme Court, and General Assignment. Such verbatim quotes are indented; indicates a new person is speaking, and they are based on notes taken by me, not on tape recordings. I have altered interviews only to mask identities.

In essence, the pages that follow are an inside view of what is happening to the coverage of Washington by the evening news programs on the three major networks. The correspondents and producers tell the story in their own words. It is an important story because television is the principal vehicle by which political and social values are transmitted to a national audience. Those who watch the evening news on ABC, CBS, and NBC--variously estimated at from thirty-five to forty million viewers daily--say they consider television a prime source of their information about the nation and the world.

Television news sets the agenda for the national discussion of issues and is a crucial component in the determination of popular attitudes toward politics. Studies have shown, for example, that voters are as interested in what they think is happening to the national economy as they are sensitive to their own pocketbooks. They are likely to form these impressions from what they see and hear on the evening news broadcasts.

News from Washington is obviously essential to an understanding of the political process in a self-governing democracy. Anything that weakens or dilutes the ability of the press to act as a watchdog of what is going on at the seat of our national government affects us all. The First Amendment--"Congress shall make no law... abridging the freedom of speech or of the press" --is historical evidence that the Founding Fathers gave the highest priority to the press in its role of keeping a critical eye on government, rather than just being a conduit for statements from those in power.

Washington is not only the seat of government for the United States but an important player on the world stage. In the federal system of government, Washington has become the principal power. Policies made in Washington in such spheres as commercial trade, nuclear technology, agriculture, banking, and finance have repercussions all over the globe. Of all the localities formerly and presently served by network news bureaus, Washington is the busiest news centre.

Wire services and daily newspapers that maintain Washington bureaus find enough of importance going on to file numerous news stories every day. Yet television, which a majority of Americans say is their principal source of news, sometimes bypasses Washington completely on the network evening news programs. The downsizing of television reportage from the nation's capital thus has serious consequences on the state of public information in a self-governing democracy.

THE CONTEXT

The present state of network news must be considered in the context of several different factors:

- All three networks were taken over by new corporate

managements, dependent upon public shareholders, in 1986. Rumors that General Electric, which bought NBC, is looking for another buyer have persisted, although GE management has continually sought to reassure the NBC staff.

- These takeovers coincided with a continuing drop in the network share of TV audiences from a once near-monopoly of over 90 per cent to barely more than 60 per cent, a result of competition from cable, home video, and independent stations.
- Network advertising revenues have been decreasing as audiences have shrunk, a problem compounded by economic downturn and the diversion of advertising revenue to cable and other forms of promotion, such as direct mail.
- The share of the television audience reached by the three network news programs fell 10 per cent in the decade between 1980 and 1990. After an uptick for the 1992 presidential election, viewership for the evening news dropped 10 per cent in 1993. More alarmingly for market researchers, the falloff was particularly steep among the eighteen- to thirty-five-year-old viewers so dear to the heart of advertisers.
- The large costs of network news divisions—$200 to $300 million a year-have been seen as less necessary to hold federal regulators at bay and are thus more vulnerable to cutbacks by corporate managers less committed to the news as a public service. Out-of-the-ordinary stories that demand coverage are often very expensive. For example, an estimated $150 million was spent by the three major networks reporting the Gulf War, and the cost of covering the Anita Hill-Clarence Thomas hearings came to an estimated $15-$20 million when preemptions of sponsored programming were figured in. Such big-figure stories have increased the pressure to cut down on day-to-day news costs.
- Extravagances in the news divisions during the

heyday of network profits in the seventies made the departments an easier target for bean counters when the lush times ended. Now that news divisions have been severely downsized and prime-time magazine shows have turned out to be profit centers, the bottom line is looking better. In 1993 the news divisions at all three major networks claimed to be running in the black. In Washington the dismissal of correspondents appeared to have bottomed out temporarily at NBC and CBS—the first to suffer severe staff reductions-but downsizing was taking a belated toll at AB C. And the trend seemed to be away from network evening news as we have known it.

- The expansion of local news broadcasts, with the technological capacity to go anywhere the networks also choose to cover, and, since 1980, the rise of CNN as a twenty-four-hour national and international headline news service have led to a reexamination of network news and all its premises.
- The restructuring of family patterns, with many women working outside the home, has disrupted the tradition of watching the evening news at suppertime. Many people now catch news on the fly.
- There is more network-described news on the air than ever — all three networks have late-night and early-morning newscasts, network morning shows all contain news segments and have expanded to the weekend, prime-time newsmagazines have proliferated to every night of the week, CNN provides round-the-clock coverage, and syndicated so-called reality programs have multiplied. But this increase in quantity has been accompanied by a decrease in the quality of serious news gathering for television.
- Not only traditional network news programs but the future of the networks themselves is in a precarious state as we advance toward the twenty-first century.

> The new Information Age is already upon us. The proliferation of the number of channels available on cable, the imminence of information brought directly into the home, the multiplicity of events that can be sold over pay-TV—all these threaten the survival of the major broadcast networks as they have existed. The downsizing of comprehensive network news is one response to the challenge of reining in costs that were more affordable during more profitable times. If there is no network, there will be no network news.

All these factors have made an impact on the network news divisions at a time when Washington by any definition is a critical player in global and domestic affairs. The realignment of power caused by the collapse of Communist regimes in the Soviet Union and Eastern Europe has made the White House and State Department the power centre of what former President George Bush and others have described as a new world order.

The president and Congress are confronted with the painful dilemma of trying to balance acute needs in the spheres of health, education, and urban poverty against an unprecedented national deficit. The Supreme Court, dominated by conservative justices, has embarked on a new course of judicial interpretations in such areas as the criminal justice system, affirmative action, and human rights.

After twelve years of gridlock between Republican presidents and a Democratic Congress, a new Democratic chief executive is dealing with a majority on Capitol Hill of his own political party, although his agenda could still be thwarted by conservative members of his party and a determined Republican minority in the Senate. Should Washington be de-emphasized as a source of TV news at such a defining moment in the nation's history?

Back in the early days of television news—dating back to the fifties and continuing through the dominant years of the sixties and seventies—sometimes as many as seven out of nine items on the *CBS Evening News* came from Washington. Washington was on a handy line that came into

New York directly. Film from abroad and across the United States had to be flown in, and the broadcast relied on wire bulletins without pictures.

Walter Cronkite, who took over as CBS anchor on April 16, 1962, was a former reporter for United Press who made a name for himself covering the first national political conventions available to a wide audience on television. He liked hard news, and especially news from Washington. Charles Kuralt with leisurely reports from "On the Road" or commentaries by Eric Sevareid fleshed out the time. Washington news was comparatively cheap and convenient.

In the Eisenhower era, news from the rest of the country was relatively calm. Also, the importance attached to the goodwill of Congress and the regulators at the FCC made the networks anxious to show off their concern for public affairs. The Washington bureau, under these circumstances, was very cost effective, and Washington correspondents became familiar faces to the captive audience watching network TV news.

CBS and NBC expanded their evening news broadcasts from fifteen minutes to half an hour in September 1963. ABC, which was rated far behind the other two networks, followed suit in 1967. The inauguration of President John Kennedy and the crush of reform legislation under his successor, Lyndon Johnson, continued to make Washington a central source for the evening news. The increased role of the U.S. military in Vietnam in 1964 became a domestic political issue as vivid scenes from the battlefield were produced nightly on the news, but the film from the battlefront still had to be flown to New York.

The introduction of electronic cameras, microwaves, and satellite transmission in the 1980s transformed broadcast journalism. Stories from all over the world could appear on the evening news on the same day they happened. Some thought Washington was still being covered too much at two or three items a broadcast. Among the decision-makers in New York there was a feeling in their bones that the American people were tired of Washington—long before the flood of

Washington scandals and the appearance of Ross Perot on the political scene. As one former network executive producer recalls:

When I would travel around the country, I always got the " Washington is a joke" speech from local news directors. These people believe that Washington is an irrelevant rat-hole where Americans send their money with no results. The credo of local news is that people don't give a damn about government—federal, state, or local—in any form. That Washington news is a fascination of the Eastern elite who are prisoners of the values along the Washington-New York corridor.

Today, those who came up from local news are in the ascendancy in New York at CBS and NBC. ABC is owned by a company that got its start in local radio and TV.

When the evening news shows enjoyed a virtual monopoly of the television audience, they could afford to be cavalier about sharing the product of network correspondents with newscasts on local stations. The best stories of the day would be held back for exclusive use on the evening news programs. All that changed when transmission by satellite enabled independent broadcast services to market reports to local stations no longer totally dependent on network news sources. Networks now had to compete with their own local affiliates.

CNN, although enjoying a limited audience on cable compared with overthe-air stations, could also sell its news output to regular local news programs. Furthermore, local stations using modern technology were able to send their own reporters to cover national and foreign stories for which they had formerly depended on the networks. In the quickly changing marketplace for news, network shows had to contend with the fact that they could no longer be simply a headline service about stories that the audience might have already seen and heard from other sources.

The popularity of network evening news shows is a subtle thing to analyse, but it is generally conceded to be as much a reflection of audience tastes in anchors as the content of the broadcast. The network evening news is presented as a highly personal experience between the audience and the human dispenser of the latest newsworthy events. Anchors are supposed to be both authoritative and likable as well as skilled at ad libbing their way through unexpected crises in the flow of the broadcast or world events.

The huge salaries, running into the millions, paid to network TV anchors indicate how vital the management thinks these personalities are to the success of the broadcast. Success, however, is measured not only by the number of viewers watching the programme but also by the demographic breakdown of the audience. Walter Cronkite, for example, appealed to older people, a set of less interest to advertisers than younger age groups. Dan Rather attracts women viewers, according to market researchers, but is said to be not as well liked by men. Peter Jennings and *World News Tonight* not only have managed to pin the largest audience, but also the greatest number of young and affluent consumers.

Working correspondents are often critical of the network anchors, who influence which news items are picked every day as well dominate the limelight. In Washington, staffers point out that at least a half-dozen correspondents could be fielded if these eight-hundred-pound gorillas gave up only $1 million of their annual take.

Chet Huntley and David Brinkley, who shared a relaxed partnership on NBC during the fifties and sixties, dominated the network news audience until just before their partnership ended in 1970. Huntley occupied the anchor desk in New York and Brinkley broadcast from Washington. They consistently ran ahead of CBS until the *CBS Evening News* with Walter Cronkite finally forged ahead of NBC in the late sixties.

Graying and looking more and more avuncular, Cronkite was voted annually in the polls as the "most trusted" man in America, until CBS hastened his retirement in 1981. His replacement was Dan Rather, a Texan who had attracted national attention as the CBS reporter on the spot when President John F. Kennedy was assassinated in Dallas. Rather subsequently covered the White House under presidents

Johnson and Nixon. His main rival for the anchor position, Roger Mudd, had also been a Washington correspondent.

The *CBS Evening News* with Dan Rather remained on top for 213 straight weeks from 1981 to 1985. Rather's rating advantage began to slip in 1987 in the competition against NBC's *Nightly News* with Tom Brokaw.

Also a former White House correspondent, Brokaw had previously anchored the morning *Today* show. By December of 1989, however, ABC's *World News Tonight* with Peter Jennings had overtaken them both, and won 185 of the next 188 weeks. ABC stayed in first place through the 1990-91, 1991-92, and 1992-93 television seasons and remained there at the start of the 1993-94 season.

Peter Jennings became the solo anchor of ABC's *World News Tonight* on July 4, 1982. Before appointing Jennings, however, News President Roone Arledge had experimented with the idea of multiple anchors. Barbara Walters, hired from NBC, and Harry Reasoner, lured from CBS, were ABC's first co-anchors. So bad was the chemistry between the pair, however, that viewers were also turned off. ABC thereupon tried out a three-person anchor system: Frank Reynolds in Washington, Max Robinson in Chicago, and Peter Jennings, a Canadian who had been a Middle Eastern correspondent, in London.

The experiment helped the ABC news division become a respectable alternative to the other two networks, but ABC remained in third place in the ratings. Among other problems, a multiplicity of anchorman appearances left that much less time for reporting the news. Arledge's idea was that an anchorman should be something beyond a mere reader of the script from the studio, but capable of reporting out there on his own. He was perhaps ahead of his time, as indicated by the recent tendency to put the network anchormen on the scene for such stories as the 1993 Tokyo economic summit and the Mississippi River Basin floods.

NBC, when it continued to lag behind CBS, in the mid-eighties tried to combine Roger Mudd (who had been hired by NBC when he was passed over by CBS in favour of Dan

Rather) in Washington with Tom Brokaw in New York. That didn't work either.

Jennings' appeal has been credited to the impression he gives of having a conversation with the audience, whereas Brokaw and Rather are said to merely announce the news. One CBS correspondent described Rather as "like watching someone have a nervous breakdown in front of your eyes." Many viewers said they were turned off by Rather's lack of ease at the anchor desk, combined with his aggressiveness in interviewing prominent Republican officeholders such as Richard Nixon and George Bush.

Stuck in the ratings race, CBS announced that beginning in June 1993, Connie Chung would share the *Evening News* desk with Rather. Chung, a veteran of anchoring local news in Los Angeles before moving first to NBC and then CBS, enjoyed an exceptionally high "Q rating," which is market research's way of measuring likability among the TV audience. Her reporting credentials, however, were not universally admired. Ed Siegel, TV critic for the *Boston Globe,* wrote: "Appointing Connie Chung to co-anchor" the *CBS Evening News* "is like appointing Judge Wapner (of the TV show The People's Court) to the Supreme Court."

Presumably Chung would provide the likability and Rather the authority. The theory was that she might help to expand the audience for the *CBS Evening News* and then possibly in the long run, after establishing her own authoritative credentials, take over alone. (At the close of the first broadcast by the new pair, Chung turned to Rather and said, "Good night, Chet." Rather replied, "Good night, David." The coy exchange, of course, replicated the famous sign-off on NBC's Huntley-Brinkley evening news, which had been off the air nearly a quarter of a century.)

The *CBS Evening News,* which had fallen into third place the previous week, got a temporary surge of 13 per cent in the ratings for the week in which Rather and Chung premiered as co-anchors. Undoubtedly, the publicity over the new pairing had stimulated sampling by curious viewers. The show had experienced a similar surge from samplers who had been following the 1991 Winter Olympics, but the ratings soon went back down.

Chung and Rather actually fell into third place during the summer of 1993, with an 11 per cent drop in CBS ratings from the period a year earlier against a rise for both ABC's *World News Tonight* and NBC's *Nightly News.* As the 1993-94 television season got underway, NBC and CBS were locked in a tie for second place, still behind ABC, although the gap was narrowing.

The system of male-female pairing at the anchor desk—commonplace in local TV news—already included Barbara Walters and Hugh Downs on ABC's highly successful 20/20, Jane Pauley and Stone Phillips on *Dateline NBC,* and Sam Donaldson and Diane Sawyer on ABC's *Prime Time Live.* (Sawyer took over the anchor desk in New York and Donaldson broadcast from Washington after early trouble with finding a formula for the programme.

Donaldson was never happy with the arrangement.) Tom Brokaw and Katie Couric were picked to anchor the magazine news-programme, Now, which was launched in the summer of 1993 under NBC's president, Andrew Lack, as one of his first acts after taking office. In all these shows, the stars do little reporting themselves for the segments they front.

The rising gender-consciousness in the land was having its effect on network news offerings. As news ratings stagnated, the Rather-Chung arrangement was another sign that network news divisions felt compelled to try something different if they hoped to survive until the end of this century, never mind into the next.

The strength of local news-programs on local affiliates and popular lead-ins (such as the syndicated talk show hosted by Oprah Winfrey, which appears on more local affiliates of ABC than those of the other networks) also influences the size of the audience for the evening news on each network.

Local stations sometimes use contests with cash prizes to lure viewers to tune in their newscasts, and these hyped ratings feed into the network news audience. Peter Jennings moved from 7 P.M., eastern standard time, to 6:30 in several markets to avoid competing with the popular game show Wheel of Fortune. The evening news, in turn, is traditionally considered pivotal in establishing audience flow into network entertainment programs in prime time. CBS enlisted help for Rather just as it was achieving first place in yearly ratings for prime-time programming.

Stephen Hess, a researcher at the Brookings Institution, polled White House correspondents in 1991, both print and broadcast, and learned that 75 per cent preferred to watch Peter Jennings. When I asked Hess what he thought was the reason, he replied that *World News Tonight* was a harder newscast than the others and that perhaps Washington journalists found Jennings' cosmopolitan air more congenial. The next day Hess called again. Perhaps he should add, he said, that Jennings broadcast at 6:30 P.M. on Washington's local ABC outlet, whereas the other two split the audience at 7:00, the earlier time also being more useful for correspondents making deadlines on stories filed back to the home office of daily newspapers. I asked a prominent contributor to the editorial page of the *Washington Post* what he watched and he replied, "Tom Brokaw." He was a Washington Redskins football fan, he explained, and preferred the sportscaster on the local news at Channel 4, the NBC-owned-and-operated station. So that is where his set was tuned at 7:00, when it was time for the *NBC Nightly News* with Tom Brokaw.

Anchors also branch out on their own to appear on network prime-time news specials. Peter Jennings has done a series on the drug problem in America. Dan Rather uses 48 Hours as a vehicle for special reports, such as coverage of Hurricane Andrew and President Clinton's health care plan. Tom Brokaw did a series of prime-time specials, including A Day at the White House, which reported on everything from the morning presidential jog to policy discussions in the Oval Office. NBC used ten camera crews and sixty people to mount the show, a major investment. Such specials, which are not unlike the print magazines that concentrate on a single topic, may indicate where network news resources are headed.

Although difference in ratings among the evening news programs is relatively small, being number one among the evening newscasts has had a strong psychological effect on ABC's Washington staff as well as a positive influence on the news division's balance sheet. Moreover, thanks to its strong lineup of other news division programs, ABC can claim that more Americans get their news from ABC than any other source.

THE NEW BROADCAST

In the competition to survive, network news has been forced to rethink what it has to offer that rival services, such as cable and local news, do not. The quality and expertise of network news correspondents is one such asset. When documentaries were still allocated exposure on prime time, correspondents could take advantage of the opportunity to show their stuff. Nowadays, the insertion of longer forms of reportage within the daily summary of the news is a way in which to convince viewers to prefer the offerings of one network over that of the other two.

These days, long form survives on the evening news in the truncated version of four-minute segments, which are usually incorporated in the broadcast in between the spot news of the day. Despite all the angst expressed by Washington correspondents, the items reported on any one of the three network evening news programs do not seem that different to the casual viewer—nor do the respective abilities of the competing correspondent corps.

Van Gordon Sauter, president of Fox News and former president of CBS News, deplored this sameness in the November 1992 issue of *Communicator*, published by the Radio Television News Directors Association: "There is an inhibiting, discouraging sameness to TV news. The journalism schools, consultants, researchers, timid corporate executives, and narrowly targeted audiences have had the impact of reducing TV news to a spongy blur existing in a narrow framework of creativity.... It is as though each city out there had three or five or seven newspapers, and each had the same format, the same target audience, the same editorial attitude, the same photographs."

His boss, Fox chairman Rupert Murdoch, agreed, including local news in the indictment: "I honestly cannot distinguish one programme from another. It's like every news director in the marketplace graduates from the same dumb journalism class." Sauter's attempts to enliven CBS News had included a sharp reduction in the number of stories originating in Washington and a formula that defined story values in terms of "moments" that could capture the audience.

There is, however, no evidence that the audience was enlarged during Sauter's watch. Moreover, his actions generated considerable unhappiness in the ranks of veteran CBS correspondents who had inherited their news-gath ering ideas from Edward R. Murrow, the pioneering newsman who had hired most of the individuals who became the nucleus of the CBS correspondent corps, first in radio and then in television.

The fact remains that it is fairly predictable that the evening news programs on ABC, CBS, and NBC will each have the same lineup of the day's major developments. They do not even look that different, with computer-driven graphics illustrating the spots introduced by an anchor sitting at a desk. Except for the personalities of their anchors, the main points of difference between these shows are subtleties: the relative competence of reporters covering the same story, the balance of features versus hard news in the coverage of secondary events, and the order in which these events are presented to viewers.

When John Chancellor retired as an editorialist on NBC's *Nightly News* in 1993, it marked the end of an eleven-year tradition on that broadcast, the only one of the three shows to sustain such a feature into recent years. CBS had long since abandoned a similar heritage developed by Eric Sevareid and Bill Moyers.

The changes occurring in evening newscasts coincide with similar changes taking place in magazines and newspapers. Evening newspapers are disappearing from the scene, newspaper circulations have ceased to grow, and weekly newsmagazines such as *Time* and *U.S. News* and *World Report* have recently undergone design changes in the way they present information.

Television is at its best when communicating live images of graphic events-floods along the Mississippi, "ethnic cleansing" in Bosnia, war and famine in Somalia, fires and looting in Los Angeles, hurricanes in Florida, a student uprising in Tiananmen Square, tearing down the Berlin Wall.

Even Washington sometimes provides such opportunities for dramatic, direct coverage, such as the Army-McCarthy hearings, President John E Kennedy's funeral, and the Anita Hill-Clarence Thomas confrontation during the Senate hearings on the latter's nomination to the Supreme Court. But news of this dramatic dimension does not happen every day, and the day-to-day flow of the news from Washington does not usually fit the limited capacities of TV to communicate complex ideas.

It is the job of the network correspondent on the evening news to explain with a very broad brush stroke what has happened in Washington that day, to put what pictures and sound bites are available into intelligible focus, to help the viewer understand what he or she is seeing and hearing when events themselves do not carry their own message.

Moreover, this has to be done in a very short period of time allocated to the spot on the total broadcast, which itself is of very limited duration. The job of the network Washington correspondent is thus both challenging and frustrating.

When the news is exciting and graphic, audiences no longer have to wait until the dinner hour for their first glimpse of daily dramas, which can be seen earlier on CNN or local newscasts.

Having lost their monopoly, the nightly network news programs thus would have needed to change whether or not there had been a turnover of network ownership or new executive producers in New York. Takeouts on important running topics in the news are one way to add a valuable dimension to the evening news.

One consequence, however, has been that there are fewer minutes available on the broadcast for hard news out of Washington.

Although some Washington correspondents carry out these longer features, such stories generally call for different talents than those possessed by "crash" reporters who scramble to make deadlines on breaking news. And correspondents who work on these longer features have less and less time to cover the general run of Washington news.

The dilemma created by these in-depth segments, now a regular feature of network evening news, is that on the one hand, they provide an opportunity for network correspondents to make use of their expertise on significant areas of the news, such as science, health, and education, but on the other hand, they decrease the resources available for coverage of the daily flow of news.

The model for these longer takeouts is "American Agenda;" the concept developed by Paul Friedman, then executive producer of ABC's *World News Tonight* with Peter Jennings. The idea for doing longer pieces has been around for a long time. Friedman himself had worked on features called "Segment 3" on NBC's *Nightly News* before joining ABC. CBS called them enterprise stories in the sixties, before abandoning them for the time being. But the execution of Friedman's "American Agenda" has accompanied the ascent of *World News Tonight* into the number-one slot in the ratings of network evening news programs.

CBS's *Evening News* with Dan Rather calls its current version of the long form "Eye on America." NBC's original longer segment, "Daily Difference," on the *Nightly News* with Tom Brokaw—after a period in which it had difficulty defining what its label meant—was renamed "America CloseUp" in imitation of its two network rivals. The general consensus was that NBC's special segments under former executive producer Steve Friedman had tended to feature a softer approach to the news. An old hand from another network thought that this had turned out to be the wrong approach at the wrong time:

When Steve Friedman introduced the "Daily Difference" on *NBC Nightly News* it was a period of international upheaval, overwhelming stories, real tough issues. "Daily Difference" was built around categories labeled by producers with no thought of what, if anything, they might mean to viewers. These special segments have become a code word for the pictorial and frothy items. Education, employment, race-these are the grist of what these longer pieces ought to be about. Done correctly, longer stories on the evening newscast can contribute a lot. But Friedman chose the soft route and NBC is slipping. There was no reason to stay tuned.

Under executive producer Erik Sorenson, the *CBS Evening News* has a tendency toward "user friendly" pieces, such as the best way to buy a used car or how to plan for your retirement. "Eye on America" is supposed to tell the audience what other people are talking about across the country.

ABC's "American Agenda" is more focused, according to two ABC producers: When "American Agenda" started, the ABC evening news was in a rut. There was weakness in the body of the show.

It was foreign-news heavy. Jennings was perceived as a foreigner. He couldn't pronounce "Ohio" the way people from there pronounce it. We wanted to make our coverage of domestic news credible.

So they created these special beats: family, health, education, environment, drugs. Correspondents and producers were assigned full time to each other.

"American Agenda" pieces by definition are supposed to offer a solution to the problem being covered. If not a solution, a point of view. It's easier to make a connection with an audience that way. "Eye on America" doesn't do that. NBC's longer pieces are really more feature-ish than the other two. "American Agenda" is a harder version of special segments. It takes a major commitment of resources to do that. When Jeff Gralnick came over from ABC to become executive producer for NBC's *Nightly News* in the spring of 1993, one of the things he brought with him was the thinking behind "American Agenda." "America CloseUp" almost immediately focused on stories that outlined not only a problem in the news but also a possible solution, one of the guidelines for "American Agenda" pieces on ABC. (Fads have a way of chasing each other on television programming.) Of course, all problems do not have solutions readily at hand, and such segments run the risk of claiming too much for a single local example of an attempt to cope with issues that are national in scope. By coincidence, just as Gralnick was bringing the formula to NBC, Emily Rooney, the new executive producer for ABC's *World News Tonight,* was telling staffers there that the problem-solution approach to "America Agenda" was a hackneyed idea in her opinion, and she proposed abandoning it.

The willingness of ABC to make a major commitment to new ideas is documented by its patience in staying with *Prime Time Live,* with Diane Sawyer and Sam Donaldson, after a rocky start. NBC, by contrast, went through seventeen short-lived magazine shows before its entry *Dateline NBC* went on the air in 1992 with a promise from management to give it time to develop an audience.

The differing approaches of the three major networks to dealing with the crisis involving the future of the evening news have perhaps been influenced by a difference in the commitment of top management to the business of broadcasting over the long term. NBC has been recurrently rumored to be on the auction block.

CBS President Laurence Tisch has been selling off CBS subsidiaries and has supposedly been waiting for the most propitious time to sell his CBS stock holdings. Capital Cities/ ABC alone among the three seems to be positioning itself for the future. It has acquired a sports cable network, ESPN, and a share of Arts & Entertainment, another cable programming service. Most interesting, it regards its whole news output as the basis for future expansion.

ABC's "American Agenda" pieces on *World News Tonight,* although subject to some changes in format, are often announced a night in advance. A regular feature of the Friday broadcast is the "Person of the Week," which attempts to provide an upbeat alternative to the sometimes negative flavour of the run of broadcast news. "American Agenda" has been part of a studied effort to keep audiences tuning in just to watch *Work News Tonight*. In the words of one ABC producer: The ABC philosophy on news is called "appointment viewing." "American Agenda" provides the opportunity to promote a piece in advance so viewers will feel they have an appointment to see it. The future is going to be newsmagazine shows in prime time that the viewers will also have an appointment to see. Especially the key demographic groups, such as women aged nineteen to thirty-nine whom advertisers love. It's no accident that "American Agenda" concentrates on family, education, health—things that particularly appeal to women.

Steve Weiswasser [then executive vice-president of ABC News] said in a recent meeting that we are producers of programs, not just newsgatherers. We have got to learn to package and repackage what we do.

World News Now, the 2 A.M. broadcast, is an example. Weiswasser talked about creating a cable component of all-night news, so that if you missed it, you can still see it. The same with Nightline and "American Agenda." These are programs with a shelf life, unlike spot news.

ABC owns rights forever to its news products, unlike the first-run-only rights to entertainment shows. A network possesses a library of raw tape. Weiswasser pointed out that Capital Cities/ABC includes a publishing division. Perhaps we can produce something like a printed guide to go along with in-school video.

The emphasis of the new regimes in New York on all three networks is on an evening news broadcast that can hope to attract audiences already beset by viewing options, ranging from local news programs, to cable services such as CNN and C-SPAN, to a host of syndicated shows—such as *Entertainment Tonight, A Current Affair*, and *Hard Copy*—that fuzz the distinction between entertainment and news. Can the audience tell the difference? Does it care as much as professional journalists?

Reporters know from experience that newspaper readers often blame the fact gatherer for opinions expressed on the editorial page; the distinction between news and editorial pages, so frequently cited by journalism professionals, is lost on many in the general audience. Similarly, some tabloid "reality" programs sold by syndicators to local stations are viewed by the audience in the same continuum as adjacent news programs, both local and network. Not all viewers are that sensitive as to when one leaves off and the other begins. In the passive environment of television-watching, TV news is sometimes lumped together as an indiscriminate whole. Indeed, the important distinctions between responsible journalism and trash are more difficult to recognize in this most invasive of mass media.

Chapter 7

News Gathering

State political reporter at *The Age*, Richard Baker, was enjoying a drink at the pub one evening when an "older bloke" told him a yarn about the seals in Port Phillip Bay. It seemed the state government had built an expensive covered platform out in the bay for the seals to loll about on. But the seals were unimpressed. They were snubbing the new platform and refusing to budge from an antiquated, tumbledown structure nearby.

The story had several fine elements for a news piece; among them, government extravagance and appealing marine mammals. After a few calls to check it out, and the dispatch of a photographer to provide a visual showing the old and new platforms, with the seals firmly ensconced on the old one, Richard had a front page story.

The next day it was covered widely by radio and television and had become one of Victoria's more memorable human interest stories of the year.

Journalists call the process of finding and developing an original item "breaking a story" and for most reporters it's what journalism is all about. Richard describes breaking news as "the most fun part of the job". It means "doing something no one else is doing and going home at night knowing that tomorrow it is going to be all over the radio and TV and at this stage you're the only person who knows about it". (Interview with Richard Baker.)

This section is about finding and developing news stories, both those initiated by reporters themselves and those assigned by the news desk.

The news day: Every day in every newsroom begins with a series of story possibilities. During the day some of these will become items for publication or broadcast. Extra stories will emerge while some of the original ones will fall out of consideration. The way in which each day's news agenda is developed is complex and, like so many other features of the industry, varies from one medium and one newsroom to the next.For instance, in a large metropolitan newsroom, most of the day's news will fall into one of four categories:

- First, there will be the predicted events, which are known about in advance and filed in the newsroom's diary. These can include sittings of parliament, council meetings and court hearings, media conferences, the release of official reports, scheduled meetings or negotiations, all sports events, the release of official statistics, regular financial decisions and events, openings, previews and pre-arranged interviews.
- *Then there are watching briefs*: These are the monitoring activities that generate news, including the calls to the emergency services, monitoring other media, stake-outs (at a scene where a newsmaker might appear) and running stories (where new developments are expected in an existing story or where the story can be developed by journalists finding new angles).
- *There are unpredicted events*: These include accidents, fires, natural disasters, attacks; things no one suspected in advance would happen.
- Finally there are stories which might be termed initiated stories. Like the example at the start of this section, they fall outside the routine news cycle and begin with a reporter's observation or a tip-off from a member of the public.

Non-metropolitan newsrooms, and those that don't have a daily output, including suburban papers, metro weeklies and so on, are likely to have a different pattern of gathering news from metro newsrooms. They may place more emphasis on initiated stories and less on events such as stake-outs or daily emergency stories.

Reporters can be given assignments by the chief of staff or editor. But newsrooms also rely on their journalists to generate stories themselves, within the framework of the organisation's specific news agenda. For instance, agency reporters need to be able to think of ways to develop new angles to stories that are already part of the news agenda because news wire services tend to stick closely to the main events and issues of each day.

Television and radio also usually stick closely to the main events of the day. This is because—with the exception of round-the-clock services— broadcast news programs are of fixed duration. The first priority for a television bulletin is to touch all the main bases of the day's events. There's usually room for one quirky or lighthearted item at the end. Radio's priority is to continually update the main stories of interest to the station's audience.

Reporters who work in radio and TV know their programs have "no back page"—in other words, there's nowhere to put the stories of minor significance that are useful fillers in newspapers. But because radio is a high rotation medium, it also has some room for stories of limited impact which can be run on a single bulletin. Online news services have the capacity to run unlimited numbers of stories. But experience suggests that the stories that receive most of the "hits"—that is, the stories accessed by the largest number of readers—are those placed at the top of the story list on the screen and which are therefore deemed to be the most significant stories of the moment.

INITIATING STORIES

At News Ltd in Sydney, pitching stories is seen as fundamental to each reporter's daily routine. If they're not walking in the door and greeting the chief of staff with at least one story idea, the day's already a failure. We tell them, if they're sitting at their desk waiting for the chief of staff to give them a story, they're not a reporter, they're a clever clerk.

We expect people to come up with ideas constantly and to follow those ideas through.

One metropolitan newsroom tests its trainees" ability to find news using a series of exercises. In one exercise, they are made to head out onto the streets without their mobile phones and come back with a publishable Covering assigned stories—such as this opening of a public garden—is a standard part of many reporters" work story. What do they find?

One reporter doorknocked nearby brothels for her story. Another went no further than a local lingerie shop for a quirky piece on the most popular item of women's underwear (the thong) and another used her skills of observation to pick up signs of domestic life in a nearby commercial building. Investigating further she found young squatters had turned the top floor into a personal arts commune.

Not all newsrooms require reporters to generate so many of their own stories. Certainly there is an expectation that reporters with their own round will come up with original ideas and break news. But general reporters may be expected to spend most of their time following up story ideas given to them by the assignments desk. Newsrooms with smaller staffs—for instance those in non-metropolitan areas—may need all their journalists to both cover a large number of stories assigned by the chief of staff as well as find their own material.

Covering assigned stories inevitably leaves a journalist with less time to dig up their own material, but it's a truism in journalism that any reporter who can pitch good stories to the chief of staff on a regular basis will be given more time to follow their own leads and will spend less time chasing the chief of staff's ideas.

The story with which we began this section came about because the reporter was an approachable person who was prepared to listen to a stranger's suggestion and check it out. Had the reporter been out sailing in Port Phillip Bay rather than having a drink in the pub, he might have noticed the unused seal platform for himself and generated the same story from observation rather than a tip-off. News stories can come about in many different ways, which are covered in the previous section of this book. But once the original idea is formulated, the process towards publication usually follows the sequence outlined below.

- From story idea to publication
- Research (this can include calls to check the story and finding an angle)
- Story idea
- Publication
- Interviews Writing and checking Sub editing
- The news conference

No matter who initiates the story idea, at some point early on in the process, it will need to be discussed by the reporter and the chief of staff or someone else in the editorial process. The reporter, the chief of staff and the editor all need to have an idea of the direction the story will take so that it can be fitted into the daily news hierarchy which determines where it will run in the paper, programme or site.

Chiefs of staff and news editors take this information to the news conference so that the various stories on offer for that day can be weighed up against each other to work out the final shape of the paper or broadcast.

Most large newspaper and television newsrooms hold at least two news conferences each day. At the morning conference, the editorial staff (which may include the editor, foreign editor, chief of staff and so on, depending on the size of the newsroom) discuss the day's potential stories, how they might be approached, who will be reporting them, any potential problems such as legal ones, and what rival news outlets might be doing. They hold another conference in the afternoon, to review what stories they have and work out a more detailed version of where the various news items will appear in the publication or broadcast.

THE STORY BRIEF

If a story is assigned to a reporter by the news desk, the reporter will be briefed on the way they should approach it. The story brief may include instructions on the kind of finished item that is expected—that is a human interest story, or a hard news item.

The reporter may be given suggestions as to the angle to take and who to interview. Working to a brief means a reporter has far less autonomy about how to prepare and write their stories than those outside the news business might imagine.

But for young reporters it can provide a useful guide to the way the finished story should read. Reporters who fail to follow the initial story brief can find themselves criticised by their news editor if their story is subsequently dropped. Journalists who generate their own stories have more control over the direction their work takes than those working on assigned pieces. They usually have the opportunity to decide how to frame their pieces and who to talk to when gathering the information needed to write them.

Chiefs of staff and editors value reporters with a positive attitude towards assignments—that is, reporters who don't try to talk down or reject the stories they're given. That doesn't mean that all assignments are potentially good stories. It means that chiefs of staff and editors know that the publication or programme has to be filled.

So reporters who want to challenge their assignments will find the process easier if they have better ideas of their own to offer. Reporters who try to "kill" stories to which they're assigned will quickly gain a reputation for negativity and laziness. Assigning editors are more likely to accept a change to the story brief if the reporter offers an alternative way of approaching it.

FINDING NEWS STORIES

News stories can be found anywhere. But to turn observations, incidents and information into news, reporters need four skills:

- They need to be able to see the potential for a news story.
- They need to know how to pitch the story to their chief of staff or editor—particularly in large metro

newsrooms where there is intense competition for space in the news pages.

- They need to know how to find an angle that will make the story interesting to their particular audience.
- And they need to be able to follow through on their pitch and deliver the story.

To find potential news stories, reporters need to develop a series of habits. First, they need to develop good contacts with people who are, or might become, sources of information. They need also to read, watch, listen to and browse as many media as possible.

That includes the local, metro and national press and broadcast media. It also includes high quality international publications, such as *The Economist,* and the most populist of media, the women's magazines, music press and mass-market magazines.

There's no point in being snobbish about which media to dip into, though a media diet consisting entirely of popular magazines is no grounding for a career in news reporting and it is important to bear in mind the different journalistic standards of accuracy and attribution that apply within different media. Consuming a wide range of media gives a journalist a better understanding of the interests of all sections of the audience.

Reading, viewing and listening widely allow reporters to put the information they use for their stories into a wider context. This is a particular issue for young reporters who inevitably lack life experience. A good general knowledge allows young journalists to add some depth to their reporting.

Journalists on daily news publications and programs are usually expected to have read two papers, listened to the morning radio news, and watched the previous night's TV news and current affairs programs in preparation for each day's work. But it's not just these daily news services that are useful to journalists. The specialist media, which cover topics as diverse as computers, health, consumer issues, motoring and so on, are a particularly good source of ideas.

They can alert journalists to trends or developments in a particular field that would be of interest to a wider news audience. Advertisements, including the classifieds, are another source of potential news stories.

Second, journalists should be observant. They should notice things going on around them and ask "why?"

Finally, journalists need to talk to people—all sorts of people. They need to be interested in other people and the things that concern them.

The editor of the Queensland regional daily, *The Fraser Coast Chronicle,* Nancy Bates, tells her reporters the best way to be a news gatherer is to avoid mixing with other reporters. She believes journalists can become too caught up in agendas and intrigues that are of limited interest to everyone else.

I find a lot of journalists tend to get a slightly groupie mentality about politicians and VIPs. They just get a little bit lost about what is really important to the person out there and what they are interested in.

Chronicle reporters are advised to get out and mix with the rest of the community and ask what's happening. When the sports reporter plays golf, he comes back with stories. And when reporters go shopping, they listen when other shoppers talk to them in the aisles in the hope of picking up story tips with their groceries.

There's an apocryphal story about a Sydney metropolitan radio news director who told his reporters to take the train to the outer western suburbs every month or so and just listen to what people were talking about to give them a feel for audience concerns.

True or not, it's a reminder that journalists need to be aware of those issues that are important to their readers, listeners or viewers. Journalists also need to know how to frame issues so that audiences can best understand them.

TTIP A successful reporter:

- Is a "media junkie" (and watches, listens to and reads as much as possible).
- Is observant and curious and asks "why?".
- Is interested in people and their concerns.

TECHNIQUES FOR DEVELOPING STORIES

In the last section we looked at some of the sources of news. These include tip-offs (as happened in the story described at the start of this section), direct observation, official hearings, media releases and so on.

Sometimes the raw material from these sources can be turned into news stories with very little effort on the part of the reporter. But to generate more original stories, journalists need to know some of the techniques that can be used to develop observations into stories or to develop new angles for existing news items. Some of these techniques include:

- *Repercussions and reaction*: News generates more news. A story of any significance will lead to break-out and follow-up stories, so reporters need to consider where they might look for reaction to a particular event or issue and its repercussions. One obvious source of repercussions is in your own local area. National and international events often create ripples that spread out across the nation, even the world. When something happens somewhere else, one of the first questions a journalist will ask is "What's the local angle?". There are also stories to be found in considering the repercussions of government decisions and asking "Who benefits?" and "Who has been left out?".

Tip

Reporters need to go beyond the superficial and ask questions about the repercussions of issues and events. This applies to even seemingly low-impact issues.

These are just two examples: First consider the fad for D-I-Y home improvements buttressed by several television "infotainment" programs and lifestyle magazines.

When it arose the fad itself was worth a "colour" (i.e. light-hearted) story. But there was also a more serious news story later on, when statistics on hospital admissions suggested an increase in injuries from more people using power tools, working on ladders and so on.

Likewise, when small, collapsible scooters first hit the market, they prompted stories about the fad itself. But again, there were more serious stories to be told about the repercussions of young children riding these scooters, often without proper protective headgear, and the number of accidents and injuries that caused. So stories can be generated from looking at events and issues and considering "What next?".

- *The other person's opinion.* Rightly or wrongly the Australian media thrive on conflict. Another way of looking at it is that they value diversity of opinion. So whenever a decision or announcement is made, there's bound to be a story in the way various groups in the community react. Try to canvass opinion widely. There are not just two sides to every story. There are usually more.
- *Going back.* Revisiting past events to see what has happened since is a regular way of generating stories, not least because it helps to fulfil journalism's role of keeping officials accountable.

It also helps answer the criticism that journalism is too concerned with the short-term news cycle and not sufficiently concerned with longer term repercussions of events. Going back might mean looking at how a community has coped with tragedy, such as bushfires. It might mean looking at how a community of refugees has settled in. It might mean interviewing war veterans. It might mean asking "Where are they now?" of people who were once well known.

And revisiting doesn't just have to revolve around people. What about changes to local traffic management or town planning? Did they work? Stories on past events need an angle to justify revisiting them. The most common angle is an anniversary of the original event, though it's not the only angle available. Some issues and events are worth tracking as they progress and these stories can be picked up at any stage along the process.

Smart reporters will keep a file of stories worth tracking. These can include the construction of prominent buildings or developments, public campaigns and so on. They can also include far more personal stories.

For instance, landmark medical procedures or emergencies often make the news at the time but are quickly forgotten. But the aftermaths of such events will often make stories just as interesting as the initial ones.

- Backgrounding events. One of the most regular, and fair, criticisms of the way news is presented is that it focuses on the *when* and *where* at the expense of the *why*. This leaves the audience unable to put events or issues into a context. So stories which investigate the reasons behind events in the news have an importance beyond their contribution to the daily news quota.
- Looking forward. Some news events are known of in advance—a dignitary will visit, a protest is being planned, a big sports event is forthcoming and so on. These are worth a preview story.
- The story behind the story. Behind many news stories there is another story waiting to be told. Sometimes that means finding a wider issue in a story that focused on an individual.

For example, an item on a single franchisee's business difficulties might lead to a broader story about problems within the company or that particular field of commerce. Conversely, big picture stories also lend themselves to items on the individuals involved. For example, consider the Olympic Games.

Of course the high profile, well-credentialled athletes will be covered. But dig a little deeper and there will often be far more interesting stories of athletes who struggled against considerable odds for their place at the starting line, even if they have only a small chance of finishing well.

It may infuriate sports fans but a disproportionate amount of attention at the Calgary Winter Olympics and Sydney Olympics went, respectively, to British ski jumper "Eddie the Eagle" (Michael Edwards) and swimmer "Eric the Eel" (Eric Moussambani) from Equatorial Guinea, neither best remembered for their sporting skill. There are other, if less quirky, stories behind almost every competition—from the craft and cooking competitions at every Easter show to junior chess titles, to the wine awards. And competitions don't just have competitors.

They have judges, statisticians, former winners and so on, all potentially worth a story. Even media coverage itself can generate good story material, such as the camera operators who train for months to run up and down the field covering the players at the footy grand final.

There's also a human story behind many official statistics; the family of the road accident victim, the person making a recovery from an accident, the small business person forced to close down, the farmers coping with land degradation. Almost any time you are presented with statistics on an issue, there's a human story that deserves to be told.

- *Local heroes*: The media are regularly criticised for too easily dividing the world into heroes and villains, and journalists need to avoid the tendency to oversimplify issues and events or stereotype individuals or groups. That said, the elevation of people or things to heroic status can be a way of creating stories, which become both a selling point for the media and a focus for the community. Heroic status can be conferred on almost anyone or anything.
- When bushfires raged across parts of New South Wales at the start of 2002, a large American helicopter nicknamed Elvis was designated the hero of the fight to control them. It helped that the name lent itself to a lot of "Elvis sighting" jokes. The emphasis on the machine may have clouded some of the serious issues the fires raised, but it provided some "feel good" stories at a time when they were needed.

WARNING

Note that it's particularly important to take great care when writing stories of this kind, because there is no shortage of examples of individuals whose high profile and status in one area has been allowed to distract the media from properly scrutinising other areas of their lives, particularly their business or professional activities.

- Individualise. Stories about the big issues—from serious medical problems to the impact of the federal or state budget—are usually more accessible if they are told from the viewpoint of one person or a small group of people. This tendency to individualise issues and events is sometimes criticised by those outside journalism.

They argue it diminishes the scale of stories and oversimplifies issues. The counter argument is that individualising issues, such as poverty, cancer, drug abuse and so on, makes them much easier for audiences to understand.

And far from diminishing the scale of such stories, individualising can give them depth by giving presenting a human face. Homelessness is more than a set of statistics. It is the destruction of individual lives and hopes.

Focusing on an individual gives the audience a chance to see that. Focusing on the individual living with or recovering from serious illness has the potential to offer hope and useful information to others in the same situation.

It can be hard for the audience to empathise with people with whom they rarely come in contact—such as asylum-seekers.

Indeed, one of the easiest ways to ensure lack of a public empathy is to cast a group of people as a faceless mass. In these cases, presenting individual stories to represent the issue serves to cut through political and official rhetoric.

- *Free plugs*: One of the first things a journalist discovers is that there's no shortage of people wanting you to give them or their business free publicity. This is an issue that warrants a good deal of discussion and the way it's handled varies from one organisation to another. Reporters have the power to give people and institutions a free plug.

At its worst this can result in uncritical, promotional pap

being passed off as news. But some of the promotional aspects of news can be seen as both fair and socially useful. When a retailer provides a destitute family with new household goods does the promotional element of the story matter as long as the story has its own value as news? Stories about an upandcoming new band or a local festival are the sort of items that are a tonic for viewers, listeners and readers. And they don't have to come across as free PR, as long as they're written with a light touch.

- *The follow-up*: We've said already that news creates more news. That's one of the reasons reporters should be avid consumers of the media— their own and their competitors". Some stories will lend themselves to one or more spin-off pieces. It's important not to simply rip off another reporter's story. Plagiarism is always unacceptable. But developing an existing item into a new one is an everyday event. It's called "doing a follow-up". This can amount to no more than a new version of an existing idea.

For example, if one of the Sydney papers runs a story on a significant increase in the number of young people serving on local councils, reporters in other areas are likely to check to see if the same can be said for their own region.

In other cases, the original story provides a starting point for a new and different item. For example, an item in the Brisbane media on the number of southerners relocating north might prompt an article in the Melbourne media on the long-term effects on Melbourne property prices of people moving interstate.

It's also worth monitoring overseas media for issues and trends that might lend themselves to a story on the Australian reaction. For instance, overseas developments in road safety and education have both generated stories about the implications for Australian experience, to cite just two examples.

Tip

- *Keep a file of story ideas*: This should include original ideas as well as stories clipped from newspapers, magazines and the Internet, or other sources, which could be developed in new directions or which are worth following up after a specific period of time. A file such as this is particularly useful on slow news days. But note that if you plan to cover a story on a weekend, particularly Sunday, or a public holiday, or during traditional holiday seasons, you should organise it in advance to make sure interviewees will be available. This is particularly important for television where you need the image of interviewees, not just a voice on a mobile phone.

- If you come across a potential story, never assume that it has already been covered. Check. It's easy for a reporter to lose a story by assuming that another journalist has already written it. But no good idea should be dismissed on these grounds without first checking with the news desk.
- Subscribe to emailed news lists, particularly lists of events in your city.

These can be a good source of news about activities worth covering.

- A certain amount of news is cyclical. This includes coverage of the main national and religious observances (including ANZAC and Australia Day, Easter, Christmas, Passover, Ramadan, New Year, Chinese New Year and others). It also includes the changing of the seasons (including the start of the snow and bushfire seasons) as well as the first day of school and so on. In these cases, your story file should include potential new approaches to familiar material.

Case studies—using contacts and ideas to generate stories

- Jane Rocca is a freelance journalist who has written extensively on music and youth issues. Since she relies on her ability to generate her own stories to get commissions, working her contacts and coming up with new ideas are essential."I make sure I maintain contact with publicists who organise upcoming events and generally keep an eye out for story ideas. Look at the opinion pages in the newspaper and see what people are writing about. This can give you a good indication of what editors want. It's about being aware of what's going on in your community." When an anti-drug campaign featured television ads showing body bags as a scare tactic, Jane developed a story on the effectiveness of the ads on their young target audience. It was a simple idea, but it involved a contemporary news issue.

- A young reporter at *The Fraser Coast Chronicle* heard that a friend of her mother's had become upset after the electricity company refused to allow her to pay her power bill using coins. The reporter turned it into a story on what is legal tender. What made the story particular interesting was its implications for all those people, especially those on a budget, who keep piggy banks just so they can pay their bills.
- Freelance journalist and trainer, Jane Cafarella, used a friend's tale about losing veggies from her suburban garden to furry, four-legged raiders for a story idea on rabbit control. And when the store-owner who sold her a piano told her about a French polisher who worked for him, Jane wrote a profile of the craftsman in question. He was 91.
- Out for dinner with a couple of friends? You are never "not a journalist". What are your friends talking about? What are their problems at work? One very experienced reporter who was out for dinner found she had trouble hearing her friends talk. She ended up with a news feature on noise limits and associated problems in city restaurants. Another reporter ended up with a page 1 investigation into conditions in a local mental health facility after listening to a friend describe her working conditions over dinner.

DEVELOPING CONTACTS

There are a few core skills in journalism. One of them is being able to spot a story and develop an angle. Another is writing.

And developing and keeping good contacts or sources is another. Contacts are more important than writing ability and there are examples of reporters with a mediocre writing style becoming valued and highly paid members of a newsroom on the basis of their contacts and therefore their ability to dig out information.

After all, someone else can always polish the story. But without good information to start with, there's no story to polish. Journalist Ingrid Svendsen describes the idea that journalism is primarily about writing as "the most common misconception" about the profession.

It's not about writing, it's about people skills and researching and finding out stuff and having the curiosity to wonder why things are as they are and having the ability to find out why a certain thing is happening. It's about contacts and knowing what is really going on and not just the official version of what's going on. (Interview with Ingrid Svendsen.)

Developing contacts probably sounds more complex than it really is. A contact is simply someone who can provide information and *anyone* can be a contact.

One of the misconceptions about contacts is that they have to be highly placed people. In fact, the opposite is often true. People in high places may hold many secrets. But they're unlikely to divulge them. And if they do, there are often strings attached which may not suit the journalist. But ordinary people often have a story to tell or have access to information and may be far more prepared to share it.

To look at just one example of this in practice, let's go back to 1978 and the aftermath of "the dismissal" of 1975, in which then governor-general Sir John Kerr sacked the Labour government of Gough Whitlam and installed Liberal leader Malcolm Fraser as prime minister. Nearly three years later, Sir John Kerr was living in Britain and would be a prize interview for any reporter able to find him.

The journalist who did manage to locate Sir John was Network 7 political correspondent, Mike Peterson, who was in Britain as one of the media contingent with then prime minister Malcolm Fraser for the Commonwealth Heads of Government conference. Peterson won a Walkley Award for his news story on Sir John and Lady Kerr at their Surrey home. He found them, where others had failed, because, as fellow Walkley winner John Hurst wrote later, he "had always believed that ordinary people—doormen, drivers, lift attendants and the like—were good sources of information if approached in the right way". Peterson asked a driver outside the official pool to put out feelers to see if any other drivers had an address for Sir John. It worked.

Journalists need to become accustomed to viewing everyone as a potential source of information and filing their contact details. You never know when they might come in handy. For example, a reporter at a suburban newspaper met a local American couple at a social function one evening in 2001. Nothing unusual there.

But it was a week before September 11. In the aftermath of the attacks on New York and Washington, the paper wanted to know how American members of its community were feeling. The couple the reporter had met socially were the first ones she turned to.

The process of building contacts can be difficult for a reporter new to the job. Where do you start? Brett Foley, a journalist at *The Australian Financial Review,* suggests keeping a notebook by the phone and writing down the name and number of everyone you speak to for every story then regularly entering the details in a hard-copy contact book or a contact file in a computer programme, preferably one with a search function. He says when you're a very junior reporter you're not "establishing a network of deep throats".

What's important is just to keep track of everybody you speak to. You might not pick a particular person as a contact because you might be on a story which is about something which doesn't seem very consequential ... But it always happens that not very far down the track, especially if you're covering general news, something will come up in their field and keeping track of those things allows you to show a bit of initiative and say you know someone. It's always handy to know the widest number of people in the widest number of capacities for you to draw on.

Ingrid Svendsen of *The Melbourne Times* says if you're new to a round, find out who's who. It's a matter of finding out who are the influential lobby groups in that area and getting in sweet with them because they know everything. They're doing submissions to government on various subjects, they're meeting with bureaucrats on the issues they're lobbying on.

They're very clued in. So they'll be able to tell you what's going on. If you're new to a town, it's a similar process. It's figuring out who's who.

Who's pushing the decision-makers in the town and who are the decision-makers—and cultivating them. In any sphere there are always decision-makers and lobbyists. It's a case of figuring out who they are and reaching them. Richard Baker suggests a reporter starting a new round should go through articles written by the last reporter on the round and note the names of people interviewed.

There will also be certain people a reporter will have to deal with while covering a round. For example, state rounds reporters have to deal with press secretaries. Richard suggests calling anyone who's likely to become a regular contact, introduce yourself, perhaps meet over a coffee and ask about the issues and events worth looking out for.

Regular contacts will often tell a reporter about things that are not yet ready to be written about but are worth keeping an eye on. A reporter might call a regular source every fortnight or so simply to check what's happening. It's important not to hassle contacts unnecessarily but to build a good working relationship.

Journalists find that people they meet casually often want to share some piece of information they reckon would make a good story. Sometimes they're wrong and the "story" is no more than a rumour unworthy of serious attention. At other times—as with the bloke in the pub and Richard Baker—they're right.

Building contacts is a circular process. Once you know someone inside an organisation or department or field, they can help to point you to other people in the same area. And once a reporter becomes known for their work, they can expect to have potential contacts approach *them.*

A reporter's friends may become sources, but it's unwise to treat sources as friends. That's because the relationship between reporters and their sources is a professional one, based on mutual interest. The reporter needs stories and information. The source wants to see stories and information used in the media. But not everything a source wants to see published or broadcast will be judged newsworthy by the journalist. And journalists can't simply take a source's version of a story at face value. They need to take in other, often rival, angles and opinions. So reporters need to maintain their access to the source without winding up in their pocket.

Ingrid Svendsen believes it's important to treat sources with integrity and to "set out the ground rules clearly at the start". The problem with making contacts is that people often feel the need to display loyalty to those contacts at all costs. And it's a balancing act between treating your contacts well and treating them with integrity and faithfully reporting what they've told you and at the same time ensuring the public's right to have the full story. Your first sense of responsibility is to your readers, not your contacts. I've had to "burn" contacts and it's really unpleasant when you have to do it. But sometimes you have to because the issue is so important that you have to tell it as it is, even if that entails "burning" a contact.

But Ingrid also says the potential for damaging relations with a contact can be minimised if they are given the chance to understand how journalists work. "Most contacts will understand that your job is to tell the full story and that their views will be fairly and accurately represented but they might not be the sole focus of the story. The story might have other angles."

ROUTINE CONTACTS

Some news sources are routine contacts for newsrooms. The most obvious of these are the emergency services-the police, ambulance and fire brigade. A reporter rostered to the first shift of the morning will usually ring the local branch of each of these to find out what has happened overnight. Some newsrooms, especially radio with its rapid turnaround of stories, will call later in the day as well.

Keep a contacts book (or electronic organiser). List the name of every person with whom you come in contact who might be useful as a source. Collect their work, home and mobile numbers plus their email details. Addresses are useful, too (for those days when your source isn't answering the phone).

WORKING WITH INFORMATION FROM SOURCES

A story can begin with information from a single source, but it's rare that it can proceed on that alone. Stories need to be given depth with confirmation from other sources and with a range of comment from different sides of an issue or argument.

It can be far too easy for young reporters to place too much faith in individual sources, without considering why a person is giving them information or without putting information into a wider context. Editor of The Courier, Stuart Howie, says he tries to instill in his largely young reporting staff the point that every story has more than one dimension. He says that sometimes even experienced reporters will talk to one person for a story and wrongly think that's the story.

It's never the story talking to one person. It's one person's viewpoint. People will only ever tell you something for their own benefit. And they will only ever tell you something from their own point of view, which is just human nature.

Stuart's advice to reporters is to get lots of points of view and work out each source's motives for their information or comment. "If you're going out on a story, talk to lots of people. The more you explore and investigate, the better the story and the more thorough your research will be and that will be reflected in what you write."

Tip

One of the skills every reporter needs is, for want of a better term, a "crap detector". Much of what they are told will come coloured by the source's self interest. Reporters must be able to tell when someone is spinning them a line and report in as balanced a manner as possible.

Information supplied by the representative of an organisation is often considered more reliable than that supplied by an individual alone. But anyone can set up an organisation and sometimes organisations are no more than a front for one person or a handful of people. When dealing with information and comment from organisations, especially little known ones, reporters are advised to check the size and scope of their membership and for whom they actually speak. This can be done by speaking to other groups in the same field, though it's important to take into account that any opinion from other groups might be tainted by rivalry.

This need for caution applies to written and online sources as much as to personal informants. Journalists need to weigh up the veracity of every piece of information they work with. For example, the newspaper files or story archives that are a routine source of background information can include errors that will be perpetuated unless the information is reassessed and checked before reuse.

GETTING PEOPLE TO TALK

Not everyone a journalist wants to talk to wants to talk to them. People often need to be encouraged to share what they know. They may also need to be reassured about the way in which their information will be treated. Encouraging people to talk is one of the skills journalists need to develop. Ingrid Svendsen says even people who are seemingly unwilling to grant an interview or provide information are often prepared to speak, providing they are given the right reasons.

Most people are desperate to tell you stuff. It's basic human nature. People can't keep a secret. Everyone wants to tell what they know. It makes them feel like they're really informed and influential. So really it's just a matter of giving them a good reason to. It's a matter of appealing to whatever it is that's going to press their buttons and make them want to tell you. Perhaps by raising this issue they can assist other people who are in a similar situation to them, or their organisation might get funding as a result of it. Or it might just make them look good and raise their profile. There's always a reason for people to want to talk.

Ingrid says it surprises her how free people are with information. But she also says good sources of information are often overlooked, and one of the features of journalism that concerns her is that often "people who are in the know are never asked".

In any story involving a dispute, the people or organisations involved should be given the opportunity to present their sides of the story. In these cases, reporters usually phrase their request for an interview in these terms—that is, "We'd like to present your side of the story." It would be churlish to pretend that this is not a form of pressure on people to cooperate.

On the other hand, not giving people on different sides of a dispute the chance to have their say produces one-sided reports. There are at least two sides to most stories and there are frequently more than two. Good journalism involves reporting as many different points of view as possible.

Some people will refuse to be interviewed no matter how the journalist phrases the request. They may have good reasons for not wanting to talk. In some of these cases the reporter simply has to find an alternative interviewee. In other cases the refusal is more problematic. The person sought may be particularly important to the story, either for the information they can provide or because their opinion is necessary to ensure the story is balanced. If they can't be persuaded, it's customary to include within the story the fact that an interview was sought, using words such as "Mr X refused to speak to ..." or "The minister was offered the chance to comment but declined."

Alternatively, the questions can be used in the story, even if there are no answers: "If Mr X had agreed to speak to us, this is what we would have asked ..." But a reporter who uses this technique needs to ensure that the questions do not contain any defamatory insinuations.

THE DENIAL

One of the difficult circumstances in which journalists have to seek out additional comment is when they have to put an allegation to a person about whom the allegation has been made.

Many stories begin with a claim which must be throughly checked out before the story can be written. An allegation can be made by one side of a dispute or it can come from a disinterested party—that is, someone with information they believe should be put before the public but with nothing personal to gain from the outcome.

For example, a whistleblower might accuse a company of dumping toxic waste. Before putting the accusation at the nub of the story to the person or organisation about whom it is being made, the reporter needs to marshal as many of the details as possible.

One reason is to see if the story is worth pursuing. Another is to have a solid foundation for the questions that the reporter will have to ask the subject of the accusation(s). Eventually the reporter must call or confront the subject for their response.

What if they deny it? Denial is hardly uncommon. But it doesn't necessarily mean that the story is wrong. Indeed, sometimes a denial simply makes a story better. Perhaps the most famous denial of an allegation in recent times is former US president Bill Clinton's insistence that he had not had "sexual relations with that woman". Did the denial kill the story? One reason it did not was that among the media, among many politicians on Capitol Hill (both Republican and Democrat) and among the US public, the denial was not considered credible. On the other hand, the media have been accused of pursuing some stories to the point of zealousness, despite a denial which was subsequently found to be correct.

If one of the parties to a potential story denies that it is true, the reporter (and their chief of staff or editor) has a series of options:

- If the balance of evidence suggests the story cannot be substantiated, it should be dropped.
- If the journalist remains convinced the story is true but does not yet have enough evidence to substantiate it, it may be worth additional research to try to verify it.
- Finally, if the journalist (and their chief of staff or editor) already have enough evidence to substantiate the story, despite the denial, then the denial becomes part of the report. Lines such as "Mr X has denied the claim" are a routine way of covering this, as are "Mr X was unavailable for comment" or "Ms Y refused to comment". In such cases the issue of defamation is an obvious concern and the journalist needs to be sure of their facts and of their ability to defend them.

It's important to remember that someone denying a story does not make it untrue any more than someone telling you a story makes it true. Each option has to be treated on its merits, bearing in mind the other available evidence, and each circumstance has to be treated with care.

On the Record/off the Record

Journalists deal with information from their sources on three basic levels:

- On the record.
- Background.
- Off the record.

A problem for journalists and sources alike is that these terms have no legal or even fixed definition. In his book, *The Journalist's Guide to Media Law,* journalism academic and lawyer Mark Pearson says that "part of the problem is that

Australian journalists have no accepted system for ranking information according to its level of confidentiality, no way of defining what expressions like "off the record" or "background only" really mean".

Of the three terms above, the first is unambiguous. If someone speaks to a journalist "on the record", it means the reporter can use the information in full and attribute it to the source.

There's less consensus about the other two. Some of the common understandings of the terms are that:

- If someone speaks to a journalist on "background" it means the reporter can use the information but cannot attribute it to the source.
- If someone speaks "off the record", it means the journalist may not use the information (and by implication they can't name the source). Some reporters take the view that if they obtain information "off the record" they can't use it at all, even if someone else subsequently gives them the same material "on the record". Others take the contrary view—that is, that they can use the information if they subsequently hear it from someone else. Journalists who take the first view often won't allow a source to tell them something "off the record", because it would prevent them from using the material if they heard it again later.

Part of the difficulty with the term "off the record" is that it is used differently by people with different levels of experience with the media. To media novices it may mean that they can speak privately, without what they say being used. But to media-savvy operators, including government officials and their minders, "off the record" can be a way of giving a reporter information that the source wants to see used, as long as they can distance themselves from it. Offering reporters information as "background" is another common ploy of politicians, who use it to try out proposed policies or positions to see how the public will react while maintaining enough "wriggle room" to bail out if the reaction is adverse.

PROTECTING SOURCES

Reporters walk a fine line between trying to get information out of people and maintaining their trust. In some cases, the source will be taking a risk, either legally, professionally or personally, by giving a reporter information.

In these cases, clarifying the way in which the information is to be reported is particularly important, both to protect the source and because the reporter might want to draw on that person in the future. Brett Foley regards clarifying the issue of whether information can be used "on" or "off the record" as very important.

A lot of the time you're dealing with people where that understanding is tacit anyway. They're very media savvy and they're aware of what they're able to say without getting themselves into trouble.

Increasingly you deal with people who say "XYZ-but you didn't hear it from me", or who go so far as to say, "You could phrase it this way to keep me out of it." You'll also come across people who aren't as savvy with the media.

You'll ask, "Can we say this on the record?" and the person might have to think about it and will say, "I guess I could get myself into trouble." In those cases you'll tell them, "There are ways we can get around that." You can phrase it a particular way or it could be not attributed and so on. But you'd also want to check that information and corroborate it before committing it to print.

Ingrid Svendsen believes that the need to exercise some care with sources who are inexperienced in dealing with the media is even more important for reporters working outside the metro dailies.

I don't think there's anything to be gained by abusing people's trust and I don't think there's anything wrong with explaining to people how the system works.

Most people don't deal with journalists every day of the week. So you ask them, "Do you want your name used? Do you want us to identify you and your agency? If you don't then do you prefer us to say "a social worker working in the drugs field?", What form of words makes you most comfortable?" If I know they're inexperienced I try to explain to them quite fully beforehand what it all means.

Wherever possible, journalists are advised to obtain information "on the record". This recommendation is enshrined in the Journalists" Code of Ethics, clause 3, which urges journalists to "attribute information to its source" wherever possible and to consider "the source's motives" before agreeing to use information supplied anonymously. Information is always more credible if it can be traced to its source. If someone offers you information as "background" or "off the record", you need to ask yourself why they are not prepared to attach their name to it.

That said, a journalist who agrees to accept information on a not-forattribution basis is bound to protect the source of that information. Clause 3 of the Journalists" Code of Ethics ends: "Where confidences are accepted, respect them in all circumstances." On rare occasions, journalists have been ordered by a court or inquiry to give up the names of confidential sources and have gone to jail or suffered other sanctions rather than do so.

Tip

Remember that many people are unaccustomed to dealing with the media and don't know the ground rules so you may need to explain these to them. This is particularly important for reporters working for local media where the relationship between media outlets and their audience is different from that in large metropolitan areas.

WORKING WITH CHILDREN

Journalists need to exercise special care when reporting on or seeking information from children. Children are often the subject of lighthearted stories where parents or guardians are present and able to give consent (e.g. stories of children at shows or similar events). In other circumstances the ethical issues can be less clear cut. The 1999 Journalists" Code of Ethics does not specifically refer to children. But the in-house guidelines of some media outlets do.

For Instance, the Age Code of Conduct Specifies

- Special care should be taken when dealing with children (under the age of 16). The editor must be informed when children have been photographed or interviewed without parental consent.

The Professional Conduct Policy at News Ltd cautions journalists not to interview or photograph children under 16 in regard to their welfare or their parents or siblings unless a parent or guardian is present and has given consent.

In addition, it says:

- Extreme care should be taken that children are not prompted in interviews, or offered inducements to cooperate.
- The News Ltd policy also instructs its journalists not to "approach children in schools" without the school's consent.
- The law requires that children involved in court cases not be identified.

GENERAL TIPS FOR ROUNDS

There was a time when being given your first round (i.e. a specific area such as courts, politics, police) to cover was a sign that you had left the incubation crib of journalism and were moving into the world of being a seasoned reporter. Nowadays, not only is it common to be given a round very shortly after arriving in a newsroom, it is equally common to have more than one round, or to be moved frequently from one round to another.

Being a good roundsperson of course requires the same skills as being a good general reporter with the added requirement of being expected to generate more stories. Because of the general pace of newsrooms today and cutbacks in staffing levels, specific preparation or training for rounds is rare. At best, in many newsrooms, the preparation may consist of being given some advice on contacts from the departing reporter and, if you are lucky, a brief introduction to some key people on the round. Other than that, good rounds reporters have to fall back on the two important qualities any journalist needs: initiative and the ability to build good contacts.

Rounds journalists are likely to spend longer with contacts than general reporters, and build up deeper relationships, which of course can create problems indrawing boundary lines between personal and professional relationships.

The journalist covering rounds needs to be vigilant about whether information being given by contacts can be used and attributed to them. For instance, police round journalists are often given background information that should not be used. Such background information, especially when based on mere speculation or opinion, can be a dangerous influence.

This chapter will look at some of the key rounds of police or emergency services, courts, local and state government, health and sport.

POLICE ROUNDS AND EMERGENCY SERVICES

Reporting emergency services, that is, covering the police, fire and ambulance services, is the bread and butter of many newspapers.

This round may conjure up images of car chases, drug raids and scoops about major crime figures but covering this round involves the same mundane routines as reporting on other areas.

The nature of police rounds varies a great deal depending upon the news organisation and the audience they are targeting. For example, tabloid and broadsheet newspapers will want different things from these rounds. Tabloids may place more emphasis on the bizarre aspects of violent crime than the more conservative broadsheet newspapers, which may be more interested in processes, structures and other organisational issues.

If you scan the pages of your local suburban or regional paper, you will be able to gauge where police reporting fits into each organisation's news priorities. Break-ins, robberies, vandalism and assaults are all the mainstays of the police round in this context.

In metropolitan areas, police are likely to hold a daily conference where they brief reporters on any newsworthy occurrences.

Regional and country journalists can use the Internet to quickly check any breaking stories with central media liaison to see if there is any relevance for their local areas. All state and federal agencies have websites with useful background information as well as contact details for specific follow-ups.

Coverage of courts and police rounds can often reflect the wider culture within a news organisation as well as that of its audience. As we noted earlier, suburban and regional organisations are often more sensitive to immediate community reactions than bigger news organisations.

This may affect things like:

- The size of headlines and language used in reports.
- The use of photographs—for example, publication of a car accident scene where a local person has died—will have major impact in a smaller community.
- The amount of detail or explicit descriptions included in copy.

Roundspeople should always ensure they are aware of any internal style or taste guidelines on issues such as these.

Adam Pearce covers police rounds for a regional newspaper. He also covers sports and general stories. Adam checks "in person" with his contacts twice each day and while some of that time is spent going through the "daybook" with the sergeant, he also spends time wandering around the station just talking with officers in different sections. Just chatting with people is never wasted time for the roundsperson or any journalist.

Adam advises reporters on police rounds to keep their "ears open, especially at the scene of incidents". For example, on one occasion, he was covering a house fire and while chatting to people at the scene, he discovered a number of emergency calls had been made before there was a response.

By following up on-the-scene gossip, he got a major story on how the local emergency response system had failed. Nina Lees has worked on newspapers in Tasmania and Victoria and is an experienced police and court reporter. She says it takes time and effort to build relationships with contacts in the field, and that a reporter has to work to build a reputation as someone who's trustworthy and efficient. Police work within a particularly strong and complex subculture and a journalist needs to appreciate this.

When it comes to building contacts, Nina suggests asking other people in the office about local personalities and finding out all you can about the sources you are going to be dealing with. She also notes that it's important to show that you value your contacts.

Getting to know the police takes a lot of work and you need to be prepared to give them a lot of attention and visit the station every day just so you are a face there. It helps them feel comfortable with you. Talk to as many officers as you can. It doesn't always have to be about work, but at the same time they must know that that is the main reason you are there. Still, keep the visits friendly and professional.

But Nina also believes that is as far as a professional relationship should go. Early on in her career, Nina made a personal decision not to socialise with contacts at all and she says if you're covering police rounds, "don't date a police officer", because you could lose your credibility.

Both Adam and Nina believe it's important for reporters to develop a wide range of sources "around the round". That gives them alternative sources of information. For instance, Adam finds union sources useful in his work.

GENERAL WRITING TECHNIQUES FOR COVERING POLICE ROUNDS OR EMERGENCY SERVICES:

- Because of the very nature of emergency stories, there will always be two key things that you will want to know and they should always be the first things to be included in your intro.

  They are:

  – *Threat to life*: Have any people been killed or injured? Was there any real threat to life? Did people have a narrow escape?

– *Damage to property*: How much, and can anyone put a specific value on it?
– Do note that your concerns should always be in that order. You would never write the following intro:
– A truck crash on the Newcity Highway yesterday led to the loss of a load of grain worth $50,000.

The 40-year-old driver was killed in the accident.

Obviously the loss of human life in this story would come before the damage to property.

- *Look for the unique angle*: That is, what is unusual about the fire or the accident. For example, non-fatal fires in buildings occur every day but if the fire was caused by a pet, a faulty appliance or a cigarette and so on, that would probably be the angle. A quick check of the back files or with more experienced colleagues in the office might reveal that a fire was the second at a particular location in a year, or that an accident happened on a notorious stretch of road and so on.
- *Remember to be specific*: In covering these rounds, it should never be a case of "many people" were hurt or there was "some" damage. Even if you can't get a specific, confirmed figure before your deadline, get as near as you can.
- *Use any drama high up in the copy*: Any acts of heroism, rescue attempts or eyewitness accounts should be included in the first three or four paragraphs.
- Avoid clichés such as "a fair cop", "the long arm of the law", "mercy dash", "rampage", "streets of fear", "tragedy struck", "trouble flared".
- Know the jargon ("multiple offenders forced entry at the rear of the premises") but avoid it in your copy.

WARNING

Covering this round you must be careful to check on the difference between speculation and fact. It is a constant danger, especially if you are close to contacts, to take material as verified. Never become dependent upon one source for your information.

- Just because you get information from a police officer, don't take it as fact.
- Take great care to avoid attributing blame. A story may *sound* all right, but think carefully about whether it in any way attributes blame to anyone.
- Be careful not to sensationalise.
- *Be legally alert*: The journalist covering police rounds must always be wary. Once someone has been charged with an offence, the reporter is very limited in what they can report. Once a charge has been laid, a criminal case is deemed to be "pending" or *sub judice*(literally, "before the judge") and a reporter publishing material which could affect a person's right to a fair trial (such as a suggestion that the accused has already confessed) could be found guilty of contempt of court. All journalists have to be very careful of publishing background material about the events or circumstances which led to an arrest.

SIEGES AND DEATHKNOCKS

There are two situations that are specific to covering emergency rounds and both involve situations of high drama and stress.

These are sieges and deathknocks. Both place immense pressure on the emergency services and journalists must recognise the crucial role they also play.

Some of the risks that journalists run into when covering sieges include:

- The risk of glorifying offenders.
- The danger of inspiring "copy cats".
- The risk of hindering police work by tying up phone lines, divulging details of police operations, or interviewing offenders.
- The risk of distressing relatives of those involved.
- The danger of prejudicing subsequent court proceedings.

In order to avoid these risks, reporters need to:

- Know their legal rights and responsibilities—that is, what you can and cannot publish.
- Rely on good contacts you can trust.
- Know the policies of your employing organisation.

"Deathknocks" or "intrudes", as they are sometimes called, are professional jargon for interviews with the relatives of someone who has recently died or been killed in newsworthy circumstances.

Justifications given for doing these interviews include:

- They help to maintain the public's interest in the story.
- The public's right to know if there is a public safety issue related to the story.
- The story may help to mobilise public awareness or support.
- Telling the public about the incident may act as a form of grief therapy for the family.

Those who object say it is an unnecessary intrusion into people's grieving. However, journalists do have to accept that much of their work is covering the events of life that others don't want to think about. This does not mean journalists are not aware of the problems associated with this kind of interview. These are often the assignments most feared by young reporters.

Some have refused to carry out such interviews on ethical grounds. Others have pretended to carry out the interview when actually they never got out of their car. Many journalists are just plain fearful of a violent reaction from distraught relatives.

But some relatives can also be quite willing to talk. In some cases, they feel a story will offer public recognition of their loved one. Others may want to warn the public about the circumstances in which the person died.

The Journalists" Code of Ethics gives journalists the right to refuse to conduct deathknocks. Clause 11 says:Respect private grief and personal privacy. Journalists have the right to resist compulsion to intrude.

Many individual news outlets also have their own ethical codes, which cover such issues.In addition to these professional guidelines, every journalist asked to conduct a "deathknock" will also consider:

- What any rival media outlets might be doing?
- Who is your audience and what are their expectations?
- What does your editor/management expect?
- What is your own ethical position?

The first three of these points may seem unfeeling, but they are part of the reality of covering news. If you do conduct a deathknock interview, there is one thing you should always take with you and that is your own humanity. Deathknocks don't have to be done in an uncaring and intrusive way. Journalists don't and shouldn't leave compassion at the door.

Stuart Howie, editor of the Victorian regional daily, *The Courier*, says his paper only conducts a deathknock when it is considered appropriate and if the public interest merits the story.

He says covering these types of stories is different for a regional paper than for a metropolitan one, because, when someone in the community dies, it is usually someone they know. Stuart says his staff are encouraged to take a "step back" from the immediate family and look for other ways of getting the information or pictures.

For example, if a young person has died in tragic circumstances, it may be less stressful all round to approach their school for information and pictures, rather than the immediate family. This same policy also suggests that journalists should always try to use an intermediary to contact the relatives. Stuart suggests funeral directors can be a good link to those intermediaries.

Remember:

- Take your humanity with you.
- Check that the people know why you are there.
- Be honest.
- Identify yourself and your purpose.
- Don't say "I know how you feel" or ask "How does

it feel?"

- Keep the interview equipment to a minimum and out of sight.
- Start with simple questions.
- Remember that many people do want some form of tribute for their loved one.

Checklists for Covering Emergency Stories

Below are some useful checklists for the standard emergency services story. In each case you should always check first whether anyone has been killed or injured.

Fires (remember no "blazing infernos" please):

- Check the extent of property loss.
- What rescue operations were/are involved? Was any special equipment used?
- Were there any evacuations?
- Check the cause of the fire, if known.
- Check the number of personnel, units or volunteers involved.

Accidents (remember you must not attribute blame in the initial report—that is likely to be the subject of an inquiry.):

- Check the location and time of the accident.
- Check the vehicles involved.
- Check cause, if known, from an official source.
- Check names of the dead or injured and whether these have been released (i.e. have the relatives been notified?)
- Check where any injured have been taken and find out their latest condition.
- Ask the extent of injuries, if known.
- Were there any rescue attempts or any heroic acts?
- Check if there were unusual weather or road conditions.
- Get any eyewitness accounts.

Crime stories:

- Check victims" names and addresses. Usually these details will not be released until relatives have been informed. Check. Don't release such details until police have informed relatives.

- Check the time and location of the crime.
- Were any weapons used?
- Check whether any goods were stolen or damaged and, if applicable, get the total value.
- Check how entry to the premises was made.
- Check circumstances of discovery. For example, who found the body?
- Get police comments.
- Get comments from neighbours, friends or victims if possible.
- Check any unusual circumstances.

COVERING COURTS

It should go without saying that court reporters require a sound basic knowledge of the law. They also need to be aware of any specific state legislation that changes the way they can report in different jurisdictions.

The Australian legal system consists of both state and federal courts. There are different tiers of court, depending on the nature, importance or severity of the case. Court reporters spend most of their time covering criminal cases in state courts, specifically:

- The Magistrates Court (also known as Local Courts or Court of Petty Sessions).
- The District (or County) court.
- The Supreme Court.

At federal level you will find the Federal Court, Family Court and the High Court.

More than any other single area of reporting, court stories are likely to have a negative impact on the people involved who will be exposed to public scrutiny regardless of the eventual outcome of their case. The issues this raises demand particular thought and care on the part of reporters.

Many journalists, particularly in regional areas, have had experience of individuals (or their families) pleading that their court appearances not be covered. Different news organisations handle this in different ways and these can include a policy that all court stories are covered or that none are or that certain types of stories are covered and not others.

Some papers have a policy that the names and addresses of people appearing in court should not be published. The sensitivities of reporting courts have also led some news outlets to adopt policies such as dropping honorifics like "Mr" for people found guilty. Reporters need to be aware of their own organisation's guidelines.

The sensitivities of reporting courts in a small community can have repercussions for reporters themselves, and Nina Lees, who covers courts in a regional area, suggests regional court reporters should have unlisted numbers and protect the details of their home addresses. She also cautions against talking about court stories in public.

Court reports must be fair, balanced and accurate. Reporting courts requires even greater attention to detail than in other reporting. The elements that need to be included in a court report of a criminal matter include:

–The full name, occupation, age and address of a person charged with an offence—except in those cases where identification is not permitted. (These details are necessary to avoid confusion between the accused and anyone else with a similar name.)

- The nature of the accused's plea—either guilty or not guilty. Note that this is so sensitive that you should check and recheck that it appears correctly in the copy.
- Full details of the charge.

It is obviously important to check the name of the magistrate or judge in a case, and of any lawyers or witnesses involved. Court reporter Nina Lees suggests going back to the Clerk of the Court to check basic details such as the accused's name and other details before writing a report.

Testimony quoted from a court case needs to be reproduced faithfully. Even small changes in the words used can change the meaning of what was said and have unwanted repercussions.

Nina advises writing down everything you hear in court, but only expect to use a fraction of it. Leave out anything you are not 100 per cent certain of, unless it is vital to the report, in which case check it until you are certain.

The terminology that applies to some cases also needs to be used accurately.

For instance:

- Committal hearings are held to decide whether there is enough evidence to send an accused person to trial. They are preliminary hearings, not trials.
- At the conclusion of a committal hearing, the accused is either discharged (not "acquitted") or committed for trial (not "found guilty").
- Reporters also need to ensure they accurately report a convicted person's sentence. If several offences have been dealt with, the accused may be ordered to serve concurrent or cumulative sentences. Concurrent means that the sentences will be served at the same time; cumulative means they will follow one after the other. If the time the convicted person spends in jail may be shortened by parole, this will affect the way the report should be phrased.

Generally, anything said in an open court is protected by privilege and may be reported. But some things cannot be published:

- An accused person's previous criminal history cannot be reported until a trial is over.
- Evidence must not be published until it is presented in open court.
- An accused person's confession must not be reported until read out in open court.
- Information given to a court in the absence of the jury must not be published.
- Any material which the judge has ordered suppressed must not be published.
- The victims in sexual assault cases may not be identified.
- Children charged with offences or otherwise involved

in court cases may not be identified, but note that the age at which someone ceases to be a child varies between states and territories. Reporters need to check this in their own area.

- Parties or witnesses to cases in the Family Court may not be identified.
- If the identity of the accused could be an issue in a case then you should not publish the image of the accused (and this includes photographs, video and also drawings).

Like other rounds reporters, those covering courts need to develop specific contacts—including clerks of courts, judges and their associates, barristers and solicitors, police prosecutors and police officers. That said, court reporters need to take care not to uncritically accept information offered by their contacts, especially police contacts.

Court reporting involves respecting court etiquette. This includes dressing in a businesslike manner and bowing or nodding at the judge or magistrate when entering or leaving the court.

It goes without saying that you should turn off your mobile phone before entering the court and that you should not check mobile phone messages or chew gum in court.

Some courts now allow reporters to use recording devices—but only to ensure accuracy, not for broadcast. Check with the judge's associate or court information officer.

GENERAL COURT REPORTING AND WRITING TIPS

- Remember to make connections on both police and court rounds. If there are 10 assault cases of a particular type on one day, find out why.
- Look for the "around-the-system" type stories—for example, the appointment of a new person to deal with indigenous issues could provide a good story. Alternatively, if there have been a number of similar cases then that might warrant a background feature. One reporter found one such story in detailing the

problems of the slow processing of domestic violence cases.

WARNING

Stay away from any colourful language. Write it straight. In particular there is no room for descriptions like "the guilty looking man fidgeted in the dock".

Defamation

While contempt of court is a particular concern for police and court reporters, all journalists need to know what constitutes defamation and the defences available.

The generally accepted definition of a defamatory statement is that it causes a person or institution to be:

- Exposed to hatred, contempt or ridicule.
- Lowered in the estimation of right-thinking people.
- Avoided or shunned by their peers.
- Stated or implied to be unfit, unqualified or incompetent for their professions.

The defences to defamation are:

- That the report is true. In Victoria, South Australia, Western

Australia and the Northern Territory, truth alone is a defence. In New South Wales you need to prove truth and public interest. In Queensland, Tasmania and the Australian Capital Territory, you need to prove truth and that its publication was for the public benefit.

- That the report is protected by qualified privilege. This defence applies to accurate and fair reports of the proceedings of parliaments and documents published with parliamentary authority, court proceedings, judicial inquiries such as Royal Commissions and, in some states or territories, council meetings and some other forums.
- *Fair comment*: This allows reviews of films, televisions and plays and sporting events provided these are fair and based on facts which are either well known or set out in the report.

Two excellent guides to media law are listed at the end of this section.

COVERING COUNCILS/LOCAL GOVERNMENT

Councils may be the lowest tier of government but they do deal with issues of major concern to many people and their activities are a staple of reporting for local papers. The proceedings of open council meetings can be reported and, in some states, qualified privilege applies to reports of these meetings. Journalists need to check the rules applying in their own area.

Council rounds reporters need:

- A working knowledge of the state or territory's Local Government Act.
- To know which departments look after specific functions.
- To know how to read a council report (but don't reproduce the jargon).
- To cultivate contacts among council officers.

TIPS FROM A REPORTER

Mary Papadakis covered local government for *The Geelong Advertiser* for several years. She concedes that "council is not traditionally seen as an exciting or "sexy" round like police rounds". But, she says, it can be. The most distinctive feature in this round is the fact that, at one time or another, council decisions will affect everybody living in the municipality. This makes the council round very newsworthy.

The contacts you use on the council round are very diverse. Contacts could include local pressure groups and other interest groups, local real estate agents, the local chamber of commerce, progress associations and resident action groups as well as sports associations and clubs like Rotary.

Depending on the story, contacts can be made simply, for example, by door-knocking residents living near the site of a proposed controversial development, or through ratepayer action groups. Council officers and councillors are always good sources. But Mary warns that it can be difficult on this round to access information other than through official channels because many councils now employ professional public relations and media teams.

Mary's survival tips for the council rounds are:

- Don't be afraid to ask questions.
- Always ask for copies of reports referred to by councillors in or out of meetings.
- Keep in regular contact with councillors, council officers and council media departments.
- Read up on ongoing issues before attending a council meeting.
- Familiarise yourself with the formalities of council meetings.
- Don't take things on face value or regurgitate the information provided in meeting agendas.
- Do your research and always look for a better story.

Mary also warns that young reporters need to work hard to turn what are essentially informative stories into stories that are interesting or entertaining. She says it can also be difficult to keep abreast of all council meetings and outcomes and be aware of a wide-range of issues including those of an environmental, social, political or economic nature.

Council stories should essentially be treated like any other story, always look for an interesting angle and make sure you are short, sharp and to the point. There is a formula to a degree in the sense of discussing motions and amendments, who voted for what and whether a decision provides scope for public comment.

The trick with council stories is also to look for a human-interest element and expand your story. Take time out to consider how a council proposal or decision will affect ratepayers, particularly their hip-pocket.

Health rounds

Anyone consuming some sections of our media could be forgiven for thinking that there is a major breakthrough or a new miracle cure every day and herein lies the first two lessons for covering the health round:

- Be sceptical. You must ask *who* is making any claim and *why*.
- Avoid the clichés.

Because this round covers a vital issue of concern to most people, it is absolutely essential that journalists strive for high standards of responsibility and accuracy.

- Don't fall for the PR and certainly don't accept any claims made in a media release. Try and find the source of the information—for instance, the leader of the university research team (though the claims of researchers should also be checked with others in the field).
- Always question who is backing the research.
- Cut out all the jargon. If you don't understand what the medical language means then certainly your readers won't understand it. Keep digging until you find someone who can explain the issue in clear, understandable language.
- Beware the words "groundbreaking" and "miracle cure".

Anyone who has worked in a newsroom will be aware of the intense public interest in any story canvassing new medical treatments. The special responsibility this places on journalists is spelt out in the Professional Conduct Policy at News Ltd:

Reports of new drugs or medical treatments must be considered with great caution. It is easy to raise false hopes or alarm among readers. Cross check all claims with responsible and neutral sources.

Mary-Anne Toy was the health editor for *The Age* newspaper for four years and she has her own insider tips for this complex round.

- Get out and see people whenever you can. Don't stay chained to the desk. Show people that you are around and that you are interested. Go to the hospitals, go the conferences and go to the Minister's launches. This all builds goodwill and this is the foundation of the round. Every contact is important, from the

Minister down to the support staff in a hospital.

- Bookmark key websites, including those of the leading medical journals.
- You need to develop good scanning skills and be sceptical: there are a lot of quacks (however well intentioned) and misinformation out there. You have to be able to take in a lot of information quickly and then you need contacts who can qualify and interpret that information for you.
- *Think of your audience*: You need to be able to explain your stories in terms that you can understand and that the public can understand. This is not about "dumbing down", this is about writing well. Most scientists and doctors are good at explaining things if you are prepared to keep asking them.

When it comes to writing health stories, Mary-Anne says reporters need to consider both the market or the audience and the timing of the story.

Some stories will lend themselves to a straight news format, like a fresh outbreak of legionnaire's disease. But a new insight from laboratory work with mice may lend itself more to a feature-style article. You need to make your judgement calls based on experience.

POLITICAL ROUNDS

John Ferguson covers the state round for the *Herald Sun* in Melbourne and has covered politics in various states for almost 10 years. He says the most important thing when covering politics in any form is to establish your credibility as a journalist and credibility comes with being accurate. The more credibility you have, the more people will want to talk to you.

John's advice to anyone starting a political round is to "learn quickly who are the most reliable sources of information" and "work out which MPs will tell you what's really going on". He says you soon learn that there aren't many. Often good sources are the backbenchers or sometimes it is the malcontents, people who may have missed out on a promotion. These are people with an axe to grind and you need to learn to balance their prejudices. When dealing with sources, you always need to know who they are and where they are coming from. You need to understand why they are telling you something.

John says that building your contacts requires "an element of lunch or coffee". He says, "You want to be able to build a relationship that has a bit of a relaxed atmosphere. If it is always going to be on the record, you can't really build a strong relationship."

John's survival tips for political rounds include:

- Be accurate and be fair but also learn not to swallow the official line.
- Learn to poke and to prod.
- Everyone in politics has an agenda and everyone has the capacity to lie.
- The higher up the chain the source, the better the info.

When it comes to writing news stories on this round, John says any kind of formulaic writing is out.

The days of formulaic news writing are gone. There is a real art to writing news properly. Clichés are to be avoided wherever possible. You have to present your news stories in different forms; you don't want to be predictable.

There are always a hundred different ways to write any story. To capture the essence of a story, I will always try to portray its urgency and I try to capture detail and build atmosphere. For example, if the Premier is making an announcement and his back is covered in sweat, then this is a sign of a man under pressure, which is something you should try and convey to your readers. I always try to include colour into my writing.

Like most seasoned reporters, John understands that journalism doesn't stop when you leave the newsroom for the night. One evening he was having dinner in an Adelaide restaurant and, looking across a crowded room he spotted a man he recognised. The man was a merchant banker associated with the collapse of the State Bank who had gone to ground and had been "missing in action" for several weeks. John didn't hesitate to get up from his dinner, phone work and arrange for a photographer to meet him outside the restaurant. He also didn't hesitate to leave his friends sitting in the restaurant for more than an hour while he waited outside. He did however get the scoop.

SPORTS REPORTING

Nothing fills as much space in Australia's newspapers and time on its radio and television news bulletins as sport. Nothing can throw politics, economics or crime off the front pages faster than the latest sporting achievement or scandal involving a sporting icon.

Australians are obsessed with sport—whether it's in the cricket or tennis or golf season over summer, or in the football season (whatever the code) in winter, or when one of our favourite sons or daughters (or teams) is winning on the international stage.

When Brisbane Broncos rugby league star Allan (Alfie) Langer (temporarily) retired in 1999, saying his heart was no longer in the game, both the Queensland Premier and the Prime Minister felt it necessary to eulogise Alfie's contribution to the game. Channel 9 said on the news that night that Queenslanders were in shock.

Mention "the first Tuesday in November" or "the last Saturday in September" and sports fans around the nation know you're referring to the Melbourne Cup (for which we're told "the nation stops") and the AFL grand final (on the "hallowed turf" of the Melbourne Cricket Ground).

Sport is big business, and not only in terms of what free-to-air and pay TV networks shell out to broadcast events and in sponsorship deals for naming rights to the big events and teams. There's also the amounts paid to the stars of the major sports in earnings, appearance money and winnings, as well as the sponsorship dollars the stars can command for endorsing products.

In winnings alone, a Leighton Hewitt, Pat Rafter or Greg Norman can take home more in a competitive week than most

Australians will earn in 20 years. Overseas, the earnings of major sporting stars—like Tiger Woods and other top golfers, Formula One racing driver Michael Schumacher, the world's best soccer players, and the baseball, basketball and gridiron stars of the US—beggar the imagination.

It's the hundreds of hours a week devoted to sports coverage on freetoair and pay TV that's a major problem for sports journalists.

Every time they sit in front of their computer terminal to compose a story about the latest exploits of the national cricket side, the Brisbane Lions AFL team, or the Wallabies rugby side, they know that most fans already know the result, and either saw the game in person or on TV.

The West Australian's David Marsh is a senior sports writer who's covered three Olympic Games and three Commonwealth Games and has been covering sport for his Perth paper for nearly 20 years. What can he write that the audience doesn't already know from watching TV?

The sports journalist can no longer simply chronicle facts in the form of a match report, with readers wanting and demanding more from their paper. For example, after Cathy Freeman won the Olympic women's 400 metres gold medal in Sydney, simply providing a description of the race was superfluous for most Australians.

To remain valid, the print journalist will need to ask the big questions: What significance her victory will have for Australian society? What will it do for Aboriginal rights? And what does the man or woman in the street say about the victory?

REPORTING AND WRITING TIPS

Reporting sporting contests, whether they're between individuals or teams, involves many of the basic tenets of good reporting on any round, like politics, business, the law courts or police rounds. But to put these stories in their unique sporting context, here are some tips for reporting and writing this important round.

- *Do your research*: Know how the game or contest is

won or lost. If, as a novice sports reporter (and all reporters will at some stage have to cover sport, even if they loathe it), you are sent to a sport you know next to nothing about, do as much research as you can beforehand. While most know the basics of the major games such as cricket, golf, tennis, basketball, baseball and the various football codes—AFL, rugby union and league, and soccer—from schooldays or casual interest, there are many sports which will be unfamiliar. Ring the local association, check the sport's websites, and establish the fundamentals before the game. If you're still ignorant of the basics, find someone in the game's administration who can fill you in before the competition begins.

- *Know the rules of the game*: Learn how points, goals or whatever are scored. Find out if the particular fixture has a referee or an umpire. Establish what constitutes a penalty, under what circumstances a player can be sent off, and how the particular sport's judiciary system operates to decide further penalties for on or off-field indiscretions. Nothing opens you to more ridicule—if only among the sub-editors back in the office—than confusing the fundamentals of the game. For instance, both rugby league and rugby union have tries. In rugby league, a team gets four points for a try, two for a successful goal conversion or penalty goal, and one for a field goal. In rugby union, it's five for a try and two for a successful conversion. Much of the scoring in union comes from penalty goals—each worth three points. Teams have scored tries in union, and been beaten because they gave away too many penalties that were converted into points.
- *Learn the language of the particular sport*: Each sport has its unique language. In golf, for instance, they talk about sub-par rounds, of birdies, eagles, albatrosses and the much-prized hole-in-one. Yachties talk about spinnakers, tacking and beating to

windward. If you don't know what they're talking about, ask. Make sure you can write your stories so that people who are unfamiliar with the finer points of the contest will understand what happened. In other words, avoid using sports jargon in your stories.

- *Cultivate contacts in every sport*: This is especially helpful in the early stages of your sports reporting career. These contacts are the sports administrators, players, coaches, trainers, physios and so on who can give you invaluable background before and after the contest that will help you to put the conflict into context. As with all rounds, you need to nurture contacts, and sometimes you also have to criticise them in the context of a story, which can lead to strained relations.
- Know the star performers in the particular sport. Know if they are carrying an injury, returning from suspension or, in the case of cricketing twins Steve and Mark Waugh in 2002, struggling to keep their places on the national team. In this context you also need to know something of sports medicine. What is involved in the various common sporting injuries, what effects will the injuries have on the champion's performance, and how long will they be out of the game? Watch the stars to see if they rise to the occasion (most do), or if they underperform. Watch for the rising star. How do they perform on debut?
- *Be aware of the context of the contest*: It might be a club game, but is an individual playing for a place in a state or national team? Are they playing just to stay in the team? Or are they making a come-back?
- Get the background on the major issues in sport. Drugs are a major issue in sport, from the rugby league star who tests positive to recreational drugs to the systematic use of performance-enhancing drugs in sports such as cycling and weight-lifting. In recent years, the big issue in international cricket

was match-fixing. At the Sydney 2000 Olympic Games, the major issues were drugs (again), and also the politics of international sport, ticketing foul-ups, and public transport. All provided major stories during "the most successful Olympics ever".

- *Know the history of the team or individual*: If it's a team sport, what's the record of previous clashes between the two teams? How have the teams or individuals performed in recent times?
- *Keep the statistics*: All sports have their statistics. It's a way of comparing performances over the years. Know the ones that pertain to your particular sport and keep them at hand. Remember the excitement when the Sydney Swans" Tony (Plugger) Lockett broke the AFL's long-standing record for the most goals kicked? *The West Australian*'s David Marsh keeps a large database of sports at home. He collects basic biographical information and up-to-date results, and has copies of the annual books that cover the major performances around the world. "At my first Olympics in Seoul in 1988, I took all of my records in several manila folders. But at the 1998 Commonwealth Games and 2000 Olympics, with the improvements in technology, where I took a PC, all my records were downloaded into two floppy disks, " David says.
- Give the "why" and "how" of the contest, but don't forget the result. What was the turning point in the event? Why did the team or individual win or lose? How did the winning team or individual exert their dominance over the competition? This is where much of your audience will have an opinion, so get it right. Did anyone break a record during the game? It's here and in post-contest interviews with participants, coaches and officials that newspaper journalists often find the story that hasn't been seen on TV or from the grandstand.
- Watch the body language of the individual or team.

Did the opposition drop their heads after the third try in five minutes in a rugby league game, or after the sixth unanswered goal in an AFL match? At what stage did they appear resigned to defeat?

COVERING MAJOR SPORTS EVENTS

Covering major events, like the final game of a competition but more particularly events such as the Commonwealth and Olympic games, poses its own set of problems. In Kuala Lumpur in 1998, Sydney in 2000 and Manchester in 2002, teams of reporters were sent from all over Australia to cover the gold-medal aspirants.

The big media groups, like News Ltd, Fairfax, Australian Associated Press and the major television and radio networks, sent teams of reporters (and photographers and cameramen) to slake Australians" insatiable thirst for news on our competitors. The major broadcast organisations pay big money for the rights to cover these events, and not having "rights-holder" access to athletes adds to the problems of a journalist from a relatively small media group.

Such organisations may send one or two reporters (and possibly a photographer) for the sole purpose of covering the performances of competitors from their local area. Not every competitor is going to win a gold medal, but there's a story in how the local hero performs against international competition, something the news agencies and major media groups are unlikely to cover unless the competitor ends up on the medal podium.

So how do you cover local competitors? The organisers of major sporting festivals like the Olympic and Commonwealth games set up internal news services to provide officials and the visiting media with coverage of every event. While this helps the journalist who has to cover several sports at different venues at the same time, it rarely provides enough detail about "local" competitors for the local paper "back home".

David Marsh had to cover several sports on his own at the 1988 Olympic Games in Seoul and at the 1990

Commonwealth Games in Auckland, New Zealand. Being the only reporter from the organisation at the Games meant being selective about which events to cover—and that meant covering events from an Australian perspective. The main sports I covered in Seoul were the swimming in the early part of the Games, and the track and field, which started at the end of the first week.

There are times when the unexpected can happen, which results in the best-laid plans being shelved. Seoul is an example, when Canadian sprinter Ben Johnson tested positive to the anabolic steroid stanazol. I was taken off my scheduled duties at the Games for more than a day to follow the Ben Johnson story.

The regional journalist faces any number of problems reporting such events. Transport to the various venues that doesn't run to the pre-arranged timetable, telephone connections that are unreliable, events that are completed after the paper's deadline (because of time differences) to name a few. Covering local competitors for regional media starts for the sports journalists long before the actual competition begins. They make contact with the competitors local to their area before they leave for the event. They get the competitors" mobile phone numbers, and organise to meet them after their main event. In this way they get "their story".

It may be a story of success or disappointment, but it will be the story the locals "back home" want to hear. Sometimes it will be a "colour" story of what the local competitor did in the Games city after their event—how they enjoyed the atmosphere of such a major event, whether the family were there to see them, what it was like to live in the athletes" village, or simply a story about a shopping spree with local athletes. These are the sorts of stories that the network and major newspaper coverage cannot provide, but will be of intense interest to "local" readers, listeners and viewers.

But, like everything associated with journalism in general, and sports journalism in particular, pre-planning, an abundance of background knowledge and reliable contacts are essential. Actually writing the story is no different to any other news story. It is your evaluation of the various commonly used news criteria that will decide how the story will flow. Proximity, for instance, will determine a major part of the lead.

While in Brisbane a win by the rugby league team, the Broncos, will be lauded as another victory to the local audience, in the "local area" of the defeated team it will be reported as a loss. At the Kuala Lumpur games, the audience "back home" was really only interested in the gold medal victories of the Australian competitors, and the rare defeats of the highly fancied, like the full-strength Aussie cricket team.

One of the main news criteria used in sporting stories is, of course, conflict. Sports events are almost always characterised as conflicts, with sporting reporters using language perhaps more at home in the "War on Terror" than in a "conflict" on the sporting field.

In team sports, for instance, unless a key player is injured, the lead will usually be who won, the score and possibly why.

Prominence is another news criteria used by sports writers in determining the angle for their story. If the star performs well—a century to a one-day cricket captain, or five or more wickets to a top bowler—they will often figure in a "double-barrelled" lead that combines the outstanding performance with the result.

Two of the other accepted news criteria, suspense and resolution, figure in every sporting story—suspense as the contest is played out (and covered progressively on radio, online or TV) and resolution when we know the result.

Other news criteria also figure in sports reports, like timeliness (it must be the latest result), interest (there is always public interest in sports results—the more public interest, the bigger the story) and clarity (your story needs to be understood by all readers regardless of familiarity, or lack of, with the sport). Human interest (the rising star), novelty (the outstanding performance or strange occurrence) and, of course, sensation (in any form) will all have a place when deciding how to construct a sports story.

Chapter 8

An Interview

News is fundamentally about people and it is people who are a journalist's main source of information from which to mould news.

The process by which journalists get most of their information from sources is interviewing. Interviews can range from structured, live to air, broadcast current affairs interviews to the much looser lifestyle and human interest interviews heard on radio and television, to over-the-telephone conversations which are the way in which many reporters gather much of their information.

Whether a conversation or a contest, confession or confrontation, interviewing is a complex exchange. What all these circumstances have in common is that at least one reporter (sometimes an entire room full) is questioning at least one other person with a view to obtaining information.

Most reporters agree that interviewing, or gathering information through an interview, is one of the most difficult aspects of the job. It is also one of the most important. As Paterno and Stein point out: "In journalism, quotes—or the lack of them—can make or break a story".

There is usually someone to assist in writing or producing your story after you have collected your information but with interviewing, you are generally on your own, asking questions of someone you have never met, about an area you may know little to nothing about. SBS journalist and presenter, Jana Wendt, compares the experience of interviewing to being "dropped by parachute into a foreign country then having to put on a four act play".

There's plenty of room for error, particularly for young journalists new to the profession and to interviewing. There are very few journalists who don't have a tale to tell about an interview that went wrong. The tips and guidelines included in this chapter are aimed at helping you to avoid the pitfalls of interviewing.

There are three main keys to success in interviewing. Most journalists will agree you need to:

- *Prepare*: Research and preparation for the interview is essential.
- *Listen:* This will encourage your interviewee, help you to focus and enable you to get the most from your interview.
- *Check*: Don't be afraid to check you have answers to all the key questions and that you have taken down the information correctly.

SETTING UP AN INTERVIEW

Most interviews begin with a phone call. This phone call may be to set up an interview time, or to obtain background information to help you to devise the questions. Ideally, you would want to conduct the actual interview face-to-face, and preferably one-to-one as well, though on-the-spot media conferences (called "doorstops") are an increasingly common method of interviewing.

Sometimes you will have to conduct your interview over the phone, or via email, either because the person you want to interview is too busy for a face-to-face meeting or because the workload of the newsroom requires reporters to complete stories as fast as possible.

Of course, sometimes all you will want is a short comment, so a phone interview will be the quickest and most efficient means of getting it. But for longer interviews, phone and email lack a vital ingredient—the non-verbal communication (or body language) which is part of a face-to-face exchange.

The telephone at least will provide you with some clues from the person's tone of voice, or if they laugh or sound abrupt, but email will not provide any of these. The latter is ideal for contacting people from all over the world, but can be even easier to ignore than the phone if the source does not want to talk to you.

What do you want from the interview?

When you set out to conduct an interview, it's important that you know *what* it is that you want to achieve. The first step should be to get a firm idea of the story and the angle, and how the interview will contribute to this. You should be able to summarise your story in about 30 words (or write a possible intro) and, if you can't, you need to spend some time getting this straight before going any further.

Author of a leading book on interviewing, Shirley Biagi, believes you should also establish the interview *why* or the goal or purpose of the interview. She asks: "Will you: Gather facts? Look for quotes? Collect anecdotes? Characterize a situation? Confirm what you know? Show that you were there?"

Once you have determined *what* you want to achieve, and *why* you need to conduct the interview, now is a good time to look at the *who* of the story. Who are the key figures involved? Who can you contact? In other words, who should be interviewed. Make a list of the sources you want to interview for the story.

Shirley Biagi also notes that time should be spent ensuring you have the best source for your story.

People become part of the news for one or more of several reasons:

- Their jobs are important
- They accomplish something important
- They know something or someone important
- They have watched something important happen
- Something important has happened to them
- They represent an important national or international trend

Sometimes the nature of the news will present the obvious choice for the interview. As we've seen already, news can come from events that are managed or that occur spontaneously, from the watching briefs or from reporters" rounds. To a certain extent, these will dictate who you speak to and how you interview them.

For instance, with a managed event such as a media conference, the person conducting the conference will be your main source. Today, doorstop interviews are probably the most common method of interviewing politicians, CEOs and other busy people.

Doorstops usually involve representatives of the different media—print, radio and television—all of them with different interests and deadlines. Political reporter for *The Age*, Richard Baker, says asking a question in this environment can be "quite Newsmakers often find it more convenient to give "all-in" interviews rather than talk to reporters individually.

Intimidating" for young reporters. But reporters have to get used to working in front of their peers. Richard says confidence comes with practice and he recommends journalists new to the job should tag along with more experienced reporters to see how these doorstops operate, and how other journalists handle them.

INTERVIEWING STYLE

The style of interviewing each journalist uses reflects not just their training but also their cultural background and personality. That means some reporters may adopt a combative style to get the answers they want, while others may find it difficult to be sufficiently pushy to get more than superficial responses.

The Editorial Training Consultant for Victoria's Leader Newspaper group, Jane Cafarella, has written of the need for young journalists, especially women, to overcome a tendency to be "nice", saying it's not the best characteristic for a journalist. She says too often these young journalists want the interviewee to like them and that makes them gullible. Jane tells her cadets that their job is "to represent the reader and to ask what the reader needs to know". She says reporters conducting interviews should always imagine the reader looking over their shoulder asking "Why?"

Editor of *The Fraser Coast Chronicle,* Nancy Bates, says a reporter needs to think about the expression on their face and the tone of their voice during an interview. Reporters shouldn't give the impression that they're on one side or another of a debate. Nancy tells her journalists, "If you are asking questions, be detached", though she concedes that "it's easier to be detached on some issues than on the ones more inclined to arouse sympathy".

REMEMBER

A reporter must accurately represent the views of the interviewee. But that doesn't mean you need to agree with them. A reporter is there to represent the public's interests, not the interviewee's.

Reporters wanting to improve their interviewing style will probably benefit from watching top interviewers in action. But it is not recommended that you copy someone else's style. Richard Baker believes a journalist's interviewing style is instinctive, but techniques can be learned.

It's only by being around a bit and getting experience that you can get the guts to say to someone "Hey hang on you're not answering my question. " You learn that and it comes with being around people and having a bit of experience and confidence.

DIFFERENT MEDIA, DIFFERENT STYLES

Always collect more information than you need, it's easy to cut out material later, but extremely difficult to pad out a story if you have not got enough information. However, this tip is only useful if you have the luxury of time. Generally, broadcast journalists have to gather just enough for what they need (sometimes only a seven-second grab) and then run to get it back to the newsroom to edit their story.

This is just one way in which different media make different demands on the way reporters conduct interviews. They also often want different *types* of responses. Print reporters often want a lot of detail as well as comment to help to expand their reports. By contrast, radio reporters usually want raw information—"When is something going to take place?" "How many people will this affect?" That's because radio news reports are brief and to the point. Television news is good at conveying the emotion of a situation, but not good at presenting large amounts of detail. Television reporters will often ask "emotional" questions, the "How did that make you feel" style of question.

The types of interviews reporters conduct, and the skills required, also vary according to the type of publication a reporter is working for. Jane Cafarella says many of the people who are interviewed by reporters working in metro media outlets are accustomed to being interviewed and they know what's expected of them when answering questions. By contrast, she says, journalists working for suburban or regional papers have to be prepared to coax information out of ordinary people who are not used to dealing with journalists.

A lot of the time the people we interview aren't newsmakers. They're not used to being interviewed. So it's not so much a question of trying to get information from people who are holding back because they've got big company or hot political secrets. It's people who either won't shut up or won't say anything. So there's a skill in drawing those people out.

THE FIVE Ws AND H

There are six questions which should be answered in every story—who, what, when, where, why and how—commonly known as the five Ws and H. Even the smallest news brief, of two or three paragraphs or sentences, should answer the first four of these questions at the very least.

The two main question types are:

- Closed (requiring only a "yes" or "nO' answer).
- Open (inviting more explanation and detail).

It is very easy to turn a closed question into an open one, simply by adding one of the five Ws and H. For instance, if you were to ask a netball player, "Do you think you'll win the game?" you would probably elicit just a "Yes". However if you ask, "*What* will influence the outcome of the game?" you should get so much more simply by adding *what* to the question.

Jana Wendt says early in her career she made the mistake of trying to make things too complicated. She believes the best advice for those starting out in interviewing is to keep it as simple as possible because there's "nothing like a simple question—the classic who, what, when, where, why and how questions".

They're a sure-fire way of getting a flow of conversation. They give you time to think about what you are being told, and any weakness in an argument, and how you might be able to draw a person out. Simple is always best.

However, occasionally you will require someone to answer a closed question to confirm important information. For instance, if you were to ask the prime minister if taxes were going to increase next year, you need a firm "yes" or "no' answer before asking for any details. Another useful question is described by Sedorkin and McGregor as the "bigger, brighter, better" question.

These are the sort of questions the public would want to ask if they were conducting the interview themselves. For instance, an interview with a police detective about a drug raid invites the "bigger, brighter, better" question. The curious journalist should be wondering: What makes this raid different, special, unusual or worthy of coverage?; What gives it that newsworthy angle?

Example: Q: Is this the biggest drug raid in this area/ state/country? A "yes" answer to this question could easily result in a front page story.

Richard Baker advises against excessive formality. He says, "If you're interviewing someone for a newspaper, magazine or E-zine, you don't want to make them feel as though they're being quizzed on *Four Corners* or *60 Minutes.* You want your interviewee to feel comfortable."

That means if you have the time to conduct the interview face-to-face (rather than by phone or email), you should try to schedule the interview in a place where the interviewee is most likely to feel relaxed. That might be their office, or a coffee shop and so on. A reporter needs to be adaptable. They also need to be patient. Richard says he would never start an interview with his toughest question.

You've got to get the interviewee at ease and gain a bit of trust. So, if it's a contentious issue, start with a few general questions—let them get their side of the story out and then work into the harder questions and then pull back. You don't want to batter them around the head because very rarely will it get you anywhere. You just want to try and seduce them into speaking honestly and without feeling that they've been driven into providing a certain answer.

Jane Rocca, who often interviews people in the entertainment industries, believes it's important not to shy away from uncomfortable questions. She says an interviewer can afford to be "a bit daring", as long as it's done with respect.

If you want to confirm a rumour or something you read about that person (for instance in the tabloids), approach the topic gently. Don't patronise the artist but simply ask what they think of a specific article. Be daring to get their opinion on something completely off the wall. If it is a music interview, don't be afraid to venture into family chit chat, religion, spirituality, drugs etc. You often get the best material by just being yourself and digging more than just beneath the surface.

In their book *Talk Straight, Listen Carefully: The art of interviewing,* Paterno and Stein say it's important to avoid "overloading" questions. One way of overloading is to pose a double-barreled question, which contains two or more questions in one. The problem with overloading a question is that it gives a "source with something to hide" the opportunity to "keep it hidden".

For example, when reporters were trying to find out if then US president Bill Clinton had had a long-standing affair with a woman named Gennifer Flowers, a well-known television reporter misused his opportunity by asking an overloaded question.

Reporter: "Was Gennifer Flowers your lover for 12 years?" Clinton: "That allegation is false." What allegation is false? That she was his lover? Or that she was his lover for 12 years? Maybe she was his lover for 11 years or seven years, in which case Clinton answered truthfully. By asking imprecise questions, reporters allow sources to wriggle out of responding to issues that are difficult for them.

Different reporters have different opinions about whether a reporter should have all their questions written down, though most journalists agree that when someone is just starting in journalism, they should at least write down their first few questions and perhaps any complex questions they might otherwise forget.

Others suggest it is more useful to have a list of key areas to be covered in the interview, rather than specifically worded questions. The concern with written questions is that journalists can, and do, stick slavishly to their lists, rather than listening and taking their cues from what the interviewee is saying.

Presenter of Radio National's *Breakfast* programme, and former presenter of the SBS television current affairs programme *Insight,* Vivian Schenker says she finds it very useful to have a list of questions, for two main reasons:

One, if your mind goes blank, but more importantly because I refresh my mind as I'm going with the sorts of areas I want to cover. I remind myself that "yes, that's still really important and I want to get back to that, but those four in the middle are much less important" and "how do I get from here to here?". I'm thinking while I'm listening and while they're talking.

Ask any experienced interviewer the secret of a good interview and they'll usually say it's *listening* to the interviewee. Vivian Schenker at ABC Radio National.

So I think it's not a bad idea to have done the preparation and the work and have an idea of what you want out of the interview, as long as you're prepared to throw it away, and as long as you listen really, really hard— not just with one ear. Vivian says the best tip she can give people doing interviews is *listen.* She says, "I'm still staggered by how many people there are who think they don't have to concentrate really hard during the interview—that if they'd done their homework, then that was the work done. To me, homework can sometimes be thrown right out the door."

Vivian also believes that the really crucial part is the actual interview, not the preparation. She says, "Preparation makes you feel more confident going in, and I would always have the first questions written down, and I would always actually have a script and 10 questions. You just have to be prepared not to ask them, and not be sorry about it."

Former *60 Minutes* reporter and ABC foreign correspondent, Jeff McMullen, agrees that the most important skill to use during interviews is listening. He says one of the finest broadcast journalists he watched was Bill Moyers.

What he really did best was listen. He never had the rapier-thrust of Mike Wallace [a veteran reporter with the US *60 Minutes*] and he's not like the great British conversationalists, but he was such a strong mind. What he really did was sit with a brilliant person and listen.

Jeff says he took that lesson on board and from then on started to structure interviews differently. He says he's never worked with a clipboard or notebook in front of him. "I would, whether I was recording a *Four Corners* interview or a *60 Minutes* interview, study the subject, plan a very elaborate interview, commit it to memory, and then throw it away."

Jeff says he did what Moyers had shown him; that you have a conversation with people, and they will tell you which ways to go in the interview. "Your own mind, your improvisational skills, will take it where you need to go. But really that's more about listening than having the "smarty-pants" questions."

These days many people who deal with the media regularly, such as business people, politicians, sports people and so on, have been given media training to help them make the best of media appearances. These people know how reporters work and how to side-step reporters" questions to get their message across.

In cases such as this, it's important not to let a person in a position of authority bluff you. Reporters need to develop the confidence and authority to stand their ground and, if necessary, tell the interviewee that they are not answering the question and ask it again.

Certainly some interviewees are intimidating, either by design or simply because of their job or position. Broadcast journalist Sally Spalding says whenever she has to interview someone like that, she falls back on a piece of advice she was given early on in her career:

One tip that someone gave me was that, if I was ever intimidated when I was going out to do an interview, just to imagine the person I was going to interview with no clothes on! I've used that a lot. But it didn't help me once when I had to interview Gough Whitlam because he was still so intimidating—naked or clothed.

Jana Wendt believes the important thing to remember when you are feeling overawed is that you *are* the media and the conduit for the interviewee's words. "They know that," Jana says. "So you may look stupid and inexperienced and overawed, but ultimately you will be delivering this person's words and attitudes and style to the general public. So if they're smart they will realise, in a sense,*your* power, even if you're a very young journalist."

Jana says the best way to deal with someone who is overwhelming is to stay focused on what *you* want to achieve in your interview with this person.

Presumably you will have done your research. Presumably you will know what the key issues are, you know what this person's vulnerabilities and strengths may be, where the cracks are in any particular argument—hopefully you know that. So you craft your questions around those key important issues.

OBSERVATION

Observation is also very important with both "hard" and "soft" news interviews. Keep your questions short and let the interviewee speak as much as possible. In broadcast interviews, people want to hear the interviewee— not you. With print, you want quotes with *their* words, thoughts and opinions—not yours.

Interviewing requires more than just accurately taking down a person's responses to your questions. It means noticing their surroundings and general demeanour, because that might be an important part of the story.

Threadbare furniture and empty cupboards may tell you more about the plight of a family where the parents are out of work than anything the family says. Similarly, anger or frustration in the voices of consumers fighting a large corporation tells you something fundamental about their position.

Checking

Before you leave any interview you should check that:

- You have correctly taken down the interviewee's name and title.
- You have covered the five Ws and H and any other crucial questions.
- You have all the interviewee's contact details.

Journalist and media adviser, Andrea Carson, says she was given two really good pieces of advice when she first started interviewing.

One was to check that she had correctly taken down all the important information such as name and title. The other was that, before finishing an interview, she should always ask if there was anything else the interviewee would like to add that hadn't been covered. Invariably, she says, this produced some very important information and some really strong quotes on an area she had not thought to ask about.

It's important to check and clarify information as you go along, not just at the end of the interview. News director at 3AW, Rob Curtain, says checking throughout the interview ensures that you have understood what the interviewee is saying. One way of doing this is to paraphrase the interviewee's responses—for example, "so you're saying ..."—and use them as questions. One thing that's important for younger reporters—particularly doing stories you may not know much about—is that you need to keep putting back to the person you're interviewing your understanding of what they are saying.

It's almost as though you are writing the story in your head and putting it back to them because then, if it sounds completely different to them from the way it should, you know you're on the wrong track.

Remember

If an interviewee says something defamatory or in contempt of court, the outlet that publishes or broadcasts the comment is just as accountable as the person who made the comment and more likely to be sued or charged. As a reporter, you are responsible for what you write or broadcast, regardless of whose words you are quoting.

It's also important to remember that the mere fact that someone (no matter how highly placed they are) says something, doesn't make it true. All claims and comments need to be evaluated and checked. How much say should an interviewee have in the final product?

There's one question reporters are regularly asked by the people they interview: "Can I see the story before it's published/broadcast?" Interviewees have every right to be concerned about the way their comments will be used. They've probably heard of, or know of, incidents where interviewees felt they were misquoted or otherwise damaged by a media report. But does that mean you should give someone the right to veto your work? In most cases the answer is "no'.

For one thing, deadlines make it almost impossible to realistically promise to check back with every interviewee before publication.

But that means the onus is on the reporter to quote accurately, with sensitivity where required, and in context. In denying an interviewee the right to revise what they have said and check the way you've used it, you are asking them to trust your professional standards.

Quoting someone accurately won't guarantee that they approve of the finished story. That's because reporters must canvass opinion widely and weigh up competing interests in their stories.

Many reporters, even those with good shorthand, use recording devices during interviews. If you have a choice about the device you buy or use, choose a digital system, either solid state or MiniDisc.

These systems allow you to mark every significant point in the recording and later find each marker instantly. This overcomes the main criticism of cassette recorders, which is that it takes too long to spool though the tape when you're writing the story.

In addition, these digital devices are highly portable and, as long as they're equipped with a good quality microphone, will record audio at broadcast or webcast quality, if high quality audio is needed.

Ensure that the machine has a microphone input as well as a line input and line output. Unless the machine has a "mic in" socket, you will not be able to connect an external microphone. If you are buying a tape machine, you should spend the extra money to get one equipped with a counter.

Many reporters record interviews conducted over the phone for backup notes. There are a couple of devices that make this simple and easy.

One is a suction cup or "inductive phone line pick up", which can be attached to the phone's earpiece. The other is a small microphone that fits within an earpiece worn by the person recording the conversation. Note that for legal and ethical reasons you should *always* tell someone when you want to record them over the phone.

Print reporters who also want to use their interviews for broadcast or webcast have to learn one of the basics of interviewing for broadcast, which is to stay silent during the interview unless they are asking a question. Print reporters often encourage their interviewees by using common phrases—"really?", "uh huh", "go on" ... and so on. But these little interruptions sound silly when the audio is edited for use on air or online as a soundbite. So, if you need to edit your interview for use as audio soundbites, keep quiet when the interviewee is talking. Using a suction cup or an earpiece microphone, both shown above, makes it easy to record phone interviews, but interviewees should always be told they are being recorded.

Chapter 9

News Writing Style

Body subsidiary points in order of importance The inverted pyramid model of newswriting starts with an *introduction* (*intro* or *lead*) which will usually be no more than 25 words and contain the key elements of the story. The *body* of the story will cover remaining details in descending order of importance. The model of writing works for print and online news. It does not work for radio and television, where stories need a strong ending.

Putting the most important details first didn't just ensure that they weren't lost if the transmission by wire was interrupted. It also allowed sub-editors to trim stories from the bottom without losing any valuable details.

This form of news writing is called the "inverted pyramid" and, as its name suggests, it turns the traditional form of story telling on its head. Instead of being left until the end, the conclusion goes at the top as the "intro". The second sentence, or "par", expands on the intro and the remaining story details are then set out in descending order of importance.

WRITING TO SPACE

Starting a story with the punch line is the opposite of the narrative way of telling a tale. But these days, long after we stopped sending stories by telegraph wire, and despite the fact that editing from the bottom is no longer so common, it remains a useful technique. For one thing it allows readers to take in the most important points of a story without reading the rest, and that's all some readers want.

In recent years, some analysts have predicted the demise of inverted pyramid writing. It was seen as outdated at a time when many newspapers were turning to a more personalised or magazine style of writing.

In addition, the compilation of newspaper pages on computer screens means reporters these days usually know the number of centimetres allocated to their story when they write it.

The day after bushranger Ned Kelly was hanged in Melbourne in November 1880, *The Sydney Morning Herald* ran the following report on the bottom of page five.

Much has changed in news delivery since then but in this report we can see the development of the style of news writing we work with today.

For one thing, though some of the language used may seem unfamiliar, the report is a factual account of Kelly's death.

And while much of the report follows the events of the day in the order in which they occurred, there is a clear hierarchy of information, with the main news elements—Kelly's death, after the failure of his hopes for clemency—placed at the top of the story.

Newspapers were not always written this way. Earlier in that century, a commitment to reporting factually was of far less importance than presenting a point of view, and the information in stories was presented chronologically or thematically rather than in the order of its significance.

In his *A History of News*, American writer Mitchell Stephens points to the role of the communications revolution of its time, the telegraph, in establishing a more factual and hierarchical style of news writing.

During the American Civil War in particular, journalists rushing to transmit their most newsworthy information over often unreliable telegraph lines had begun to develop the habit of compressing the most crucial facts into short, paragraph-long dispatches, often destined for the top of a column of news ... From here it was not a long distance to reserving the first paragraph of their stories, the "lead", for the most newsworthy facts and then organizing supporting material in descending order of newsworthiness.

That means they can write to fit the space and the story needn't trail off at the end because it's unlikely to be trimmed by the sub-editors. Certainly, if you read some news stories these days, particularly in the metropolitan newspapers, they do not follow the inverted pyramid style. But the basics of the style are far from out of date. They're still a staple of tabloid news writing and of news delivered online or to portable hand-held terminals.

As we'll see shortly, different media apply the hard news model in different ways. But the basics of the style remain much the same and it's with these basics that reporters begin learning to write in news style.

STRUCTURING THE NEWS STORY—FIVE Ws AND H

In news writing, brevity is a virtue, but not at the expense of the facts. Making sure they've covered all the main elements of a story is one of the first things reporters have to learn. Lucky for them there's a mantra for checking the main points. It's the five Ws and H and it stands for:

Who What When Where Why How

These are the questions that the readers/audience will expect to have answered in the story:

- Who (or what or how many) did (or will do) something? –What did (or will) they do? –When did they (or will they) do it? –Where?How? And Why?

THE INTRO

In most cases, the intro will contain the *What* and the *Who:* either someone doing something or someone saying something. The *Who* can involve a person's name, an explanation of who a person is, or both. If the subject, or one of the subjects of the story is very well known, their name will form part of the intro. But if the *Who* is not a household name, that can. This intro contains the What and When, but the detail of the Who (the name) would just slow down the intro and can be left to the next par.

In this case, the Who belongs in the intro, because it involves a household name.

An aged pensioner from Sunshine is the winner of last night's $20 million lottery draw.

Olive Yang said...

Premier Fay Dushki said last night she would not be quitting politics, despite her $20 million lottery win.

be left until lower down the story and a tag is used in the intro instead, as in the example below.

The *Why* often involves the greatest amount of explanation so that, too, will usually be part of the body of the story, not the intro.

Example: The angle

Before you can write the intro to the story, you have to settle on the approach or *angle* you are going to take. You can see from just the simple example above that there's usually more than one possible angle, and the choice you make will be dictated by the nature of the story itself and the audience for which you are reporting.

In choosing an angle, the reporter is shaping the raw information and turning it into *news*.

WARNING

It's not news, for example, to report the lottery draw as a linear sequence of events, as in:"State lottery officials presided over draw 203 last night. They drew the winning ticket followed by those that would receive the five secondary prizes. The owner of the winning ticket has been revealed to be the state premier, Ms Fay Dushki ..."

Choosing a news angle means finding the most newsworthy element of the story and putting that at the top. The angle a reporter takes to a story will also influence the way they conduct the interviews and the quotes they choose to use.

To develop your skills in choosing angles and writing news intros, compare the ways in which at least two different news outlets approach the same story each day.

Different Media Outlets—Different styles

While "inverted pyramid" writing sets out information in a hierarchy, from most to least important, the way in which it's applied varies considerably according to the news style of the paper or programme. The style of writing at a tabloid is different from that of a broadsheet. The metro, suburban and regional papers will all have different approaches. Radio, television and online will be different again.

There's a metropolitan broadsheet style, which can be found not just in those papers directed at the educated, white-collar readership but also in those like-minded broadcast services including the ABC and SBS. Tabloid style is a little racier, more populist. The smaller, more commuter-friendly format of tabloid papers encourages the use of shorter stories. "Short, concise and sharp" is how the Victorian Leader Newspaper group's Jane Cafarella describes the style of her suburban tabloids. She says their stories don't include a lot of detail, just "the bare facts" told in a manner that is "as interesting and snappy as it can be".

Radio and online news are news in a hurry. They offer rapid turnaround services for people who want to find out what's going on, be brought up to date with events and feel that they're in touch. Paradoxically, while online news services generally exploit the medium's potential for the use of images and graphics, the audience seems more focused on the text.

Research conducted by Stanford University and the Poynter Institute tracked the eye movements of a group of Web news users and found that they were drawn first to text and only later to photos and graphics. The style of television news is driven by the need to integrate pictures and narration.

News agencies, such as Australian Associated Press, provide stories to subscribers who can either use the stories as provided or rewrite the copy, often including material of their own. That means news agencies have to keep their product fairly unvarnished, so that it appeals to the broad base of users. AAP's Melbourne bureau chief, Joanne Williamson, describes its style as "fair, accurate and tightly-written".

We try to be factual, take no sides, straight down the middle basically. But not so it's dull and uninteresting. We also try to ensure that there's some flair in the writing. Because we have such a wide and diversified subscription base, there's no point in doing it in *The Age* style when it's also going to other clients.

To illustrate some of these differences between various news styles, we've chosen to write the fairytale "Little Red Riding Hood" as a hard news story. It's not an entirely original idea but it is a timeless and effective way of illustrating news style.

Readers familiar with the tale, published by the Grimm brothers in the 19th century, will recall that it begins with Little Red Riding Hood being dispatched by her mother to take cake and wine to her sick grandmother who lives in a house in the woods. As the narrative unfolds, Little Red Riding Hood encounters a wolf, which then speeds over to granny's, devours the old lady before donning her clothes and getting into her bed to wait for the girl.

In the Grimms" version, the story ends happily (except for the wolf) after a huntsman rescues both the girl and her grandmother by using a pair of scissors to open up the wolf's stomach.

This form of story telling, which has been successfully used to send generations of small children off to sleep with wild nightmares, is far too slow and boring for hard news. Instead, we need to start with the conclusion. But, as we've seen already, the conclusion we choose will vary depending on when the paper, site or programme is published or broadcast, and also the nature of the media outlet and its audience.

The examples below represent a typical hard-news lead in the main news formats. We've taken a few liberties with the story (which you would *never* do in real life) to allow us to give it a location, use quotes, and to project the original tale into "follow-up" news items for non-daily papers. To avoid repetition, we've written just the intro to some versions of the story.

TABLOID DAILY

A girl and her grandmother had a miraculous escape after being eaten by a wolf in Oakville forest yesterday.

Both the 10-year-old and her frail grandmother were ripped alive from inside the savage beast's stomach.

Covered in entrails, the girl was carried from the scene of the terrifying attack by local hero, ranger Brad Gore. The little girl's grandmother,

Mrs Betty Hood, 82, also survived the horrifying ordeal.

Brad Gore said he had been on the trail of the carnivorous canine for some weeks and had been alerted by loud snoring from inside the house. Gore said he used scissors to cut the little girl and the old woman out of the wolf.

"The old lady was more dead than alive when I got her out," Brad said.

"When I went into the bedroom, I found the wolf in her bed. I was going to take a shot at him but then I thought it might not be too late to save Mrs Hood and the kid."

Covered in bandages and heavily sedated in her hospital bed, Mrs Hood was too traumatised to comment on the attack.

STYLE TIPS

- Emphasise the drama/human interest elements of the story.
- Emphasise the pictorial elements.
- Keep the story brisk and to the point. The lead should be short and punchy; a maximum of 25 words, preferably fewer.
- Use words that everyone can understand. Write your copy so that it has a "readability" age of 12 to 14 years.
- Newspapers generally use the past tense and terms such as "yesterday" or "last night" because they are reporting events that have concluded. But there is an increasing trend, in newspapers, towards the use of the present tense, because it can make events seem more current. Your choice of tenses will be guided by the story itself and by house style.

- Use the active voice, wherever possible, and strong verbs (i.e. "ripped" rather than "lifted" in this example) and nouns.
- Use quotes to liven up the story.

Note: The first of the shaded items also applies to other print news media listed below. The remaining shaded items apply to most news media— print, broadcast and online. Note also "Taking the story further" at the end of this section.

BROADSHEET DAILY

Metro police yesterday warned residents of Oakville to be vigilant against roaming wolves from the nearby forest after a near-fatal attack on two residents. Their warning followed an incident in which an elderly woman and her young granddaughter were initially eaten by a wolf and then cut free by a passing ranger. The woman, 82-year-old forest resident, Mrs Betty Hood, is recovering in St Oakville hospital. Last night, officials described her condition as serious but stable. Her granddaughter, 10-year-old Red Hood, did not require hospital treatment and was reunited with her parents after being rescued. The ranger, Mr Brad Gore, said "The old lady was more dead than alive when I got her out, but the little girl was in pretty good shape."

He said he had been hunting the rogue animal for some months and it was just a matter of luck that he had found him when he did. Mr Gore revealed he had thought of shooting the wolf but realised there might still be time to save the victims. It is expected Mr Gore will be nominated for a state bravery award.

Style Tips

- Consider the market for which you are writing.
- Remember that readers are likely to have already heard the details of a story such as this on other media (e.g. radio and television) so you need to look for a slightly different angle.
- Consider including wider issues as part of your report.

Suburban or Regional Daily

Oakville identity Mrs Betty Hood, aged 82, is recovering in hospital after being attacked by a roaming wolf. The beast also attacked her 10-yearold granddaughter, Red Hood. The pair was eaten by the animal, but rescued shortly afterwards by a passing forest ranger.

Style Tips

- Focus on the local angle or the local identity.
- Personalise the story for local readers using terms like "us" or "our" where appropriate.
- Use the standard features of tabloid writing style, including short, punchy sentences.

Suburban or Regional Weekly

Local forest ranger, Brad Gore, has been hailed a hero after saving a grandmother and her granddaughter from a wolf this week. Mr Gore went to the aid of Mrs Betty Hood and Red Hood after he heard unusually loud snoring coming from her house in a remote part of Oakville forest. Inside, he found a wolf dressed in the elderly woman's clothes and sleeping in her bed ...

Style Tips

- Find a different angle from the one(s) that will have been used by the daily press. Usually this will mean looking for an angle in the aftermath of the initial event.
- The same need to make the story relevant to the local community, and personalise it for the audience, noted above, applies here too. So does the use of tabloid writing style.

RADIO—VOICER, PRERECORDED (NEWS RADIO FORMAT)

Newsreader: An elderly Oakville grandmother is recovering in hospital after she was cut free from the stomach of a wolf.

Sonia Clack reports the animal also ate a young girl, but she was rescued relatively unharmed.

Reporter: Police can't remember the last time a wolf-attack was this vicious. They say the beast stalked 10-year-old Red Hood as she was walking through Oakville forest taking some cake and wine to her sick grandmother.

He then broke into the elderly woman's house and ate her before disguising himself in her clothes and waiting for the girl. The pair was saved by local ranger, Brad Gore, who cut them free with scissors. The Old Lady Was More Dead Than Alive When I Got Her Out. Mr Gore says the girl seemed okay, despite her ordeal. Sonia Clack, Oakville.

Style Tips

- Radio and television stories start with an intro, which usually includes the main news point(s) and sets up the rest of the report.
- Wherever possible, radio news likes to include the voices of newsmakers themselves—in this case the ranger. These small interview segments are called *soundbites* or *grabs*. In fact, some commercial FM radio news services rarely run reporters" voicers, like the example above. Their stories mostly consist of an intro followed by a soundbite.
- Write short, punchy sentences, or sentences that have easy places to pause for breath. Remember, you have to be able to read your script aloud.
- Use the active voice and the present tense, wherever possible.
- Radio and television stories can't be allowed to trail off at the end in the way some newspaper or online reports can. Instead they need a conclusion, to alert the listeners/viewers to the fact that the story has ended and another one is about to begin.
- Radio uses conversational language and contractions such as "can't" and "he's", etc. FM radio news takes this even further. An FM service, with a young audience, might personalise the story and use very

colloquial terms such as "cops", "guys", "granny" and so on.

ONLINE—METRO MEDIA OUTLET

News prepared for online delivery is structured so that readers can scan the headline and then drill down to more detailed versions of the story if they are interested.

In this form of writing, it is important that the headline tells the gist of the story. It can't be enigmatic or cute because readers won't get the point straightaway. In a newspaper, a reader can take in the story at the same time as reading the headline.

The precis will often serve as the first paragraph of a longer story, so it needs to stand alone and set up the rest of the piece.

HEADLINE

Police have warned residents of Oakville to be vigilant against attacks by wolves from the nearby forest.

Their warning follows an incident in which an elderly woman and her young granddaughter were initially eaten by a wolf and then freed by a passing ranger.

FULL STORY

The woman, 82-year-old forest resident, Mrs Betty Hood, is recovering in St Oakville Hospital where her condition is described as serious but stable. Her granddaughter, 10-year-old Red Hood, did not require hospital treatment and was reunited with her parents after being rescued.

Ranger Brad Gore said he was alerted by strange noises from the house. He used scissors to cut the victims out of the wolf's stomach. "The old lady was more dead than alive when I got her out, but the little girl was in pretty good shape, " he said. He said he had been hunting the rogue animal for some months and it was just a matter of luck that he had found him when he did. Mr Gore revealed he had thought of shooting the wolf but realised there might still be time to save the victims.

Style Tips

- The style used for an online news story will be influenced by the nature of the originating medium (i.e. whether it's a metro, suburban or regional newspaper or broadcast site). Many newspapers post the newspaper versions of stories online with few changes. Broadcasters have to ensure scripted stories work as text, which includes turning soundbites into quotes or indirect speech. Some newspapers and broadcasters may sub-edit the copy to ensure that references to locations and people make sense to an audience that can range from local to global.
- The headline should be a clear pointer to the story.
- The first par may need to both stand alone and serve as the story intro.
- Some sites also require a separate story precis of a single par.
- Different online outlets have different ways of handling time references. Both the present or past tenses may be used, depending on the site and the story.
- Online sites tend to use newspaper-style quotations and attribution.
- Try to include at least one still photograph. Stills play a greater role in identifying stories online than they do in print. Some outlets would compile a photo gallery to accompany the story.
- The issue of whether to include links to external sites is a matter of house style. But note that if you do link out it is usually better to link to an external site's *home page* rather than using a *deep link* to within the site. This is for legal reasons. Deep linking can create ambiguities over who created the copy being linked to and can bypass advertising that site owners use to generate revenue. Deep links should be restricted to appropriate information sites and used only with thought and care. Any external links should have a purpose within the full story and should be

editorially responsible. Think about where you are taking your audience.

- Consider "value adding" to the story by including additional background information and interview transcripts as separate pages linked from the main story.
- Consider opening a readers" forum on the story and inviting email responses.
- Not all information is best presented as text. The online environment lends itself to using bullet points and displaying information in graph or table form, where appropriate. You might also attach a map of the area.
- Our example is free of potential defamation or contempt of court. But reporters working in an online environment need to remember that while their site may originate in one state, it may draw a substantial audience in other states and this has legal implications.

In particular, journalists handling court reports need to respect any restrictions that might apply in any particular part of the market regarding the identification of the accused. The same issue arises in television and in print, where journalists working on national bulletins or publications have to remember the restrictions that apply in individual states within the viewing or circulation footprint.

SPECIAL-INTEREST MEDIA

A financial newspaper or news agency would, naturally, look for an angle of interest to the business community. For example, when the financial media report natural disasters, it is usually in terms of the insurance implications.

In the case of this story, they might take one of the following approaches. Landowners in the outer suburban area of Oakville are concerned that their property values may fall after a savage attack by a wild animal on two local residents.

An elderly woman is recovering in hospital after being eaten by wolf which also devoured her 10-year-old grandchild. The pair was rescued by a local ranger. However, the incident highlights the danger to surrounding properties posed by rogue animals. President of the Oakville Realtors Association, Ms Shelley Novella, said repeated pleas to council to eliminate the problem have had no effect. "We are concerned that this attack and the widespread attention it has received will drive away potential new residents," she said.

The Utility Scissor company received the sort of publicity you just cannot buy when its product was used in yesterday's headline-grabbing rescue of an elderly woman and her granddaughter in Oakville ...

The financial press, programs and sites are the largest specialist news outlets, but they are not the only ones. You might like to imagine how, for example, the agricultural press or a medical magazine might handle the above story, or how it might be reported in a paper aimed at older people.

Style Tips

- Look for an angle that fits the objectives of the specialist media outlet.
- Seek out interviewees who can present a different perspective from that offered in mass-audience news outlets.

TELEVISION NEWS

Television news is a picture medium and so the way in which this story would be written would be driven, to a large extent, by the type of pictures available. In this case, we can assume the news crews would have rolled up at about the same time as the ambulance came to take the injured to hospital. That means they would have shots of the grandmother being taken out on a stretcher, and the girl being escorted to the ambulance.

They'd probably have the body of the wolf being removed. They would almost certainly have scored an interview with the ranger and one of the emergency service officials. They might have a comment from the girl or her family. They would probably try to get shots of the two victims being taken *into* hospital and they might also have some helicopter shots of the forest.

Finally they'd check the station library for shots of roaming wolves, preferably in the same environment as the one in which the attack occurred.

For the purposes of this exercise, we are going to assume that the two victims were so traumatised by their experience that they were unable to talk to reporters at the scene and also that police kept reporters away from the girl. We can assume that a number of media organisations would be chasing the family, chequebooks in hand. But that's another story.

- Mrs Hood being taken into ambulance outside cottage
- Wolf's body being removed Photo of girl
- orest track
- Exterior of house
- Brad Gore showing scissors
- Gore interview file shots of wolves
- More shots of crime scene
- Gore interview
- Reporter's piece to camera

Most television stories begin with a presenter's intro, followed by a reporter's package. There are other story formats, though the variations are too detailed for inclusion here. Television scripts are set out in two columns, to cover the words (the narration, captions and so on), which go on the right-hand side of the page and the pictures, which go on the left.

Our example is written in the television equivalent of broadsheet style. *Newsreader* An elderly Oakville grandmother is recovering in hospital after she was cut free from the stomach of a wolf. Sonia Clack reports the animal also ate a young girl but she was rescued relatively unharmed.

Police say they can't remember a wolf-attack as vicious as this one. They say the beast stalked 10-year-old Red Hood as she was walking through Oakville forest taking some cake and wine to her sick grandmother. He then broke into the elderly woman's house and swallowed her before disguising himself in her clothes and waiting for the girl.

The pair was saved by local ranger, Brad Gore, who cut them free with scissors.

THE OLD LADY WAS MORE DEAD
THAN ALIVE WHEN I GOT HER OUT

Mr Gore says the girl seemed okay, despite her ordeal.

The ranger says he'd been hunting the rogue animal for months and he was lucky to find him when he did.

I was just passing the house when i heard an animal snoring. that's what alerted me. With news of today's attack still filtering through the community, police are warning oakville residents to be on the look-out for more wolves from the forest.

- Interview with police spokesperson
- Grandmother being wheeled into hospital
- Police taking granddaughter home

THE BEST PROTECTION AGAINST
THESE ANIMALS IS PUBLIC VIGILANCE

- Tonight, Mrs Hood is in a serious but stable condition in St Oakville Hospital.
- Her granddaughter is recovering at home with her parents.
- Sonia Clack, Oakville.

Style Tips

- Television news shares the conversational writing style of radio (and some online services). But it's not enough to add pictures to a radiostyle script. Television stories need to be written to their pictures, not least to maintain continuity in the visual part of the narrative.
- Don't make the viewers wait too long before they hear and see an interview segment (soundbite). These help to break up the narration and add pace to the story.

- Television stories need a conclusion and this usually includes a reporter's sign-off (or "tag").

BREAKING OUT OF THE "PYRAMID" NEWS STYLE

Of course, not all news stories these days are written in "pyramid" style. The computer software programs now used in newspaper production mean that reporters often know the amount of space allocated to their story as they write it. That means there's less need to crop stories from the bottom, which gives reporters more freedom in constructing the story, and it has encouraged some reporters to adopt a more expansive style of writing.

THE NON-PYRAMID PRINT STORY

This type of format has slipped into journalism under the influence of literary traditions. *New journalism,* as expounded by writers like Tom Wolfe, has also encouraged some journalists to deliberately "toy" with readers by delaying the news angle or by starting their stories with background information or description. Australian writer and journalist, Bob Jervis, also argued that deliberately creating information gaps or delays in supplying information could itself act as an enticement to readers.

Told in non-pyramid style, our wolf-attack story might go something like this:

Forest ranger, Brad Gore, had no idea what he might find when he went to the rescue of Oakville grandmother, Olive Hood, yesterday.

Certainly the loud, guttural snoring from inside the 82-year-old's bedroom had been sufficient to shock his adrenalin system into full alert.

But it wasn't until he pulled back the delicate, pink lace which enveloped the grandmother's bed that the full horror was revealed ...

A final word of caution: This style is probably best left to more experienced writers who are confident in their own approach to news.

ISSUES OF BALANCE AND FAIRNESS

By now you might have realised that most stories lend themselves to a wide variety of different angles, and the ones reporters choose are determined in part by their own approach to the story and also by the nature of their audience.

In framing angles, and in writing their reports, journalists also need to bear in mind the need for balance and fairness, enshrined in the codes of ethics and practice that inform the work of Australian reporters.

Warning

One of the lessons journalists learn early in their training is the need to set aside their own opinions and report fairly, paying due attention to the different opinions in society on the issue at hand. Of course, journalists" own opinions do creep into reports, most commonly in the choice of interviewees. But outside of the opinion pages of the newspapers or similar clearly flagged segments of broadcast programs, journalists are expected to keep their own opinions in check.

That means that, among all the acceptable angles for our wolf-attack story, there are a few that would warrant an immediate rewrite.

For instance:

- Roaming wolves should be immediately cleared out of Oakville forest after an attack on an elderly woman and her granddaughter.
- This style of writing is called "editorialising". The writer is standing on a metaphorical soapbox shouting their own opinion. It's tedious and almost always unacceptable.

TAKING THE STORY FURTHER

We've spoken earlier about the ways in which news stories generate other stories—including breakouts, follow-up news items and features.

Our example of the wolf-attack on Little Red Riding Hood and her grandmother is no exception.

Breakouts

Newspapers often supplement some of their news stories with breakout reports. These can be separate news items on different aspects of the main subject including background reports. Alternatively they can be brief "value adding" pieces, such as fact boxes or a sequence of "vox pop" comments from ordinary people asked to give their opinion on the issue.

An item such as our example could easily warrant any of the these.

- A Fact box could include short bullet points on
  - Information on earlier wolf-attacks
  - The number of wolves estimated to live in the forest
  - The size of the forest and other wild animals living there
  - The number of state forests that are home to wolves, and so on.
- A Backgrounder could cover similar material but in story form rather than as bullet points. Or it might profile forest residents and their views on the risk from wild animals.
- Vox pops would be several short comments from local people giving their opinion on the attacks.
- A box beside the main story could detail the number of serious wild animal attacks in the state or country over the past 12 months. Or the breakout box might cover the regulations that protect wildlife living in close proximity to people.

THE FOLLOW-UP

This story definitely lends itself to a follow-up and the perfect time would be when either victim speaks to the media for the first time. This would be a particularly good story for the tabloid press and commercial television. You've heard this type of story many times before.

A tabloid newspaper version would go something along the lines of:

- An 82-year-old grandmother yesterday told how she

thought she would die when a wolf attacked her while she was lying sick in bed.

- Mrs Olive Hood had been suffering from anemia and was too weak to resist when the animal burst into her home and devoured her ...

On television, the story would begin:

- *Newsreader:* An elderly woman has spoken for the first time about a terrifying attack by a wolf, which nearly claimed her own life and that of her granddaughter ...

FEATURES

Of course, a news story of between 200 and 600 words can do only so much justice to a riveting human-interest story such as this one.

This is the type of item that cries out to be given the feature treatment.

In this case, it might begin along the lines of: As she prepares to celebrate her 83rd birthday, Oakville grandmother Betty Hood knows she has more to celebrate than most people her age.

Her physical injuries are fading but 82-year-old Oakville grandmother Betty Hood is still reliving the terror that swept over her when a wolf gripped her in his powerful jaws.

As the jaws of a wolf snapped shut on her, Oakville grandmother Betty Hood's biggest fear was that her 10-year-old granddaughter would be the beast's next victim.

REMEMBER

The angle you take to a story will depend not just on the story itself but also on the nature of the publication or programme and its audience. The intro needs to be punchy and make the audience want to know more.

BASIC GUIDELINES

It's important to recognise that there is no single formula for news writing. Different outlets require different approaches. But no matter what the outlet, the main characteristics of news writing remain much the same. Here are some of the guidelines for writing hard-news stories.

- News writing is concise. People turn to the news pages or news programs or sites to get the facts, fast. So reporters need to tell the gist of the story in the first couple of sentences and then elaborate in the body of the item. That way, people who have neither the time nor inclination to read beyond the lead will still have been given the main elements of the story. Keeping copy concise, while still presenting all the essential facts, means sticking to these rules:
  - Don't use many words when one will do.

Examples

Avoid at this point in time *Instead use* now got under waybegan, was an employee of worked for crisis situation crisis at an early date soon in excess of more:

- Delete unnecessary adjectives and adverbs. Sometimes adjectives and adverbs just weigh down your writing, clogging it with unnecessary words. An over-reliance on these qualifying words can be a sign of poor writing style. That noted, your relationship with adjectives and adverbs will depend greatly on the kind of news outlet you work for. Tabloid news style makes more use of adjectives and adverbs than broadsheet news style. Indeed, tabloid news favours descriptions such as "*violent* sequel", "*brutal* arrest". It also likes alliteration (i.e. the repetition of a letter at the head of consecutive words) e.g. "terrorist tragedy" and "flood fury as wild waters keep rising".

Examples

Avoid ran *quickly Preferred* ran or sped *Avoid* the *noisy* protesters *Preferred* the protesters shouted abuse shouted abuse:

- Eliminate other unnecessary words.

For example, the words "that" and "which" can often be cut out with no loss of meaning.

Example

Delete the word that from this sentence. Infrastructure Minister Freya Yang said that the new road works were essential.

- Use short, easily understood words instead of longer alternatives.

Examples

Instead of exacerbate *Use* worsen *Instead of* commencement *Use* start *Instead of* employees *Use* workers *Instead of* employment *Use* jobs

- *Avoid repetition*: Don't use the same word twice in a single sentence if you can avoid it.
- News writing requires language with a bit of edge. Use strong verbs and nouns.

Examples

Tip

Most of the rules listed here can be set aside if there is a compelling reason to break them. But sidestepping the rules only works when it's done thoughtfully, rather than out of ignorance.

Avoid: The company *attributed* the job cuts to the poor economic environment.

Avoid: The team captain *said* officials *paid insufficient attention* to the poor condition of the ground when they scheduled the game.

- *Stronger wording*: The company *blamed* the job cuts on the
- *Stronger wording*: The team captain *accused* officials of *ignoring* the poor condition of the ground

More Rules

- Avoid using clichés. We say this advisedly because, in reality, clichés do creep into news writing. One reason is that news writing favours brevity and some clichés are the shortest way of conveying an idea. But others are simply silly or overworked. For instance, at the time of writing, the word "raft" had become the term of choice for journalists needing to describe a group of non-physical things such as a "raft of proposals", "raft of measures" and so on. When this happens to a word, someone should put it out of its misery. At the very least, individual reporters should think before automatically reaching for the trendy but meaningless term of the moment.

Examples

Avoid gunned down in a hail of bullets bit the dust *Avoid* *Avoid* dawn of time ground to a halt...etc. *Avoid* lost in time Of course, if an interviewee uses a cliché, you can include it in the quote. But you should avoid writing them yourself.

- Avoid clichéd intros. Just as certain terms have become over-used, so too have certain formulas for leads. British writer Philip Norman identified several "clunky" styles of intro that he reckoned usually stopped him from wanting to read any further.
  These included:
  - "Such and such is alive and well and ..."
  - "I have seen the future and it ..."
  - "Just when you thought it was safe to ..." (*The Weekend Australian,*

January 22–3, 2000: Features p. 8).

Another over-worked intro is the kind that begins "You don't often see ...".

- Avoid tautologies: A tautology is saying the same thing twice. Sports presenters, who do a lot of live commentary, sometimes reach for tautologies in the heat of the moment, as in, "There goes Freddy, the tall, lofty, Argentinian ..." But anyone who has time to think about what they're saying or writing has little excuse.

Examples

Don't use razed to the ground *Alternative* razed (it means the complete destruction of something)

- *Don't use* past history *Alternative* history
- *Don't use* true facts *Alternative* facts OR truth
- *Don't use* completely empty *Alternative* empty
- *Don't use* 2am in the morning/*Alternative* 2am OR two O'clock in the

5pm in the evening morning/5pm OR 5 O'clock in the afternoon (am and pm convey morning or afternoon/evening)

- *Avoid mixed metaphors*: A metaphor is a term or phrase used to describe something to which it's not literally related. Familiar metaphors include "the iron curtain", "a horse of a different colour", "the hand that rocks the cradle", "one foot in the grave". A mixed metaphor occurs when two of these descriptions are jumbled together.

Example

Mixed metaphor the hand that rocks the grave:

- Avoid the "bleedin" obvious". Some statements are so self-evident that they are not worth writing.

Example

Avoid constructions which labour the obvious:

- *Don't use*: If the Australians don't make enough runs, they'll end up losing this match.
- *Don't use*: One thing is certain, only time will tell (*or simply* time will tell).
- *When artist*: Joe Bloggs was alive, he was an outspoken environmentalist.
- *Alternative*: *(The version on the left states the obvious "When Joe Bloggs was alive". A small amount of rephrasing will fix this.)* Throughout his life Joe Bloggs was an outspoken environmentalist.
- *Alternative*: The Australians need... runs for victory.
- *Alternative*: There isn't really an alternative. If you reach for an expression such as this, it means you've run out of sensible things to say and you need to think again.

Example

- *Don't use* helping police with their enquiries
- *Don't use*: At this moment in time an inquiry is ongoing with officers conducting residential interviews on a face-to-face basis.
- *Alternative* being questioned/interviewed by police
- *Alternative*: Police are asking local people if they saw anything.
- *Don't use will facilitate*: *Alternative* will help to assist

• Avoid euphemisms. Journalists sometimes have to temper the way they write to avoid causing unnecessary distress or offence. But there is no point in taking this to extremes.

Example

Avoid Passed on, gone to meet *Alternative* Died (and, on rare his (her) maker, etc occasions, passed away)

- Attribute thoughtfully. Quotes are an important part of any story. They help improve its audience appeal by introducing the voices of newsmakers themselves. In broadcast and online journalism, listeners and viewers have the chance to hear the actual voices of those making the news and the inclusion of soundbites in stories also punctuates the reporter's narration.

When quoting someone either directly or indirectly, you often need to attribute the remark, for example: "The economy is in good shape," the prime minister said. In most cases, the verb "said" (or "says" if you're using the present tense) is the most appropriate one to use when attributing information.

It's the shortest word for the occasion. But the verb you use when attributing remarks needs to be chosen carefully because it can convey a loaded meaning, depending on the circumstances. There are occasions on which the alternatives, including "claimed", "agreed" and so on, are acceptable or preferable. But the choice needs to be made with some care.

In print journalism, the news comes first, then the attribution. Anything controversial needs to be attributed to an authoritative source so it does not give the impression that the journalist is writing their own opinion or that of their news organisation.

Examples: Direct quotes (also applies to indirect quotes)

- The economy is in good shape," the prime minister *insisted*.
- My opponent will double parking fees in the inner city," Councillor Caselli *claimed*.
- My opponent will double parking fees in the inner city," Councillor Caselli *revealed*.
- The economy is in great shape," the treasurer *averred*.

Indirect Quotes

The prosecutor *alleged*, cricket star Laura Tiger, had been driving with a blood alcohol level of.09. *Insisted* is fine if the person being quoted is being insistent for some reason, such as countering criticism, but it's a stronger word than "said", not a simple substitute.

In cases such as this, *claimed* is preferable to *said* because *said* would imply the statement was correct rather than an allegation.

The term *revealed* implies a statement is true and that the information was previously secret. Use it with caution. In this case, *claimed* is more accurate.

Occasionally the word *averred* can be used to make a point, particularly in a slightly humorous situation. But in most circumstances the word is not one you would use in daily conversation and "said" is preferable.

In court reports, the word *alleged* is important to convey the fact that something is an accusation and not a fact until proven in court.

The term *alleged* can be used in some other, similar, circumstances ("Police arrested 10 protesters *alleged* to have crossed their lines").

But it should not be used to try to reduce the defamatory implications of a statement ("the *allegedly* corrupt politician") because it doesn't work. The treasurer *denied* the economy was in poor shape. Take great care with the word *denied* because it gives credence to whatever it is that's being denied. The example opposite would be the correct wording if the treasurer were responding to claims that the economy was in poor shape.

But, in other circumstances, it would likely lead readers to assume that there *was* something wrong with the economy. Other verbs that need similar care include "commented", "stated", "laughed", "sighed" and so on. Terms such as "declared" and "chuckled" should be reserved for the novel in your bottom drawer.

News writing shouldn't be colourless. But don't use words in an effort to be clever without thinking about what they really mean or the implications they might convey. One thing all the above examples make clear is that language is not neutral.

Even quite simple words can require political choices. Journalists need to think about the words they use and what they imply to ensure that they are not unwittingly putting emphasis on a particular position, backing a cause, or slighting a person or group of people.

Certainly, there's no shortage of lobby groups prepared to monitor news outlets" use of language and push for changes.

The types of language use that require special attention include the following:

- Disabled persons" lobby groups have fought to have news organisations adopt certain terms and reject others. As a result, the word "handicapped" is rarely used now. "Disabled people" is used.
- AIDS lobby groups have fought a largely successful campaign to have the media avoid terms such as "AIDS sufferer", "AIDS victim" and "AIDS carrier" in favour of "person with AIDS" and so on.
- Mental health is another area in which the media have been urged to take special care with their reporting standards and use of language. Lobbyists in this area have urged that terms such as "insane", "lunatic" and "mental patient" be avoided.

- Many media outlets now follow the requests of Aboriginal communities in respecting cultural sensitivities, particularly with regard to the naming or showing images of people who have died.

Inclusive Language

Using language with care means using language which is inclusive rather than exclusive. It means avoiding terms which are gender specific—such as airline hostess or fireman—in favour of gender neutral terms, in this case flight attendant and firefighter. Apart from anything else, gender specific terms usually sound rather old-fashioned these days.

Equally unacceptable is language which assumes that one particular race, nationality, religion, sexual orientation and so on, is normal, at the expense of everyone else.

Most of the codes of ethics and practice applying to the Australian media make reference to the need to avoid stereotyping particular members or sections of the community.

For example, clause 2 of the Journalists" Code of Ethics says: Do not place unnecessary emphasis on personal characteristics, including race, ethnicity, nationality, gender, age, sexual orientation, family relationships, religious belief, or physical or intellectual disability.

But careful writing requires more than just avoiding the most obviously prejudicial terms. It means writing in a way that gives credence to more than one idea or position.

To take one example, it is common to read or hear that police were "forced to use" tear gas, capsicum spray or some other deterrent to pacify an individual or group of people. The word "forced" sounds dramatic, which is why it's used. But it also paints a picture of the person or group in question, which is usually open to dispute.

It's just as easy, and more honest, to write "police used capsicum spray to ..." and leave the justification to a quote, if explanation is required.

Another circumstance in which loaded language is common is in the reporting of industrial disputes. Stories that suggest that workers are "holding (employers) to ransom" or "bringing (employers, the country, etc) to their/its knees" reflect a one-sided view of a dispute.

Reporters need to think about the meaning— both intended and implied—of what they write. They also need to consider the inferences audiences might draw from their reports and try to write in a way that eliminates any unwanted confusion or conclusions.

Chapter 10

Beyond the News

Traditionally, the "six marching men" who lead journalism are Who? What? Where? When? Why? and How? By the time young journalists have written two or three news stories, however, they probably have discovered that those six questions are not adequate.

Thus, if they grow up to be Josh Getlin of the *Los Angeles Times*, they might begin one of their stories this way: "Kansas Sen.Bob Dole twice confronted Vice President George Bush 'man to man' in the Senate chamber Thursday, angrily demanding an apology to his wife and later accusing Bush of reducing the GOP presidential race to 'groveling in the mud.'"

In these forty words Getlin gives us not only a *who* but also a to *whom* (*Bush*), who becomes another who for another to whom (*Dole*'s wife). We also have a how *often* (twice) and two in what *ways* (man to man, angrily), each of which could also probably be identified as a *how*. In addition, there are three *whats* (confronted, demanded, accused), a *to what* (groveling in the mud), and the usual *where* (in the Senate chamber) and *when* (Thursday). The *why*, the reason for the confrontation, is revealed in the next paragraph (the result of a statement issued by Bush's state campaign chief).

News stories, in other words, are often much more complex than novices first assume when they begin the study of journalism. Nevertheless, to the extent that the story is simply the presentation of news, it conveys knowledge of witnessed or verifiable events or situations. Moreover, to the extent that the story is a news story, it carries the assumption that each fact will be understood by the readers for whom the piece is written. In addition, in many instances, the communication of news is all that is needed to satisfy the primary function of journalism: to provide people with the knowledge they need to make good, timely decisions.

Consequently, for instance, if we have been accurately and clearly told that the dam has burst, each of us can quickly and independently decide to run to the hills. Most of us, if we have been accurately and clearly told that one of the candidates for mayor has been engaging in illegal campaign tactics, can quickly and independently decide not to vote for him.

In fact, in a large portion of our personal and public affairs, once we have received the news, we possess all that we need to know to make good decisions. We understand what has happened, is happening, or is about to happen. We can easily determine the quality, the usefulness or importance, of this knowledge. And the choices available to us are so clear-cut that we have no difficulty in selecting the one that seems best for us or for the community.

NEWS ALONE MAY NOT BE ENOUGH

These choices, however, are not clear in all instances. As a result, to accomplish their general objective of attempting to provide people with the knowledge they need to make good practical decisions, journalists sometimes attempt to give the public more than the news. News is the basic genre of journalism, but it is not the only one.

According to Getlin's story, for instance, one of the things that had angered Senator Dole was the part of the statement issued by Vice President Bush's campaign chief that accused Dole of "cronyism."

Will the readers understand what this is all about? Since the reference is to another event now long past, the writer assumes they will not, and he adds an explanation: "The statement's 'cronyism' charge referred to investigations of former Dole aides involved in obtaining a Small Business Administration contract to supply food to the Army. Dole has acknowledged trying to help one of the aides get the contract but was absolved of any wrongdoing by a House investigation". Here we have something that is not a part of the immediate event being reported. Here the writer has moved beyond news to another genre of journalism.

This second genre has been given several names. Curtis MacDougall, for instance, called it "interpretative reporting" and, in 1938, wrote a textbook with those words as its title. In spite of the fact that only a few pages of the book were actually devoted to that subject, the popularity of the book—by 1982 it was in its eighth edition—gave the name wide acceptance.

Other writers preferred to call it "backgrounding" or "news analysis," which, as Gary Atkins and William Rivers point out, merely identify two of the techniques sometimes employed. Those two writers themselves decided to drop a syllable from the MacDougall term and use the name "interpretive" (instead of "interpretative") reporting. For the sake of simplicity, that same designation will be used here.

EXPLAINING THE NEWS

The basic function of interpretation is to explain whatever in the simple news story might not be readily understood by the intended readers, listeners, or viewers. Whereas the writer of the simple news story uses narration and description, the interpretive writer uses, primarily, exposition, although sometimes additional narration or description may be enough. (In the Getlin example, for instance, the narration of background information was adequate for explaining the reference to "cronyism.")

Sometimes interpretive reporting is added to and made a part of the simple news story; at other times, an entirely separate story—or even several stories—may be primarily interpretive reporting. In all instances a separate or separable basic news story does exist. The interpretive material is always "something more," something added to the basic news story.

The ultimate goal of interpretive material is the same as that of the basic news material: to provide the people of a community with the knowledge they need to make good, timely decisions. Thus interpretive material is not added to the news primarily to make the public more erudite or to entertain them. It is included as a contribution to their practical decision-making knowledge.

MEANS FOR EXPLAINING THE NEWS

Many techniques of interpretation, in addition to providing background information, are employed to help people understand the news. Some of the more widely used are the following:

DEFINITION OR TRANSLATION OF A TERM

Sometimes the explanation requires only a word or two, as when the media first pointed out that Soviet General Secretary Mikhail Gorbachev's new policy of glasnost means "openness." Other times, the explanation cannot be handled so briefly. For instance, in a *Los Angeles Times* report stating that some scientists fear a computer virus is spreading, the key term was defined this way:

A computer virus is nothing more than a programme—the instructions that tell a computer which functions to perform. But a computer virus differs from ordinary programs in one key aspect: It can reproduce itself.

In this way the computer virus is aptly named. By copying itself and attaching to innocent-looking programs, it can rapidly spread from one set of software or a floppy disk to another, usually through an electronic network. In malicious hands, it can do enormous damage long before it is detected.

CAUSES

Often, the causes of an event are so definite and generally acceptable that they are merely the answers in the early paragraphs of most news stories to such basic questions as *who* (caused the event), *what* (caused the event), or *why* (did the event take place). Thus, in a simple news story about a house fire, the fire chief might be quoted as saying that children (who) caused the blaze because they set newspapers on fire (how) because they wanted more heat in the house (why). When the causes are disputed, complex, or otherwise puzzling, however, the interpretive writer must search out those causes for the readers or viewers. What caused a legislator to vote for a bill she had previously opposed? What caused the financial crisis in Brazil in 1998? Or consider the explanations provided by Linda Feldmann of the *Christian Science Monitor*. She reported that, although Americans had contributed generously to famine relief for Ethiopia in 1984, they were not doing so in 1987-88.

Why the difference? She suggested many causes: The "I thought we fixed it last time" attitude, rebel sabotage of aid, bad publicity during the earlier famine, less media attention to an event similar to one that was already widely covered, the feeling of Americans that they should take care of the hungry in their own country, the stock market plunge in October 1987, and the new tax laws that reduced incentives for giving.

EXAMPLES

To cover the great variety of persons and circumstances that might fall under them, most laws, codes, and regulations have to be expressed in general terms. Because the public often find generalities difficult to understand, the media often explain general events by giving specific instances. The 1987 changes in the U.S. Tax Code provided an extensive opportunity for the use of this device. Thus *Newsweek* explained one of the modifications this way:

There's now a larger marriage tax for working couples with similar incomes. Congress repealed the five-year-old tax credit for working couples, along with many special-interest write-offs.

This hurts if your earnings are roughly equal, because joint returns thrust you into a higher bracket. For example, take two people, each with taxable incomes of $25,000.

As singles, they might pay a combined federal tax of $9,488. As a couple, however, the tax on their joint income comes to $11,052. Adding insult to injury, their income is now too high for them to take a tax deduction on contributions to an IRA.

The story is different if one spouse earns a lot more than the other. Joint returns assume that each of you earned one-half of the money, which can drop a high income into a lower bracket. An example would be two people showing taxable income of $5,000 and $45,000. If they file as singles, the total tax comes to $12,282. If they file jointly, it falls to $11,052.

Consequences

Sometimes causes and effects are so closely and clearly linked that they all become part of the basic news story report of what happened. For instance, when a truck loaded with scrap overturns on a freeway, five cars, attempting to avoid the debris, crash into one another. At other times, however, the effects of an event, although probable, have not yet taken place. In such situations the media can help the public understand the event by indicating some of the consequences that are likely to flow from it.

For instance, soon after the Public Service Company of New Hampshire, unable to obtain a license to put the Seabrook nuclear power plant in operation, filed for bankruptcy, Timothy Aeppel of the *Christian Science Monitor* explained some of the likely results. Because one utility has, in fact, been forced into bankruptcy, he said, the efforts of other utilities to recoup investments in nuclear power plants may be strengthened.

"Utilities often argue that if they are pressed to absorb too many losses, they might be forced into bankruptcy. The implicit threat has been that brown-outs and higher utility rates could follow".

The possibility may seem more likely now that utility bankruptcy has actually taken place. Another possible consequence of this one utility bankruptcy, Aeppel says, is that "public utility commissions across the country might become less demanding of utilities".

This cause-and-effect device helps the readers or listeners understand the significance, the impact of an event. The simple news report that a man in Florida was sent to prison for rape as a result of a deoxyribonucleic acid (DNA) test finding was made more meaningful by the *U.S. News & World Report* explanation that, even more accurately than through the use of literal fingerprinting, this "genetic fingerprinting" could convict criminals without eyewitness testimony and soon would be able to do so without having the defendant at hand.

Next Steps

This device is similar to consequences but indicates a more highly formalized process. For example, the day after Lieut. Col. Oliver North, Rear Adm. John Poindexter, and two others were indicted for conspiring to defraud the United States by illegally providing the Nicaraguan rebels with profits from the sale of American weapons to Iran, the *New York Times* described the many steps yet to be taken in what was expected to be a long, drawn-out legal battle.

Likewise, news stories about committee votes in legislative bodies will often include explanatory material indicating the many steps still to come before the bill will become a law, and stories about the early stages of athletic tournaments will outline the games still to be played before a team is crowned as champion.

Comparisons and Contrasts

Normally, readers or listeners can be led to a greater understanding of one thing through a comparison or contrast with something with which they are already familiar. Thus, in a news story concerning recent experiments in nuclear fusion reaction, the writer mentioned that the nation's most energetic microfusion laser has 100,000 joules of energy, and then he clarified what a joule is: "A joule is roughly the energy of a flashlight switched on for one second".

At greater length, by comparing and contrasting television 3-D with motion picture 3-D, Michael Rogers explained how a segment of the television programme "Moonlighting" would be able to achieve a three-dimensional effect: Most 3-D movie-makers mimic nature by using two cameras, spaced slightly apart, to produce left and right images. When the movie is shown, both images are projected at the same time—producing double vision if the viewer isn't wearing special glasses to sort out the pictures.

The "Moonlighting" 3-D segment will rely on a different trick: the illusion of 3-D can also be created with a single image if the film speed is increased and one eye sees a dimmer image than the other.

Therefore the "Moonlighting" episode will be taped at a slightly faster pace, and one of the lenses in the cardboard glasses will be tinted darker.

The advantage of using a single image for network television is that people who don't get the special glasses won't think their television sets have suddenly gone awry. In some instances, however, both of the elements being compared and contrasted are generally unknown to many members of the public.

For instance, when Richard Gibson explained a new supercomputer (model Y-MP) introduced by Cray Research by comparing and contrasting it with an older model (X-MP), only the readers well versed in computer technology would have fully appreciated the comparison, but they, of course, may have been the very persons for whom the story was intended.

Although the devices mentioned earlier may not include all the means used by communicators to help readers understand and grasp the significance of events, they do include those that are used most frequently. They are the same means (although perhaps with different names) that are used to explain theoretical knowledge, such as science and philosophy. In journalism, they are simply put to a different purpose.

Often, of course, they are used in combination and at a greater length than the examples illustrate. If the event is exceedingly difficult to explain, the interpretation may be as long as—and thus published in—a book and, as a consequence, may follow the event by several months.

Although normally employed to explain an event that has taken place, interpretations may also be used to explain an event that has not happened but that might happen if the people and their leaders do not make the right choices. Jonathan Schell *The Fate of the Earth* —especially the first long section, "A Republic of Insects and Grass," which tries to help us understand what a nuclear holocaust would be—is an arresting example.

And, although the examples given here are from written verbal sources, interpretation is not restricted to words nor to the print media; visual and aural materials are often used in the media with great effectiveness. No matter what the variations, however, journalistic interpretive material retains the basic characteristic of all journalism: it exists to help people make good, timely practical decisions.

EVALUATING EVENTS AND SITUATIONS

The third journalistic genre—often called evaluation or critical writing— retains this same general objective. Ideally, it is employed in situations in which simple newswriting and interpretive writing do not convey adequate knowledge to the readers to enable them to make good practical decisions.

Even after people are well informed about an event and are helped to understand that event, they still may be in doubt about whether the event is good or bad, whether it is something they should tend toward, support, take advantage of, or something they should stay away from, oppose, or try to ward off.

It is the task of the journalists who write criticism to judge events and situations and to offer the public the critics' evaluations and their reasons for them.

Most people immediately associate the term "critical writing" with the arts: with criticism of books, motion pictures, music, dance, and other creative efforts. And certainly the best of such criticisms are classic examples of this art. For example, when the former New Yorker critic Pauline Kael reviewed the movie Tootsie she presented the relevant basic information about the film: the title; the acting, directing, and production credits; a partial plot outline, and the like. She also did a superb job of interpreting the film.

She explained some background issues that could often compromise the quality of a motion picture, especially that many writers had had a hand in producing the script: "When the screenplay had to be submitted to the Writers Guild for arbitration over the issue of who should get the screen credit, three large cardboard boxes were needed to transport the more than twenty scripts."

She placed the film in the context of a half-dozen other of "the best screwball comedies." She helped the readers understand star Dustin Hoffman's acting by comparing and contrasting the ways he handled three different roles in the film. Then, finally, she made clear her own judgment on the quality of the film, evaluating each of the major actors and, although she was not entirely happy with the climactic scene—it "needs reverberations or an aftermath—it's just shucked off"—concluded that, on the whole, "The picture is marvelous fun."

Moreover, the evidence she supplied to support her judgments was more than adequate. Readers who might have been seeking an evening of pleasant enjoyment were aided in their personal decision making by the knowledge Kael gave them. In spite of its strong association with the arts, however, criticism is not limited to that area or even to personal affairs. Public persons and their acts and proposals, public regulations, bills, court decisions, and similar matters often possess an ambiguity that must be resolved before people can decide to support or oppose them. Which of the nominees for United States Supreme Court justice deserve public support?

Which of the candidates for president, for senator, representative, governor, mayor, city council? Which bills before the Congress, the legislature, the council are best for the country, state, or town? Does the latest report about the ozone layer, the trade deficit, or the Supreme Court's decision concerning the First Amendment rights of high school students indicate that things are going well or ill?

Some people, after receiving the basic news facts and explanations, are able to judge those persons and events for themselves and by themselves, and they are able to do so quickly and wisely. But most people find it helpful to know what others are saying and to examine the reasoning that leads them to their conclusions. The critical material in the mass media provides this assistance.

JOURNALISM CULMINATES IN PERSUASION

The need for persuasive writing is based on the recognition that even when people are well informed about what is happening, when they understand what is happening and are able to determine whether it is good or bad or best or worst, even then they may not be able to decide what should be done about what is happening. It is the task of persuasive writing to provide knowledge about what should be done and even, on occasion, to motivate people to do what should be done.

On April 1, 1988, for example, the Labour Department reported that, although the national unemployment rate had dipped to 5.6 per cent, the lowest level since May 1979, the jobless rate for blacks had increased from 12.6 to 12.8 per cent. Most readers probably had no difficulty determining that the increase in black unemployment is a bad thing, not only for blacks but also for the entire country. But what should be done about it?

Should minimum wages be lowered, with the hope that increased hiring would result? Should embargoes be slapped on imports, with the expectation that domestic production and employment would increase? Should public works programs be initiated? Should job training programs be expanded? The possibilities are numerous, but what specifically should be done? Decisions have to be made. Even the decision not to do anything is a decision.

Although, in this case, the general public can do little directly, they can rally behind one or more courses of governmental action. That mysterious force called public opinion, can have a powerful effect, but only if it is aroused and directed. To achieve such an intellectual movement is one of the tasks of the journalistic persuasive writer.

On some public matters—especially the election of persons to fill executive, legislative, and judicial positions—the decisions of the people do have direct effects. Media endorsements, at least when they are well argued, help the public make these choices. When Sig Gissler was editor of the *Milwaukee Journal,* he said:

We simply recommend, or state a preference, for two main reasons. One is to stimulate thought and discussion. The other is to provide some guidance, not in the know-it-all sense but rather as a sharing of judgments based on research. Most readers don't make public affairs a full-time job. Our editorial conference does, investing much time and effort in sorting out issues. Consequently, our election suggestions can play a useful role.

What Gissler said about the members of his editorial conference applies also to most full-time journalists who are persuaders: columnists, broadcast commentators, editorial cartoonists, and the others. All earn their living by thinking and communicating about public affairs. When they do their jobs well, those persuaders perform an important public service by helping the people make both personal and public decisions.

If we recognize that persuasive communication primarily attempts to determine what should be done about some person, event, or situation, we can see that the answer sometimes involves decisions on a great number of possibilities. For example, faced with large and increasing deficits, Congress, in 1985, passed Public Law 99-177, better known as the Gramm-Rudman-Hollings Act.

Two years later, partly to avoid constitutional challenges, the law was revised; the Balanced Budget Reaffirmation Act of 1987 established new targets and extended the date for achieving a balanced budget until 1993. But what should be done to reduce the deficit, which the Congressional Budget Office (CBO) projected would be $183 billion for fiscal year 1988? The CBO, required by the Congressional Budget Act of

1974 to submit an annual report on budgetary options, listed some alternatives.

In fact, without making any recommendations—it is prohibited by statute from doing so—it set forth in some detail 26 possible cuts in national defence spending, 26 in entitlements, 7 in agricultural programs, 38 in nondefense discretionary spending, and 8 in federal work force costs. In addition, it described 25 means of revenue enhancement. Thus, on this one issue of deficit reduction, this one source alone presented 130 options for the consideration and decision of Congress and, supposedly, public opinion. In 1988, numerous persuasive journalists were attempting to provide additional guidance on decisions about budget surpluses.

journalists were described as the persons who have at least some control over the content of the journalistic product. But who is the journalist when a reporter quotes another person, especially a news source who offers explanations, utters criticisms, or proposes courses of action?

This happens with great frequency. For example, when Los Angeles County Assessor John J. Lynch sent a letter warning that he might strip churches of their tax-exempt status if they provide shelter to undocumented refugees, reporters Glenn Bunting and Paul Feldman turned to the Reverend Philip Zwerling of the First Unitarian Church and obtained this evaluation: "Mr. Lynch is acting in a very un-American manner and his strategy is better suited to the state in Poland than to that in California."

When *Christian Science Monitor* reporter Barbara Bradley asked Georgetown University law professor Paul Rothenstein to comment on the news that President Reagan's former political director Lyn Nofziger was guilty of illegal lobbying, she obtained this reply: "Because of Mr. Nofziger's high political profile, this will have a great preventive effect."

A *Chicago Tribune* reporter obtained this evaluation of the U. S. Supreme Court decision denying damages to evangelist Jerry Falwell for a parody in *Hustler* magazine: "Richard Schmidt, legal counsel for the American Society of Newspaper Editors, hailed the ruling as 'a great victory for free speech'".

Are the reporters or are the persons quoted by the reporters the real journalists? Both are; both have important control over the useful knowledge that is communicated to a public. The former are full-time journalists; the latter are occasional journalists. But all are journalists.

Journalists are not only those who own or are employed by the media of mass communications. All those who provide journalistic knowledge—including some free lance writers, public relations practitioners, advertisers, participants in call-in shows, writers of letters to the editor—belong in that category. To ignore this is to misunderstand the true nature of journalism.

ONE OF THE DANGERS OF JOURNALISM

But the fact that interpretation, criticism, and advocacy can be incorporated into news reports does give the media owners and operators a great and potentially dangerous power. If those in control of a journalistic medium wished to do so, they could influence the people's attitude toward public affairs by including only material that agreed with the view of the medium's managers.

Paradoxically, the policy of many American media—again, newspapers in particular-to maintain an evident distinction between news and "opinion" material may increase the power and the danger.

People tend to read news stories less carefully and critically than they read obvious critiques and editorials. Thus when a news story quotes judgments—especially those representing only one side, from reputable sources, and not too contrary to accepted values—the readers do not erect the same defenses that they build when they read explicit opinion articles.

Most journalists try to abstain from exploiting this power by insisting that a judgment in one direction must confront one or more judgments in other directions. Even then, however, a problem may occur, not because of the full-time journalists but because of media manipulators who know how to twist the conventions of the press to their advantage.

As many scholars have pointed out, one of the persons most adept at using the media to his own advantage was Senator Joseph R. McCarthy of Wisconsin. About persons and institutions—especially the State Department—he would make judgments that the press thought it dared not ignore.

And he warded off the desire of journalists to compose balanced stories by releasing his statements so close to deadlines that the reporters, driven by the fear of competition or the unavailability of other sources, thought they could not delay their stories long enough to obtain additional viewpoints. Jack Anderson and Ronald W. May (1952, 266) dramatize the situation that existed in the 1950s:

Say you're an editor of a big afternoon paper. It's fifteen minutes before the deadline for the final home edition—the edition that goes into people's homes and makes up 95 per cent of your circulation. And you've got no hot stories.

Sure, there's an automobile wreck, and a mayor's announcement, and maybe a riot in faraway Iran—but these aren't exactly banner headlines in a big city. So what do you use for an eight-column black "line" in the Night Final?

By this time you're scratching around, desperate. And then the wire editor pushes across a piece of yellow paper, marked WASHINGTON (AP). And you read: "Sen. Joseph R. McCarthy (R. Wis.) charged today that Ambassador-at-Large Philip Jessup had an unusual affinity for Communist causes. In a speech on the Senate floor, the Wisconsin senator said he has the proof for his sensational charge."

Quickly you scribble a headline across the copy and mark it "P. 1." Then you stuff it in the capsule and send it up the airtube to the composing room. And you've got your Night Final banner headline! There, in a nutshell, you have 99 per cent of the reason for Joe McCarthy's success.

The introduction of computers has made present-day newsroom procedures much different from those of the McCarthy period, but most of the pressures and many of the conventional beliefs still exist. In particular, the existence of deadlines is still used as a reason, and sometimes an excuse, for publishing incomplete stories, even in situations in which a delay would not place a publication at any conceivable disadvantage.

Thus, when the *Milwaukee Journal* published a front-page article containing adverse criticisms of the local Roman Catholic archbishop by the leader of a small conservative group, reader-contact editor Thomas Heinen agreed with those who objected that the story was deficient, but then added: "That doesn't mean the story, which was written on deadline with limited time for additional telephone calls, was incorrect as published."

Most widely discussed, however, as the reason for journalists being trapped into reporting one-sided criticisms is their desire to be objective. Even when they personally believe that the judgments being expressed are grievously wrong, and even when they cannot obtain any counterbalancing statements, reporters believe the goal of objectivity requires that those "wrong" judgments be set forth without any indication of the reporter's own evaluations of them. This difficulty will be discussed in the chapter on objectivity.

Although the various types of journalistic communication sometimes raise difficulties, the solution to those difficulties does not lie in attempting to do away with them. Publishers, editors, and station managers could prohibit their reporters, commentators, editorial writers, critics, reviewers, and documentary producers from presenting disputable material. The result, if such discipline could be maintained, would not only be a devitalized, but also an unrealized, journalism.

A great part of the ultimate achievement—providing the knowledge people need to make good, timely decisions—would be cut off at the knees. On many subjects, members of the public, in order to make up their own minds, need access to and consideration of the judgment of others.

For many of the journalistic media, especially those that direct their messages to the masses of readers, listeners, and viewers, the persuasive genre is often employed reactively rather than actively, especially when public affairs issues are at stake.

Instead of initiating their own proposals for solving current problems, too many editorial writers simply react to proposals made by others. If a community is suffering from poor student achievement or if a state faces a budgetary shortfall, the writers will usually wait for the governor or appropriate legislators to set forth possible solutions, and then will oppose or support those suggestions.

If the State Department announces that a foreign country is not living up to international agreements, most editorial writers will wait until the President or other government officials describe a possible solution and only then will step in, launching their praise or condemnation.

Of course, the more complicated and distant the issue, the more reasonable it is for editorial writers to hesitate to leap into murky waters. Unfortunately, though, the tendency to be reactive rather than proactive often extends to local affairs.

Locally, editorial writers can often be as knowledgeable about the issues facing the city or the town as the elected officials of a community. Journalistic media pride themselves on being known as "the fourth branch of government." They can deserve that title if they contribute new proposals to the public forum and if they encourage the people themselves to join in the debate about public affairs.

PERSONAL AFFAIRS PERSUASION

In matters of personal affairs, on the other hand, the journalistic media extensively advocate courses of action. Much of this is done by columnists, both syndicated and staff, by hosts on radio call-in programs, and by the writers of newsletters. The topics range over the gamut of personal concerns: finances, sex, child care, home repairs, etiquette, health, automobile maintenance, interpersonal relations, and the like.

Unfortunately, viewed strictly from a journalistic perspective, a good portion of this material involves an inefficient use of the mass medium. For example, Andrew Leckey, who writes on personal finance for the *Chicago*

Tribune, led off one of his columns with this query from a reader: "I'm a newlywed and trying to get ahead financially. My husband and I own 400 shares of Burndy Corp. and wonder what its future looks like long- and short-term."

Leckey replied that the stock was good, gave reasons for his thinking so, and advocated "holding or buying for short- or long-term goals". Other pieces in the personal-writing category can be almost voyeuristic.

Ann Landers began one of her columns with a long letter from a woman who, nine years ago, had married a man she had known for four years. This was the man's third marriage, and she said he had supplied good reasons for his previous divorces. But the woman discovered that the man had lied to her, and she began to distrust him.

He was making so many sexual demands that she became physically and emotionally ill. His high-school-age daughter was having sex in an open car in front of school, his son had stolen money and was thought to have burned a car to collect the insurance, and another son was living with a prostitute.

Three years ago, she continued, the man had divorced her and moved in with a woman 20 years younger. The writer said she now doubted her ability to evaluate men and wondered what she should do.

Ann Landers suggested that, from now on, the writer learn a great deal more about boyfriends before considering marriage. Two major problems are suggested by these and similar examples of personal affairs advice. First are the risks involved when a journalist gives personal advice to persons the journalist doesn't know and, except in live broadcasting, to persons the journalist can't question or engage in dialogue.

The more personal the problem, the greater the danger the adviser might give counsel that is actually harmful, like the doctor who prescribes medicine over the telephone to a patient the doctor has never seen. One way to avoid this is by giving advice that is general and innocuous, but in thus doing something harmless, the writer also provides responses that are close to useless. Both generality and uselessness work against the goals of journalism.

The second problem grows out of a paradox. For the persuasive writer to give good personal advice, the writer needs to know the specific characteristics, situations, background, and objectives of the person seeking the advice. Thus it undoubtedly helped Leckey to know that the person he was advising was a newlywed concerned about her financial future, and the joint owner of 400 shares of Burndy Corp.

And it probably helped Ann Landers to know the many details of the marriage of the woman who had asked her for help. But the more these columnists know those individuals and the unique details of their situations, the more the writers' advice about what should be done, if it is to be appropriate, applies only to those distinct individuals.

Although a large number of persons may find it interesting to peek in on discussions of the personal concerns of others, catering to such interests is not the function of journalism. Strictly as journalism, therefore, much personal affairs persuasive writing involves, at best, an inefficient use of the mass media.

Media that reach many thousands of persons are providing practical help, in some instances, only to very few persons. Among the thousands of readers of the *Chicago Tribune* there are not likely to be many other newlywed brides who are joint owners with their husbands of 400 shares of Burndy Corp, nor, among the much more numerous readers of Landers' syndicated column are there likely to be, many, even any, other readers who had experiences identical to those of the woman who wrote to Landers.

There are some exceptions, of course—some questions on such topics as home repairs or gardening that might have a degree of commonality—but, generally speaking, personal affairs persuasion does not contribute to the journalistic roles of the mass media. Such persuasion is best and most efficiently done on a one-to-one basis. People with sexual problems should go to sex therapists or doctors, those with financial problems to accountants or lawyers, those with family problems to ministers or social workers.

It is important to recognize, however, that the claim that the mass media are usually not the best place for personal affairs persuasion does not mean that all personal affairs journalism should be excluded from mass communications.

The reportorial and, to a lesser extent, the interpretive genres of journalistic writing serve both public and personal affairs. But, since the ultimate question in personal affairs is "What is good for me?" (in contrast to the ultimate publicaffairs question, "What is good for the community, for the commonweal?"), the standards for determining whether something is good or bad and for analyzing what should be done have a great personal and individual component.

Taste, feelings, private inclinations play a great part, and these are not well suited to public debate. The person does need to know and understand what is going on in his or her life and in the surrounding world, and, having this knowledge, the individual may wish to consult experts of his or her choice, but this is best done within the boundaries of interpersonal communication and with respect for privacy.

An exception should be noted for the situations in which the personal welfare of a large number of individuals is so common and linked together that personal affairs persuasion is appropriate.

Efforts to persuade young people to never start or to stop smoking, to promote exercise, healthful diets, and appropriate medical care could have far-reaching, beneficent effects.

THE HIERARCHY OF JOURNALISTIC GENRES

Perhaps it would be helpful to consider the point just made from another perspective. The four journalistic genres of reporting, explaining, evaluating, and advocating possess a logical, cumulative order. They provide the knowledge that we the people need, first, to know what is going on, then to understand what is going on, then to evaluate what is going on, finally to determine what should be done about what is going on.

Often journalists need to provide only the first type of knowledge; once we, the people, know what is going on we can often supply the rest of the knowledge ourselves. Once we have been informed that our favourite route from home to work will be under repair for the next three months, we don't need any journalist to explain to us what this means, to tell us whether, at least temporarily, it is good or bad, or to urge us to find a detour.

Less often we need both information and the interpretation that helps us understand that information, but, having that, we then can judge the event and decide what to do about it. If we read that a Thai restaurant that has opened in town serves food that is hotter than Szechuan cuisine, those who like spicy food now have information of which they can take advantage.

Still less often is there a need for persuasion after the public has received adequate reports, interpretations, and evaluations. This is most obvious in the area of the arts. If a drama critic, for instance, gives us information about a new play, explains portions that might confuse us, and gives a strong, reasoned evaluation of the play, the critic does not also need to try to persuade us to go see it if it is good or stay away if it is poorly done.

On personal issues, we are usually quite capable of making those decisions for ourselves. In fact, in the journalistic situation, one in which (by definition) the critic is addressing a mass of readers, viewers, or listeners, the critic is frequently incapable of adding any useful persuasion on personal issues. Each member of the public is an individual with private good involving unique factors.

Let's say, for example, the critic gives the play a rave review. In spite of that, many people might decide, often for reasons the critic cannot penetrate, that the play is not a good one for them to see. One man may like only musicals, and this play is not a musical. One woman, who likes plays of this type, may have an ill parent whom she does not want to leave. One man may think the decor of the theater is so revolting that he cannot tolerate being there.

One woman may think the leading man looks like an old boyfriend she now dislikes; another is planning to marry in six months and wants to save every dime for the wedding and honeymoon.

The journalistic critic, the mass-communication persuader, cannot be aware of all these contingencies, and, even if he or she could become aware of them, there would be no efficient way in which the persuader could deal with all of them in one of the mass media.

Of course, it is possible that all these people could be individually persuaded by friends or relatives to overcome their reluctance to see the play, but the means would not be journalistic persuasion but interpersonal persuasion.

JOURNALISTIC PERSUASION

In some instances, on the other hand, idiosyncratic differences are ignored, and the journalist attempts to persuade masses of people on personal issues.

In many such cases the good to be achieved seems so important that it transcends all individual objections. This occurs most often in a situation in which the public already agrees on what should be done; they are not yet, however, moved to action.

We probably have all experienced the circumstance in which we know we should do something, yet we do not do it: stop smoking, show parents our love, exercise, wear our seat belt while driving, install a smoke detector in our home, aid starving children. One of the more famous examples of mass media, personal-issue persuasion was just such a piece. In an effort to dissuade automobile drivers from speeding, J. C. Furnas wrote, "—And Sudden Death." It was published in the *Reader's Digest* in August 1935, and millions of reprints have been distributed since then.

PUBLIC AFFAIRS MOST NEED JOURNALISTIC PERSUASION

Yet the differences between public-affairs persuasion and personal-affairs persuasion are essential for an understanding of the broad field of journalism. The most important of those differences stems from this: public affairs issues are and ought to be publicly debatable. They are and ought to be subject to multiperson, public persuasion.

They are issues that affect entire groups, entire communities, *even those members of the groups or communities who are not interested in the issues.* Many persons in the United States may not be interested in revisions in the Federal Tax Code, yet those revisions affect them whether they are interested or not.

Even if a person's income is so low that he or she does not have to pay any tax, that person is affected by the provision in the tax code that exempts low-income people from having to pay income taxes.

Even if the revision under consideration pertains explicitly only to those involved in offshore drilling for oil, all of us are benefited or disadvantaged, at least to a small extent, by any exemption or penalty applied to that small portion of the population.

Good citizens will make their decisions on the basis of whether a proposed course of action is good, not solely for them individually but also for the group or community, for what is sometimes called the common good.

Whether or not that is the goal in mind, however, the decisions on public issues, since they affect the welfare of the group or community, do, in fact, affect all who are members of that group or community. And thus it is good that any persuasion concerning those public issues comes at least from all who represent distinct positions on the issues.

This is not true when private affairs issues are involved. Should I learn to roller skate? My family, well aware of my physical capacities and temporal limitations, might try to persuade me that I should or should not. But this is no subject for public debate. Those who do not know me would waste their time trying to persuade me, and I would waste my time paying any attention to what they have to say.

A company that rents roller skates might run ads aimed at convincing the public that skating provides ideal exercise and a way to share fun with friends and family. But if I feel compelled to resist those suasions, I do not also feel compelled to debate the issue in public with the advertiser. Private issues are often the basis for interpersonal discussions rather than general public persuasions.

ADVERTISING AND THE JOURNALISTIC GENRES

Much advertising is primarily news. That is, many ads simply tell the public that some items or services are available for sale at a location that is open at specified days and hours or that can be ordered from a specific business. Most supermarket, catalogue, department store, automobile, and entertainment ads are of this type.

Usually, of course, the item or services are described or pictured as attractively as possible. In general, in fact, advertisements are similar to many editorials or opinion columns in that the writers select and present the factual knowledge in ways that support the views of the writers or of the organizations that employ them.

By the very fact that advertisements, editorials, and opinion columns are labeled as such, the readers are alerted to the possibility that the news content is selected to advance the cause of the writers. The reporting, in other words, is not what is often referred to as "objective."

Nevertheless, advertisements predominantly present knowledge in the form of information that helps large numbers of people make good decisions about issues that are facing them. To help compensate for the lack of objectivity in the reporting content of ads (and of editorials and columns), the reader or listener usually will be able to compare and evaluate other available ads or opinion pieces.

Many ads also include the journalistic genres of explanation and evaluation that are no different from what we find in other areas of journalism. But if they also employ explicit persuasion, that persuasion relies heavily on either the other journalistic genres or the later communications of sales people. The latter, being interpersonal, is not journalism as we have been using that term.

Thus, the more advertising aims strictly at *personal* affairs persuasion, the further it moves away from journalism. The more decisions need to be based on individual criteria the less the media of *mass* communication become the efficient means by which the grounds for making those decisions can be conveyed to readers, listeners, or viewers.

Let us take, for example, the merchants who are attempting to sell lamb chops, ten-speed bicycles, Picasso prints, or tickets to a rock concert. News, explanation, and evaluations may be of value, but persuasion, which aims at urging individuals to action, cannot take into consideration all the factors that may affect the decisions that those individuals will have to make.

Interestingly, advertising is often claimed to be enormously influential in the decisions that people make. And, to some extent, it is. But the influence in personal decisions, at least as far as journalism and thus the mass media are involved, comes rarely from the advertisers' efforts at persuasion.

This surprises the many who recognize that advertising is a powerful and effective category of journalism. But its strength comes more from the attractiveness and selectivity with which the facts are presented and from the selective use of the other genres of journalism, such as explanation and evaluation, than it does from any explicit use of persuasion.

When we turn to public affairs decisions, the situation is significantly different. Prior to that, however, we need to bring to the surface two points that have so far been swimming under water.

DISTINCTION MAY NOT REQUIRE SEPARATION

First, although the journalistic genres are distinguishable, they are not always presented in separate articles or programs. In fact, critical and persuasive pieces almost always include some news and often include some explanatory material.

This is most evident in newspaper and magazine editorials, in persuasive columns such as those by William Safire or Cal Thomas, in film documentaries such as Leni Riefenstahl *1937 Triumph of the Will*, in television documentaries such as the 1960 CBS Report "Harvest of

Shame," and in books such as Allan Bloom *The Closing of the American Mind*.

Efforts are often made to keep evaluation and persuasion (often simply called "opinion") out of news and interpretive reports, and some media, newspapers in particular, are criticized if they fail to do so. No efforts, on the other hand, are made to keep news and interpretation out of critical and persuasive articles.

The 1987 revision of the Society of Professional Journalists' Sigma Delta Chi "Code of Ethics" states, "Sound practice makes clear distinction between news reports and expressions of opinion," but this usually works, if it is achieved at all, only in one direction: explicit statements of opinion may be excluded from news reports, but news reports are rarely excluded from opinion articles. The mere fact that two things can be and ought to be distinguished from one another does not necessarily mean that those two things must be separated from one another.

DETERMINING WHAT IS "FIT TO PRINT"

Second, the same criteria used for evaluating what news is "fit to print" can be employed in determining what material in the form of the other journalistic genres ought to be printed, screened, or broadcast. For example, a piece of persuasion would be most fit to appear in a specific journalistic medium if it advocated a decision on an issue that was vital, that affected a large proportion of the audience of that medium, that had to be decided urgently involving something close at hand that could be effected directly, and that could reach the audience only or most probably through this specific medium.

The only major qualification is this: these criteria apply primarily to personal-affairs journalism. Clear, thorough reporting often provides all the knowledge that readers, listeners, or viewers need to interpret the event or situation, evaluate it, and decide what needs to be done. Likewise, reporting plus interpretation sometimes make criticism and persuasion unnecessary, and reporting, interpretation, and criticism sometimes make persuasion unnecessary.

If we turn this around, we then see another set of criteria for determining what is fit to print: the less reporting alone is adequate for enabling the public to make good decisions, the greater is the need for the subsequent journalistic genres; the less reporting plus interpretation are adequate, the greater the need for criticism and persuasion; the less reporting, interpretation, and criticism are adequate, the greater the need for persuasion.

These genres of journalism are most completely realized and most highly respected in public affairs journalism. Why is this so? And is the presentation of effective public affairs journalism an unattainable ideal for the mass media or is it a realistic and achievable goal? It is now time to try to answer these questions.

Chapter 11

The Object of Journalistic Objectivity

When journalists and journalism scholars write about "objectivity," they often disagree, sometimes quite radically. For instance, Denis McQuail says objectivity is "both necessary and impossible," and J. Herbert Altschull says that even discussions of objectivity are useless. Donald McDonald, however, claims that objectivity "is well within the possibility of the mass-communications media despite many practical difficulties."

Beginning in 1926 and through revisions in 1973, 1984, and 1987, the members of the Society of Professional Journalists included in their Code of Ethics the statements that "Objectivity... is a standard of performance toward which we strive. We honour those who achieve it." But in the 1996 revision of the code, the word "objectivity" disappeared entirely.

What are we to make of this? These and other commentators seem reluctant to explain what they mean by the term. Thus once again, we need to look beneath the term itself and attempt to locate some of the realities to which it refers.

We are not discussing "objectivity" in any universal, unqualified sense. Rather, we want to consider only how the concept applies to journalism. Moreover, since objectivity is almost always discussed in reference to news (rather than to interpretation, evaluation, or persuasion), it is best if we further narrow our focus to that single alley of journalism that deals with news gathering and news dissemination—to what is frequently referred to as objective reporting.

At this point, the first question we must examine is whether objective reporting can be, in any way, possible. If there is no way in which it is possible, we can close the book on the subject, for, as Aristotle pointed out long ago, "Concerning things... which cannot possibly exist or take place, no counsel can be given".

SOME IMPOSSIBILITIES AND SOME POSSIBILITIES

Those who say that journalistic objectivity is impossible because we cannot know the *whole* truth about any event, person, or circumstance are, of course, correct. None of us is omniscient. We see a man take a step toward the street. But we do not know the whole truth about him or this event. We do not know the clothing he might be wearing under the clothing we see, nor do we know the number of threads or stitches in any of it.

We do not know the number of hairs on his head. We do not know where he is going or why he is going there (perhaps even he doesn't know). We do not know what effect that one step has on his muscles, his blood pressure, his nerves. Our knowledge of even this one, simple event is enormously limited.

Since we cannot know everything, we cannot report everything. More than that: it is quite likely, because of lack of space, time, pertinence, and other factors, we will not report everything that we *do* know.

If this is what is meant by those who deny the possibility of journalistic objectivity, they are correct, but they are also missing the point. It is true that we cannot know and convey the "whole truth" about anything. That, however, is not what journalists are trying to do. They seek to mine a limited piece of land.

The task of journalism reporters is to obtain and communicate only the knowledge that would be practically useful in enabling people to decide what to do or avoid doing in the situations in which imminent choices need to be made.

Most reporting involves gathering and conveying knowledge about events, persons, or situations that are outside the reporters. Instead of gathering information about and writing about themselves, reporters usually attend to persons, activities and situations that exist independently of them, to something that for reporters is "out there."

Here we must confront two closely related questions. First, is it possible that reporters can ever know anything outside themselves as it really is, unencumbered and unaffected by the fact that it is they who know it? Second, is it possible that reporters can be sure that what they think they know outside themselves does, in fact, really exist? Perhaps a single example will answer both questions.

If one were a reporter covering a joint session of Congress on Tuesday, January 23, 1996, and a person who has been introduced as the President of the United States is speaking and says, among other things, "In our schools, every classroom in America must be connected to the information superhighway, with computers and good software and well-trained teachers," and no one has claimed that the person speaking is not really the President of the United States, and no one is claiming that what he is saying is something he would never say, is it possible that no matter what the reporter thinks of President Clinton, the Congress, computers, schools, the weather outside, the reporter's own family relationships, and much more—is it *possible* that the President is indeed speaking before a joint session of Congress?

And is it *possible* that he is indeed saying, "In our schools, every classroom in America must be connected to the information superhighway, with computers and good software and well-trained teachers"? And is it *possible* that the reporter can know that the President is speaking these words? And is it ever *possible* for the reporter to communicate at least what the President is doing in such a way that what he says corresponds to what he knows, which, in turn, corresponds to what is "out there"?

None of the critics of journalistic objectivity denies those possibilities. In fact, they might point out, unless there really are some things outside ourselves and unless we can really and truly know at least some things about those things and at least sometimes accurately state what we know, there would not only be no need to discuss objective reporting but also no need to discuss journalism itself.

Or at least there would be no point in discussing journalism as it has now been frequently defined. The definition declares that there is such a thing as knowledge, that at least some knowledge conforms to reality and, once known, can help people make good practical decisions. If such is not what journalism is, those who say otherwise must furnish a new definition.

So far, therefore, we can say this much about the realities that underlie the words "objective reporting": it is an effort to know and communicate knowledge about events, persons, and circumstances outside the persons who are gathering and conveying this knowledge, and at least sometimes it is possible to do this so that what journalists think they know does in fact really exist and what they say does in fact really correspond to what they know.

This does not contradict the notion that journalists can neither know nor communicate everything about anything. Nor does it even deny the widespread claim that it is impossible for reporters to do this all the time. But if it is possible to do it at all, then it still may be worth striving for.

THE REAL CHALLENGES TO OBJECTIVE REPORTING

Not yet, however, have we reached the real difficulties implicit in the notion of objective reporting. If pressed on the point, nearly all those who question the possibility of objective reporting would admit that there are things that exist outside the individual person, that we can know at least some of those things, and that we can make statements that accurately express what we know about those things.

But the complete operation of news gathering and newswriting is not that simple. In a letter to *Quill*, Charles L. Klotzer reminds us that "every reporter always knows more than is included in any report." Then he describes half of the additional difficulty: "The writer selects which facts to include and which to delete whether on the basis of irrelevancy or more suspect motives. Such selection is the core of subjectivity... and is the working practice of every reporter on every story at any time."

And the other half of the difficulty? In addition to the possibility of subjectivity due to judgments concerning the inclusion of some facts and the exclusion of others, there is also the possibility of subjectivity due to the organization of news stories. Which facts will come first or early in the story and which will come later or last? For more than a century, most newspapers have organized basic news stories according to the principle of the inverted pyramid, in which the most important material is presented first and the other material follows in order of decreasing importance.

Thus, as part of the very nature of news gathering and news dissemination, reporters must choose what to include and what to exclude and, of what they choose to include, what will come first and what will come later. Choices. Choices made by human beings, by persons who have different standards of judgment, different likes and dislikes, different feelings about and reactions to the events that are taking place.

Events do not report themselves. Someone chooses which events to report, what to include in those reports, and in what order to present the elements of those reports.

As no two persons are exactly alike, neither will their choices be identical. It is not possible, therefore, many maintain, that there can be any uniformity, any lack of bias, any absence of personal influence in this activity.

Is there any way to remove choices from the selection and organization of knowledge? Not, say those who deny the possibility of objective reporting, as long as human beings are doing it. And news reporting, they remind us, is done by people, not by machines.

MAN AND THE MACHINE

We can contrast the work of the news reporter with its

choices to the function of some machines that actually do a certain type of reporting.

Automobile speedometers report how fast a car is traveling and odometers how far a vehicle has traveled. Grocery store scanners report what items were purchased, how much was charged for each, the total bill owed, the amount submitted, the amount of change, if any, and very often such other items of information as the date, the store at which the transactions took place, and the amount that was deducted if coupons were submitted,

We can have no doubt that these are objective reports. The one produced at the grocery store is particularly interesting because it not only normally records a number of purchases but also provides us with a printed record of the purchases, of the "events" that took place. In addition, although a machine is involved, people are also involved.

The sales slip provided to us could be called an objective report for it lacks the qualities sometimes ascribed to subjective reports. Although a sales clerk prepares it, it is not about the clerk; it is about events that are "out there." It does not express the emotions, the likes or dislikes, the preferences, the values of the clerk who produced it. Although persons are involved in the event, the report itself is impersonal.

Positively and more important, the choices about what is to be included in the report and the order in which these items are presented are not in the hands of the clerk. These choices are determined by the programme prior to the events themselves. The programme can be designed to list the items purchased in the order in which they are placed on the counter or in alphabetical order or from the most expensive to least expensive.

The programme can be designed to include the time of the purchases, the name of the checker who was handling the purchases, the number of the counter at which the purchases were recorded. All of these and hundreds of other possible choices concerning inclusion and arrangement are made prior to the event itself. If there has been no malfunctioning in this entire operation, nearly all customers willingly accept the entire sales receipt as an objective report of an event: the purchase of items at a grocery store.

Thus, if "objective reporting" is taken to mean a type of news gathering and news presentation that is about a person, event, or situation that is outside the reporter rather than within or about the person who is the reporter and that is presented with choices concerning selection and arrangement unaffected by the preferences of the reporter, then the grocery sales slip is an example of that type of reporting. This statement does not include everything meant by objective reporting, but at least it is a start.

Even at this point, however, we may have merely pushed the source of subjectivity back one step, from the checkout clerk to the programmer.

It is the latter who makes the choices, who decides which items and in what order those items shall be chosen for communication. And the programmer, objectors might point out, is subject to all the risks of bias and arbitrariness characteristic of subjectivity.

But that one step between programmer and clerk is important. Only the latter is in actual and direct contact with the event of the day. For the programmer, everything is conditional. *If* a can of salmon is purchased, the programmer decides, it will be listed in such and such a way, at a certain point in the record, with a specified charge. But the actual event may not include the sale of a can of salmon.

The programmer is analogous to the grammarian. *If* one is going to write a complete sentence in English, the grammarian tells us, at least a subject and a predicate must be present and they must be in one order if the sentence is declarative and in a different order if the sentence is interrogative. But the grammarian does not produce the event, the written sentence. Only the author does that.

The grocery store sales slip, of course, is not an example of journalism, because, if for no other reason, it is not an example of mass communication. Is there, however, anything similar in journalistic news reporting to the sales slip with its predetermined selection and organization? Indeed there is, and in great quantity, although its existence is largely ignored in discussions of objective reporting.

LOOKING AT THE FINE PRINT

Newspapers publish a great amount of statistical data. These data were customarily printed in small, agate type (about 5.5 points) and were thus referred to as "agate material."

Today, the kind and quantity of agate material vary greatly from newspaper to newspaper, of course, but publications that give heavy attention to business and sporting events devote much of their news space to this type of content.

It is not unusual for metropolitan papers to devote three, four, or more full pages to reports of yesterday's activity on the stock exchanges, the bond markets, the mutual funds, and the commodities exchanges; and from many inches to many columns of space to box scores, team and individual standings, and many other athletic summaries and ratings.

Some publications also find room for birth notices, marriage license and divorce listings, the names of recent high school and college graduates, persons cited for driving while intoxicated, tables of campaign expenditures reported by political candidates, yesterday's high and low temperatures in cities throughout the country, and much else.

Many editors decide, for instance, that their papers will publish, in alphabetical order, the names of all the stocks traded on the New York Stock Exchange the preceding day and, for each one that was traded, information about the number of shares traded, the highest price, lowest price, and closing price.

Once this policy has been determined, the papers continue to provide this information until readers are informed that some different policy will be in force. This information is provided to readers each day after a day in which the New York Stock Exchange was in operation, and the data are presented no matter what the personal, the subjective preferences of all those who are involved.

One editor might be distressed, for instance, because the stock of the company that owns his or her paper dropped precipitously the preceding day; he or she might prefer that this information be concealed from the general public. But if objectivity is to prevail, that news will appear and in its predetermined order along with all the other listings.

Some newspapers make it a policy to publish, in a predetermined order, all the persons arrested during the preceding week for driving under the influence of alcohol. If the editor of the paper is one of those who were arrested, objectivity requires that his or her name be included with all of the others.

Such publicity might shame the family, make the paper's campaigns in favour of sobriety appear hypocritical, cost the editor his or her job; journalistic objectivity will accept no excuses. The name will appear, and in the order that had been previously determined.

Does this seem to be mindless, fill-in-the-blanks journalism? Well, it is certainly very much like the machine reporting—the operation of an automobile speedometer or a supermarket scanner—referred to earlier. Much of the work, in fact, is or can be done by computers. For instance, in each instance that a stock is sold, the number of shares that change hands and the price realized are entered into a computer; these machines have been programmed to do all the rest.

However, there is a significant difference between the most mechanical of the machine operations and the most machinelike of human operations. Assuming that in neither case is any mechanical breakdown involved, the former—the operations of a speedometer or gas gauge—differs from the latter—the accumulation of information about stocks bought and sold—in this respect: only in the latter can human intentional misrepresentation be possible. In the operation of a speedometer, the information fed to the reporting instrument—the dial—comes itself from other mechanical operations.

A person controls the event being reported by controlling the speed at which the automobile is traveling, but the *reports* of the events are, thereafter, totally mechanical. In the stock market example, however, people enter in at two stages: first, they do the buying and selling, thus determining the event: the number of shares traded and the price involved. Second, a person, by entering these data into the computer, also carries out the first step of the reporting. In both, unintended inaccuracies are possible, but the very fact that inaccuracies can exist in both situations prevents inaccuracy from being a clearly differentiating factor.

If all of the equipment is working properly, the speed at which an automobile is traveling—the event—must be reported as it is actually happening. Because no human intervention is involved, no lie is possible. But under the same conditions, the price at which a stock is traded—the event—can be entered by a person as some number different from the true number. Or a person, by deciding not to enter into the computer any reference at all to the stock, can fail to do what the person and the paper promised to do. Either directly or by omission, therefore, the person can choose to lie.

One of the most stringent forms of journalistic objectivity, therefore—the one in which both order and selectivity are predetermined—remains a peculiarly human activity, for falsification is still a possibility.

The criteria used for determining inclusion and organization are, of course, regularly subject to fine tuning. In the 1990s, for example, many business-page editors began to use boldface type to emphasize those New York Stock Exchange issues whose prices, as the *Wall Street Journal* explains, "changed by 5% or more if their previous closing price was $2 or higher." In general, however, these refinements tend to increase the usefulness—or at least the interest value—of this objective reporting.

This strict type of journalistic objectivity is exemplified in still another class of news presentation, that in which the event is verbal and is re-presented in its entirety. Widely employed by mid-nineteenth-century newspapers, this form of story still appears in those media that consider themselves publications of record.

Complete verbatim texts of presidential inaugural addresses, Supreme Court decisions, budget messages, and the like, would be instances of this form of journalistic objectivity. In such material, no portions of the verbal event are omitted, and it is the presenter of the material, not the journalist, who determines the order in which each sentence is to appear.

But such agate material and verbatim texts are not what journalism scholars usually have in mind when they discuss the possibility of objective reporting. Instead of looking at the areas where objective reporting might be located, they focus on the types of stories in which it is probably impossible to find it.

Indeed, objective reporting is not likely to exist in the reports of events that involve a great amount of controversy. Political campaigns, economic disputes, foreign and domestic policy disagreements, environmental debates, religious arguments, and similar events lack any consensus either on what particular data should be included or excluded or on the order in which the included items ought to be presented.

In addition, those issues often arouse strong feelings not only among the participants in the discussions but also among the journalists covering the events. Furthermore, except for the re-presentation of complete speeches or other texts, the closer the event comes to being broadly unique the smaller the possibility that there would be any predetermined agreement about how it should be covered.

On the other hand, routine weather, auto accident, house fire, metropolitan burglary, obituary stories—the very ones that come closest to the agate material and verbatim texts discussed earlier—are not the examples chosen by those who deny the possibility of objectivity.

Why this happens is not difficult to understand. Routine stories do not win Pulitzer Prizes. They pose little intellectual challenge. Most often, they are handled by neophyte reporters. One story is so much like all the others of the same type that they lack any distinctiveness; they hardly seem worth discussing.

Most of them, in addition, are concerned with what was previously described as personal affairs—rather than public affairs—news. News helps the public make good decisions about what should be done, but personal affairs news assists in the making of personal decisions, decisions that each person can make for himself or herself; personal affairs news does not lead to decisions that require a consensus. Heated controversy, therefore, is less likely to occur.

But personal affairs news *is* a type of news. It can be useful to enormous numbers of people. The media give it large amounts of space and time. More important, the possibility of objective reporting in at least this type of news keeps alive another, much more important, issue: if objective reporting is at least sometimes possible, must we also conclude that it is, therefore, desirable?

"Objective reporting" can be used as a shorthand term to describe a way of gathering news and a manner of conveying news. News gathering can be considered objective when the knowledge is about persons, events, or situations outside the reporter, when that knowledge does correspond to what is really "out there," when it is gathered on the basis of criteria established prior to the time when this particular knowledge is acquired, and when the criteria are made known to and are not rejected by those to whom the knowledge will be communicated.

News presentation can be considered objective when the type of knowledge just described is conveyed truthfully and in a manner that is detached, impersonal, and devoid of any additional value judgments. This is possible. But the mere fact that something is *possible* to do does not, of course, necessarily imply that it is good to do.

Perhaps some of those who say objective reporting is impossible really mean that objective reporting leads to such harm that it would be best to abandon it. In other words, for them, what is impossible is not objective reporting but rather the *good use* of objective reporting.

And, indeed, in many situations it is not possible to achieve the totality of objective reporting. Thus, when we consider whether objective reporting is desirable, it would be helpful if we considered possibility and desirability separately. In the situations in which it is not possible to achieve the totality of objective reporting, we can ask whether it is desirable to aim at as much of it as *is* possible.

One of the great problems of striving for objective reporting when controversial public affairs are involved is that, although reporters themselves may be truthful, unbiased, and impersonal in reporting an event, they may still communicate one or more falsehoods to the readers or listeners. This can happen because the quoted portion of the report contains one or more lies.

Many critics leveled this accusation against the late Senator Joseph McCarthy (R.-Wis.) in the early 1950s. Senator McCarthy, they claim, perpetrated many falsehoods that journalists, maintaining their sense of objectivity, dutifully and accurately conveyed to the public. The reporters did not lie; McCarthy, it is claimed, did. The reporters merely extended the source's lies to a much wider public.

In a strong attack on this and some other characteristics of objective reporting, Theodore L. Glasser says, "Objective reporting virtually precludes responsible reporting, if by responsible reporting we mean a willingness on the part of the reporter to be accountable for what is reported." But journalists are aware that they have two stages of responsibility in reporting a verbal event.

One is the responsibility for reporting the event itself accurately, for conveying to readers or listeners the actual words used. The other is the responsibility for the truth of the statements made by those words. Objective reporters do not assume the second responsibility, but they do assume the first. Thus objectivity does not totally preclude responsibility.

Nevertheless, we dare not ignore Glasser's criticism. Indeed, can any good come from those reports that, under the claim of objectivity, communicate lies? If the job of the reporter is to provide knowledge that will help people make good decisions, how can they make good decisions when what they are being told is not true?

Perhaps the best reply was given by John Stuart Mill in his essay *On Liberty*. Mill reminds us that, sometimes, what journalists consider to be lies may not be lies at all; the speaker may be right and the journalists wrong. Or, Mill adds, even if the statements are lies, there may be some truth mixed in. Or, even if the statements are total lies, the public must know about them so that they can be refuted and so that the liars can be accurately judged for their defects of character.

Mill was assuming, however, that there were both time and opportunity, first, to reveal what truth, if any, was embedded in the quoted statements or, second, to set forth the evidence that would show the people the falseness of those statements. And many public liars know that, in the rush of practical affairs, neither adequate time nor opportunity may be available. Often, the truth never seems to catch up with the falsehoods.

Yes, say the adherents of objective reporting, but at least sometimes we can unveil a falsehood by turning to another source who will speak the truth. We can maintain our own impartiality and detachment by quoting other people "out there." If the Democrats say one thing, we simply turn to the Republicans for a reply. In fact, we don't have to determine who is speaking the truth; we merely set forth the opposing viewpoints and then let the public decide.

But this assumption that journalists can provide their publics with the truths they need to know by presenting "both sides" of a disagreement outrages some critics of objective reporting. Narrowing ideological disagreements to only two sides distorts the realities of actual situations.

In fact, it tends to elevate the dominant viewpoints and ignore the unconventional ones: presenting only the views of those who favour and those who oppose a balanced budget omits the views of others, for instance, who want a budget surplus. As J. Herbert Altschull says:

The code of objectivity assists power in the capitalist world to maintain social order and to fix limits to departures from ideological orthodoxy.... It safeguards the system against the explosive pressure for change. So long as "both sides" are presented, neither side is glorified above the other, and the status quo remains unchallenged. Dissent is permitted, even encouraged, under the code of objectivity, but its limits are proscribed.

Even when the media present more than just the pro and con positions, they often fail to present a truly balanced account of alternatives. For instance, sometimes the supporters of one or a few positions are well organized, well financed, and insistent upon having their viewpoints publicized, whereas others lack one or more of these qualities.

In the 1990s, the National Rifle Association was one of the former, while organizations opposed to the private ownership of handguns lacked some of these characteristics. In addition, editors may find it difficult to locate a person who will set forth a particular point of view.

Edward W. Conlon, for instance, who has written about the daily grind of a New York City police officer for the *New Yorker*, has done so under a pseudonym. Sometimes, no recognized spokesman exists, as has long been true of the United States prison population.

Or people are afraid to step forth and offer themselves as spokespeople, as was long the case for the gay rights community and for victims of sex crimes. In other instances, speakers for one position—such as Federal Bureau of Investigation or State Department officials—are restrained by the need to preserve confidentiality, whereas opposing speakers are not.

In addition, in trials and ethics hearings, the accusers are given the opportunity to present their viewpoints before—sometimes days and weeks before—the defenders can assert their positions. Also, the glib or well educated usually do a better job of communicating their viewpoints than do the halting or uneducated.

It is understandable that, with all this in mind, many people would cry out against the desirability of objective reporting. Ignoring the routine stories in which it can be achieved, they point to the complex public affairs in which total success is impossible and claim that any attempt to cover those stories objectively is only a pretense. For such major and important stories, in fact, objective reporting is not only impossible but even, they say, misleading.

OBJECTIVE REPORTING AS A DEFENCE AGAINST CRITICISM

Gaye Tuchman faces many of these objections with the suggestion that claims of "objective reporting" are merely tactical devices by which journalists ward off criticism. In a highly respected article, she says that "the correct handling of a story, that is, the use of certain procedures discernible to the news consumer, protects the newspaperman from the risks of his trade, including critics". Thus, to minimize the penalties imposed by deadlines, libel suits, and superiors' reprimands, the reporters will adopt procedures that they can claim mark their work as "objective."

They will set forth conflicting possibilities, pile up facts to support truth claims, use quotation marks to distance themselves from any opinions, and structure stories according to an accepted sequence, such as beginning with the usual formula: who, what, where, when, why, and how.

Tuchman says these procedures do not actually guarantee objectivity. But linking them with a respected professional quality helps journalists compensate for the fact that their special professional knowledge is not respected by news consumers. In doing this, she says, journalists are like members of other occupations who "develop ritualized procedures to protect themselves from blame". Journalists are using a word, "objectivity," as a means of defence.

Although her argument is interesting and deserves the attention it has received, she sets forth objectivity as a defence and not as a possible journalistic goal. Defenses, of course, are intended to be temporary. Once an attack or an evident threat of attack has ceased, there is no longer any need for the defence.

On the other hand, if the attack continues unabated and, in fact, even seems to grow larger and more fierce—as the growing accusations of media bias would indicate is taking place—then it is not a good form of defence and ought to be discarded. (This might account for the disappearance of the term "objectivity" in the Society of Professional Journalists' Code of Ethics.)

If objective reporting—at least as much of it as is possible—does have any truly positive and journalistically intrinsic value, therefore, we must search elsewhere in order to find it.

OBJECTIVE REPORTING AS PART OF THE JOURNALISTIC MIX

Much of the controversy over journalistic objectivity arises from the failure to recognize that there is more to journalism than news reporting. News reporting is so highly esteemed by members of the Fourth Estate that the words "reporter" and "journalist" are often used interchangeably. But news reporting is only one ingredient in the cake. Explanation, evaluation, and persuasion are also part of the mix. To ignore them is, often, to produce a totally inedible concoction.

Indeed, the more complex and controversial the event, the more likely will be the public need for something beyond the presentation of facts alone. As Douglass Cater said in his detailed analysis of the media's handling of the Senator Joseph McCarthy accusations, "Faced with a phenomenon as complex as McCarthyism, the 'straight' reporter has become a sort of strait—jacket reporter.... His initiative is hogtied so that he cannot fulfill his first duty, which is to bring clearer understanding to his reader."

Altschull said criticisms of Senator McCarthy were limited to the editorial pages, and, because few people read the editorial pages, their influence was limited. But news analysis and news comment stories—by-lined and printed on news pages but separate from the objective news reports—are common. It is not beyond possibility to place editorials, suitably identified. For instance, when the *New York Herald Tribune* on October 25, 1951, wanted to convince its readers that Dwight D. Eisenhower should be the Republican candidate for President, it did so with an editorial at the top and centre of page 1.

On April 11, 1951, the *New York Journal American* devoted two front-page columns to expressing its outrage when President Truman removed General Douglas MacArthur from his Far East commands. And on March 22, 1991, the *Milwaukee Sentinel* began a page 1 editorial with the reminder, "For seven days, the Milwaukee Sentinel has published front-page editorials urging readers to pressure their elected representatives to support a seven-day waiting period for the purchase of a handgun."

In fact, exclusive reliance upon objective reporting has been declining since the 1950s. One reason is the need by the broadcast media to fill time during the nonstop coverage of major events. Instead of repeating again and again the limited available facts, those media turn to experts and partisans for explanations and evaluations of what is going on.

This was particularly evident during the early days of the Gulf War. During that period the print media also broke away from the limitations of objectivity and began to add—usually in by-lined stories—background and critiques not only of the events but also of those who had control over information about those events.

The people were repeatedly warned that the war news was censored, and they were cautioned to read, watch, and listen with that in mind. Commenting on government restrictions concerning information about military operations in Iraq and Kuwait, for instance, Max Frankel, executive editor of the *New York Times*, was quoted as saying, "We are not getting any information that really fully and properly describes the magnitude.... We don't know how many are participating, how much ordnance is being dropped. It's hard to remember this is a nonstop, massive operation, the likes of which we may not have seen before".

It is significant that this and other similar material were appearing in the *news* sections of newspapers. It was not restricted, as it had been during the Senator McCarthy period, to comments "buried" on littleread editorial pages.

In general, it is not objective reporting that prevents journalists from providing us with the knowledge we need to make good decisions. Rather, it is the failure of both journalists and their publics to make good use of *all* the journalistic resources.

THE POSITIVE GOOD OF OBJECTIVE REPORTING

To say that objective reporting is not necessarily counterproductive still leaves unanswered the question: What good, if any, is it? It is true that now, in the coverage of complex public affairs, it is not possible to achieve the totality of objective reporting. At the present time we do not have a publicly accepted set of criteria on the basis of which the selection and organization of facts can be arranged.

But what is possible is for reporters to turn their attention to persons, events, or situations outside themselves, to acquire knowledge about them that is accurate, to convey that knowledge truthfully, impersonally, and devoid of any explicit or intentional value judgments.

This is not the whole of objective reporting, but it is a good part of it and a goal that is worth striving for. The people are well served if they are provided with information gained in this way. Even in the most controversial events, such bare facts are the material the public needs for active citizenship. As Jorgen Westerstahl has said:

The requirement of objective news reporting is intimately related to Western democracy and to one of its basic principles, the freedom of opinion... citizens need to be informed of what is happening in the world around them. News reporting must be factual and impartial in order to provide a foundation for independent and rational decision making.

It is important to mention that, although it may often be advisable to segregate the objective reporting from other genres of journalism—explanation, evaluation, persuasion—this is not a universal necessity. We can recognize this most easily if we view journalistic work from the perspective of the journalist who sets out to write a piece of persuasion, an editorial, for example. A persuasive editorial explicitly expresses opinions. It is not objective in the sense described here. Nevertheless, that editorial will normally include some content that sets forth the factual situation upon which the writer's opinions are based.

That reportorial portion of the editorial can be—and should be—objective reporting. That is, it should have those portions of objective reporting that are possible to incorporate in even the most contentious material. And what is true of the editorial is equally true of all journalism.

Magazine articles, in particular, are most likely to be a combination of journalistic forms, as any glance at the *Nation*, the *Atlantic Monthly*, or the *New York Times Magazine* will reveal. In all those instances in which reporting is involved, that reporting should be as objective as is possible.

OBJECTIVE REPORTING AND THE EMOTIONS

It is sometimes said that, in attempting to be as objective as possible, journalists should strive to be dispassionate. Whether it is possible and desirable for objective reporting to be free of feeling, to be free of emotion, depends on the meaning one assigns to these words.

Most helpful is what Aristotle says about the emotions. If one follows the Aristotelian tradition, then no truly human and alert person is ever free of emotions.

In the *Rhetoric*, for example, Aristotle defines emotions as "those states which are attended by pain and pleasure, and which, as they change, make a difference in our judgments".

Thus, if a person is not angry, that person is calm, but *both* anger and calmness (one painful and the other pleasant) are emotions.

Likewise, if a person is not fearful, that person is confident, both of which are emotions. Every person, he said, must be one or the other.

If everyone, including both journalists and their readers, viewers, or listeners, must always be in one or another emotional state, how, then, is it possible to avoid emotions in the presentation of news?

To answer, one must distinguish between the existence of emotions and changes in emotions, and between the data that cause emotions and the persons who present those data.

Let us say that a fictitious Mr. Jones is retired and has all of his funds invested in a single company. The dividends he has been receiving from the company's stock are the principal source of his income. For years, the stock market listings have informed him that the company is doing quite well. Thus, today, when he opens his newspaper, he feels confident.

But then he notices that the price of the stock has dropped precipitously, and when he turns to another objective listing, he learns that the company has omitted its usual dividend. His confidence changes to fear. He will probably have to endure painful financial strictures.

Were all of the stock market listings prior to this fateful day unemotional? No. His study of the stock market report each previous day had given him a feeling of confidence. If anything, the repeated reassurances he had received from reading the financial pages probably increased his confidence.

Moreover, the day's news, which changed his emotion from confidence to fear, did not change his state from an unemotional to an emotional one. All along, he had been in an emotional state, and he now continued to be in an emotional state.

Thus, when we say that an objective news report is unemotional, we cannot mean that it has no effect upon the feelings of readers and listeners. The report is a stimulus that either maintains an existing feeling or changes that feeling to another feeling. It does not move people from a nonemotional to an emotional state.

And what applies to the reading and listening public can be said equally about the journalists themselves. They, too, when normal and alert, are never unfeeling machines. Both journalists and public, however, are sometimes affected in such a way as to bring about a change in the *type* of emotions they are feeling.

Painful emotions sometimes motivate evident exterior actions that will liberate people from painful feelings and replace them with pleasant feelings, as when one escapes from a fearful object.

The dash to safety replaces painful fear with pleasant confidence. In some other situations, merely the passage of time can bring about a change of feeling, as when a feeling of anger, as days go by, is replaced by a feeling of calm.

What is the cause of these changes in emotion? For the reading, listening, and viewing public, it could be the journalists themselves, as is most evident in television news reporting. In addition to the spoken words, facial expressions and other body language also convey the reporter's feelings to the public.

The American television journalists who reported the assassination of John F. Kennedy, for example, found it enormously difficult to control indications of their own feelings, and the feeling of shared grief intensified the sorrow felt by their viewers. But even if the reporters had controlled indications of their own feelings, they would still have affected the emotions of their viewers, this time by holding somewhat in check the degree of their personal feelings.

In most instances, however, instead of the messenger, it is primarily the content of the message that affects the people's emotions, as when, to use our previous example, Mr. Jones receives word that the company on which he has relied for much of his income will no longer pay a dividend.

It is also true that reporters can intentionally shape the telling of the message so that the very process of communicating affects the feelings of the public. The use of emotionally loaded words, for instance, shifts matters so that the cause of emotions is neither the content of the message nor the messenger but the very phrasing of the message itself.

If a newspaper reporter would say, for instance, that a source "replied with a sneer," the word "sneer" might arouse anger in the readers who admire that source. Thus objective reporters attempt to use emotion-neutral language: they simply write, for instance, that the source "said" something and then quote what was said. But what if the source did, in fact, reply with a sneer? Then we must rely upon something beyond objective reporting to let the readers know this fact. Objectivity alone does not guarantee that everything that needs to be said is, in fact, said.

When we say, therefore, that an objective news report is unemotional we mean that whatever effect it has on the public—and it will have *some* effect—is not due primarily to the reporters but rather to the data outside the reporters that the latter communicate to the public in otherwise emotion-free language. Not everything can be conveyed in such a language, but, as inspection of agate material reveals, it is possible to do so with some types of content. That is enough to establish it as a possible goal for which journalists can strive.

OBJECTIVE REPORTING IS NOT ALWAYS DESIRABLE

Because objective reporting directs the public's attention to persons, events, or situations *outside* the reporter, there will be some situations in which objective reporting is not desirable. This will happen most clearly when the reporter himself or herself is a part of the event being reported. For example, the September 9, 1940, issue of the *Chicago Daily News* carried Helen Kirkpatrick's account of the bombing of London during World War II. It began this way:

> London still stood this morning, which was the greatest surprise to me as I cycled home in the light of early dawn after the most frightening night I have ever spent. But not all of London was still there, and some of the things I saw this morning would scare the wits out of anyone.

This account violates several of the characteristics of objective reporting. It is partly about the writer instead of being totally concerned with events outside the writer.

It is expressed in the first person, and it sets forth the writer's feelings and judgments about the event. But this subjective report provides useful knowledge about the consequences of warfare, knowledge that objective reporting would not have been able to convey. Similar characteristics can be found in the story by United Press reporter Russell

Jones that was published on November 15, 1956, about the Hungarian rebellion:

Life as the only American correspondent left in shattered Budapest is sometimes frightening, sometimes amusing. But mostly it is a continuous feeling of inadequacy both as an American and as a reporter who helplessly watched the murder of a people.

At other times, what the public most deserves is not objective reporting but rather temporary or partial silence. For example, when one party in a dispute launches a criticism against a second party, the entire story can sometimes (not always, of course) be delayed until the journalist has obtained a reply from the latter.

Lou Cannon of the *Washington Post* suggests that this is what Daniel Schorr, then of CBS News, might have done when, in July 1975, Air Force Colonel L. Fletcher Prouty told Schorr that Alexander Butterfield had been a CIA spy in the White House. Butterfield could not be reached immediately for a reply because he was on the West Coast looking for work. Schorr did not wait; he put the story on the air immediately.

He gave the competitiveness of his network with NBC as his reason for not delaying the broadcast of Prouty's remarks. But rarely is the public served (in fact, the public is usually not even aware of, and thus not impressed) by the game of "me first."

By itself objective reporting is not always fair. It may need to be supplemented by other journalistic genres. But it should not be made even less fair than it has to be.

OBJECTIVE REPORTING RECONSIDERED

Critics who claim that objectivity is impossible because no reporter can know the whole truth about any person, event, or situation are partly correct. No reporter is omniscient. And, of all that is knowable, reporters never attempt to know everything but are selective in the knowledge they attempt to obtain. If they are good news gatherers, they make their selections on the basis of what they judge will be most useful for the public to know when making practical decisions. And, just as they do not attempt to know everything, normally they also do not communicate everything they do know, and for the same reason: some of it is not useful knowledge for the public.

Those who say that objective reporting is possible are also partly right—if they mean that there are some things about a person, event, or situation that reporters can truly know. They can know that a certain senator said, "I am a candidate for the presidency of the United States," and can honestly and accurately report that statement—and much else that they know.

Even in the selection and organization of what they choose to know and of what they choose to communicate, reporters can be objective journalists if we mean by this that they establish *prior to* the events that they cover the criteria on which they base their observations and communications.

Let's consider, for example, the sports reporters who will communicate to readers the information normally included in the box scores for a basketball game. From experience they have learned what the readers want to know and thus, among all the possible bits of knowledge, the specific pieces that they should choose to include: the names of all the players for both teams who actually participated in the game, the number of field goals attempted by each player, the number of field goals made, the number of free throws attempted, the number made, and so on.

Although these journalists have feelings, desires, and biases, this format helps them set aside those subjective elements as they go about carrying out an objective investigation. No matter how much they like a certain player, his name will not be included if he did not play in the game.

And if the format dictates that the players will be listed in the order in which they are announced to the crowd, then the organization of this material is also determined. Even if a reporter has a favourite player and would like to list him first, the objective journalist will not do so if that player is not the first one whose name was announced.

In doing this, reporters can be objective in the same sense that scientists and other objective data gatherers and communicators are objective.

Before conducting any experiments, a biologist, for example, will choose a number of options that he or she knows from experience will be accepted by his or her peers: that measurements will be made according to the International (metric) System rather than the U.S. Customary System; that a certain number and type of class intervals will be employed; that a certain degree of accuracy will be used in measuring continuous variables; that a certain level of significance will be acceptable; that the report will be written in English or in some other chosen language, and the like.

As the mathematician R. T. Hayslett Jr. has said about his own field, often thought of as one where great objectivity can be achieved, in all computations "some assumptions need to be made." Likewise, in the choices and organizations predesigned for agate material, journalists can accomplish the same degree of objectivity that most people find acceptable in scientific endeavors.

Even those who say that objectivity is impossible but worth striving for are partly correct. For the coverage of complex and controversial public affairs, total objective reporting is not possible because there are no accepted criteria for the selection and arrangement of material.

But objective reporting is a complex process; thus, even when achieving the totality is not possible, it may be possible to achieve some of the elements. Even in the most contentious affairs, reporters can be accurate in their observations and truthful in their statements.

They can direct the public's attention to the object of the story rather than to the writer. They can exclude any explicit statements of judgment or advocacy. Thus, even when insuperably difficult, objective reporting—at least that much of it as it is possible to achieve—may be a goal worth pursuing, for objective news underlies nearly all the other types of journalistic writing. But whether it is achieved completely or only partially, objective news is not always fair.

For example, agate material may show that a quarterback on a professional football team completed only three of the eighteen passes he threw. But if seven of those passes went right into the hands of intended receivers but were dropped, the agate material, though accurate, does not give a fair account of his ability.

And even where fairness is not involved, readers often need more than completely objective material. On November 16, 1996, for instance, many papers reported in their stock market listings that, on the previous day, International Business Machines stock advanced $8.125 to close at $145, a nine-year high. Why this leap in price?

The agate material did not give investors the answer. They had to turn elsewhere, perhaps to interpretive reporters, who pointed out that, on the same day, Merrill Lynch & Co. announced that it was raising its target price for the stock from $150 to $195. In general, therefore, journalistic objective reporting can be both possible and desirable. But, by itself, it is not the paragon of all journalism.

Chapter 12

New Journalism

New Journalism was a style of 1960s and 1970s news writing and journalism which used literary techniques deemed unconventional at the time. The term was codified with its current meaning by Tom Wolfe in a 1973 collection of journalism articles he published as *The New Journalism*, which included works by himself, Truman Capote, Hunter S. Thompson, Norman Mailer, Joan Didion, Robert Christgau, and others.

Articles in the New Journalism style tended not to be found in newspapers, but rather in magazines such as *The Atlantic Monthly, CoEvolution Quarterly, Esquire Magazine, New York, The New Yorker, Rolling Stone,* and for a short while in the early 1970s, *Scanlan's Monthly.*

Various trends and tendencies throughout the history of American Journalism have been labeled "new journalism." Robert E. Park, for instance, in his *Natural History of the Newspaper,* referred to the advent of the penny press in the 1830s as "new journalism."

Likewise, the appearance of the yellow press, papers such as Joseph Pulitzer's *New York World* in the 1880s, led journalists and historians to proclaim that a "New Journalism" had been created. Ault and Emery, for instance, said "Industrialization and urbanization changed the face of American during the latter half of the Nineteenth century, and its newspapers entered an era known as that of the 'New Journalism.'

"In 1960 John Hohenberg, in *The Professional Journalist,* called the interpretive reporting which developed after World

War II a "new journalism which not only seeks to explain as well as to inform; it even dares to teach, to measure, to evaluate."

During the sixties and seventies the term enjoyed widespread popularity, often with meanings bearing manifestly little or no connection with one another. Although James E. Murphy noted that '"...most user of the term seem to refer to something more specific than vague new directions in journalism" Curtis D. MacDougal devoted the Preface of the Sixth Edition of his *Interpretative Reporting* to New Journalism and cataloged many of the contemporary definitions: "Activist, advocacy, participatory, tell-it-as-you-see-it, sensitivity, investigative, saturation, humanistic, reformist and a few more."

The Magic Writing Machine—Student Probes of the New Journalism, a collection edited and introduced by Everette E. Dennis, came up with six categories, labelled new nonfiction (reportage), alternative journalism ("modern muckraking"), advocacy journalism, underground journalism and precision journalism. Michael Johnson's *The New Journalism* addresses itself to three phenomena: the underground press, the artists of nonfiction, and changes in the established media.

Journalists recognized as using the style include Norman Mailer, Joan Didion, Truman Capote, P. J. O'Rourke, George Plimpton, Terry Southern, and Gay Talese. Hunter S. Thompson was a major practitioner of new journalism and gonzo journalism, his own particular style.

Thompson's first book, *Hell's Angels: The Strange and Terrible Saga of the Outlaw Motorcycle Gangs,* is a more conventional piece, and shows the beginnings of a more memoir-based approach to reportage. Gay Talese's 1966 article for Esquire, *Frank Sinatra Has a Cold,* was an influential piece of new journalism that gave a detailed portrait of Frank Sinatra without ever interviewing him.

New journalism writers brought new approaches to areas already covered by the mainstream press. The psychedelic movement was something that many of the writers of the period covered, such as in Tom Wolfe's *The Electric Kool-Aid*

Acid Test. The Vietnam War was another common topic, as was the political turmoil on the homefront. Terry Southern's Grooving in Chi documented the 1968 Chicago National Democratic Convention for Esquire Magazine in new journalism manner.

New journalism's techniques were also applied to less obvious subjects, such as financial markets (by George Goodman under the pseudonym Adam Smith, in essays originally published in New York Magazine and later collected in a book called *The Money Game*.)

Some authors of conventional fiction switched to writing in the style of new journalism, such as Truman Capote's *In Cold Blood*, and Norman Mailer's *Armies of the Night*. However, neither author ever agreed to their style's comparison to Wolfe's school of narration, nor did many others who have been retrospectively promoted as being members and therein associated. Much to the contrary, many of these writers would deny that their work was generically relevant to other new journalists at the time.

EARLY DEVELOPMENT, THE SIXTIES

How and when the term New Journalism began to refer to a genre has not been clear. Tom Wolfe, a practitioner and principal advocate of the form, wrote in at least two articles in 1972 that he had no idea of where it began.

Trying to shed light on the matter, literary critic Seymour Krim, offered his explanation in 1973. I'm certain that [Pete] Hamill first used the expression. In about April of 1965 he called me at *Nugget* Magazine, where I was editorial director, and told me he wanted to write an article about new New Journalism.

It was to be about about the exciting things being done in the old reporting genre by Talese, Wolfe and Breslin. He never wrote the piece, so far as I know, but I began using the expression in conversation and writing. It was picked up and stuck. But wherever and whenever the term arose, there is evidence of some literary experimentation in the early 1960s, as when Norman Mailer broke away from fiction to write

Superman Comes to the Supermarket A report of John F. Kennedy's nomination that year, the piece established a precedent which Mailer would later build on in his 1968 convention coverage (*Miami and the Siege of Chicago*) and in other nonfiction as well.

Wolfe wrote that his first acquaintance with a new style of reporting came in a 1962 *Esquire* article about Joe Louis by Gay Talese. "'Joe Louis at Fifty' wasn't like a magazine article at all. It was like a short story. It began with a scene, an intimate confrontation between Loius and his third wife..." Wolfe said Talese was the first to apply fiction techniques to reporting.

Esquire claimed credit as the seedbed for these new techniques. *Esquire* editor Harold Hayes later wrote that "in the Sixties, events seemed to move too swiftly to allow the osmotic process of art to keep abreast, and when we found a good novelist we immediately sought to seduce him with the sweet mysteries of current events." Soon others, notably *New York,* followed *Esquire's* lead, and the style eventually infected other magazines and then books.

THE SEVENTIES

Much of the criticism favorable to this New Journalism came from the writers themselves. Talese and Wolfe, in a panel discussion cited earlier, asserted that, although what they wrote may look like fiction, it was indeed reporting: "Fact reporting, leg work." Talese called it.

Wolfe, in *Esquire* for December, 1972, hailed the replacement of the novel by the New Journalism as literature's "main event" and detailed the points of similarity and contrast between the New Journalism and the novel. The four techniques of realism that he and the other New Journalists employed, he wrote, had been the sole province of novelists and other *literati.*

They are scene-by-scene construction, full record of dialogue, third-person point of view and the manifold incidental details to round out character (i.e., descriptive incidentals). the result... is a form that is not merely like a *novel*. It consumes devices that happen to have originated with the novel and mixes them with every other device known to prose. And all the while, quite beyond matters of technique, it enjoys an advantage so obvious, so built-in, one almost forgets what power it has': the simple fact that the reader knows *all this actually happened*. The disclaimers have been erased. The screen is gone. The writer is one step closer to the absolute involvement of the reader that Henry James and James Joyce dreamed of but never achieved.

The essential difference between the new nonfiction and conventional reporting is, he said, that the basic unit of reporting was no longer the datum or piece of information but the scene. Scene is what underlies "the sophisticated strategies of prose." The first of the new breed of nonfiction writers to receive wide notoriety was Truman Capote, whose 1965 best-seller, *In Cold Blood*, was a detailed narrative of the murder of a Kansas farm family. Capote culled material from some 6000 pages of notes.

The book brought its author instant celebrity. Capote announced that he had created a new art form which he labelled the "nonfiction novel." I've always had the theory that reportage is the great unexplored art form... I've had this theory that a factual piece of work could explore whole new dimensions in writing that would have a double effect fiction does not have—the every fact of its being true, every word of its true, would add a double contribution of strength and impact. Capote continued to stress that he was a literary artist, not a journalist, but critics hailed the book as a classic example of New Journalism.

Wolfe's *The Kandy-Kolored Tangerine-Flake Streamline Baby*, whose introduction and title story, according to James E. Murphy, "emerged as a manifest of sorts for the nonfiction genre," was published the same year. In his introduction Wolfe wrote that he encountered trouble fashioning an *Esquire* article out of material on a custom car extravaganza in Los Angeles, in 1963. Finding he could not do justice to the subject in magazine article format, he wrote a letter to his editor, Byron Dobell, which grew into a 49-page report detailing the custom car world, complete with scene construction, dialogue and flamboyant description. *Esquire* ran the letter, striking out "Dear Byron." and it became Wolfe's maiden effort as a New Journalist. In an article entitled "The Personal Voice and the Impersonal Eye," Dan Wakefield acclaimed the nonfiction of Capote and Wolfe as elevating reporting to the level of literature, terming that work and some of Norman Mailer's nonfiction a journalistic breakthrough: reporting "charged with the energy of art"

A review by Jack Newfield of Dick Schaap's *Turned On* saw the book as a good example of budding tradition in American journalism which rejected many of the constraints of conventional reporting: This new genre defines itself by claiming many of the techniques that were once the unchalanged terrain of the novelist: tension, symbol, cadence, irony, prosody, imagination. A 1968 review of Wolfe's *The Pump House Gang* and *The Electric Kool-Aid Acid Test* said Wolfe and Mailer were applying "the imaginative resources of fiction" to the world around them and termed such creative journalism "hystory" to connote their involvement in what they reported. Talese in 1970, in his Author's Note to *Fame and Obscurity,* a collection of his pieces from the 1960s, wrote:

The new journalism, though often reading like fiction, is not fiction. It is, or should be, more reliable as the most reliable reportage although it seeks a larger truth than is possible through the mere compilation of verifiable facts, the use of direct quotations, and adherence to the rigid organizational style of the older form.

Seymour Krim's *Shake It for the World, Smartass* which appeared in 1970, contained "An Open Letter to Norman Mailer" which defined New Journalism as "a free nonfictional prose that uses every resource of the best fiction." And in "The Newspaper As Literature/Literature As Leadership" he called journalism the *de facto* literature of the majority, a synthesis of journalism and literature that the book's postscript called "journalit."

In 1972, in "An Enemy of the Novel" Krim identified his own fictional roots and declared that the needs of the time compelled him to move beyond fiction to a more "direct" communication to which he promised to bring all of fiction's resources.

David McHam, in an article titled "The Authentic New Journalists," distinguished the nonfiction reportage of Capote, Wolfe and others from other, more generic interpretations of New Journalism. Also in 1971, William L. Rivers disparaged the former and embraced the latter, concluding, "In some hands, they add a flavour and a humanity to journalistic writing that push it into the realm of art."

Charles Brown in 1972 reviewed much that had been written as New Journalism and about New Journalism by Capote, Wolfe, Maiier and others and labelled the genre "New Art Journalism," which allowed him to test it both as art and as journalism. He concluded that the new literary form was useful only in the hands of literary artists of great talent.

In the first of two pieces by Wolfe in *New York* detailing the growth of the new nonfiction and its techniques. Wolfe returned to the fortuitous circumstances surrounding the construction of *Kandy-Kolored* and added:

Its virtue was precisely in showing me the possibility of there being something "new" in journalism. What interested me was not simply the discovery that it was possible to write accurate nonfiction with techniques usually associated with novels and short stories.

It was that—plus. It was the discovery that it was possible in nonfiction, in journalism, to use any literary device, from the traditional dialogisms of the essay to stream-of-consciousness...

THE EIGHTIES

In the Eighties the use of New Journalism saw a decline, several of the old trailblazers still used fiction techniques in their nonfiction books. But younger writers in *Esquire* and *Rolling Stone,* where the style had flourished in the two earlier decades, shifted away from the New Journalism. Fiction techniques had not been abandoned by these writers, but they were used sparingly and less flamboyantly.

"Whatever happened to the New Journalism?" wondered Thomas Powers in a 1975 issue of *Commonweal*. In 1981, Joe Nocera published a postmortem in the *Washington Monthly* blaming its demise on the journalistic liberties taken by Hunter S. Thompson. Regardless of the culprit, less than a decade after Tom Wolfe's 1973 New Journalism anthology, the consensus was that New Journalism was dead.

CHARACTERISTICS

As a literary genre, New Journalism has certain technical characteristics. It is an artistic, creative, literary reporting form with three basic traits: dramatic literary techniques; intensive reporting; and reporting of generally acknowledged subjectivity.

AS SUBJECTIVE JOURNALISM

Pervading many of the specific interpretations of New Journalism is a posture of subjectivity. Subjectivism is thus a common element among many (though not all) of its definitions. In contrast to a conventional journalistic striving for an objectivity, subjective journalism allows for the writer's opinion, ideas or involvement to creep into his story.

Much of the critical literature concerns itself with a strain of subjectivism which may be called activism in news reporting. In 1970 Gerald Grant wrote disparagingly in *Columbia Journalism Review* of a "New Journalism of passion and advocacy" and in the *Saturday Review* Hohenberg discussed "The Journalist As Missionary" For Masterson in 1971, "The New Journalism" provided a forum for discussion of journalistic and social activism. In another 1971 article under the same title Ridgeway called the counter-culture magazines such as *The New Republic* and *Ramparts* and the American underground press New Journalism.

Another version of subjectivism in reporting is what is sometimes called participatory reporting. Robert Stein, in *Media Power,* defines New Journalism as "A form of participatory reporting that evolved in parallel with participatory politics..."

AS FORM AND TECHNIQUE

The above interpretations of New Journalism view it as an attitude toward the practice of journalism. But a significant portion of the critical literature deals with form and technique.

Critical comment dealing with New Journalism as a literary-journalistic genre (a distinct type of category of literary work grouped according to similar and technical characteristics) treats it as the *new nonfiction*. Its traits are extracted from the criticism written by those who claim to practice it and by others. Admittedly it is hard to isolate from a number of the more generic meanings The new nonfiction where sometimes taken for advocacy of subjective journalism. A 1972 article by Dennis Chase defines New Journalism as a subjective journalism emphasizing "truth" over "facts" but uses major nonfiction stylists as its example.

AS INTENSIVE REPORTAGE

Although much of the critical literature discussed the use of literary or fictional techniques as the basis for a New Journalism, critics also referred to the form as stemming from intensive reporting. Stein, for instance, found the key to New Journalism not its fictionlike form but the "saturation reporting" which precedes it, the result of the writer's immersion in his subject. Consequently, Stein concluded, the writer is as much part of his story as is the subject and he thus linked saturation reporting with subjectivity. For him New Journalism is inconsistent with objectivity or accuracy. But other have argued that total immersion enhances accuracy.

As Wolfe put the case: I am the first to agree that the New Journalism should be as accurate as traditional journalism. In fact my claims for the New Journalism, and my demands upon it, go far beyond that. I contend that it has already proven itself *more* accurate than traditional journalism—which unfortunately i saying but so much... Wolfe coined "saturation reporting" in his *Bulletin of the American Society of Newspaper Editors* article. After citing the opening paragraphs of Talese's Joe Louis piece, he confessed believing that Talese had "piped" or faked the story, only later to be convinced, after learning that Talese so deeply delved into the subject, that he could report entire scenes and dialogues.

The basic units of reporting are no longer who-what-when-where-how and why but whole scenes and stretches of dialogue. The New Journalism involves a depth of reporting and an attention to the most minute facts and details that most newspapermen, even the most experienced, have never dreamed of.

In his "Birth of the New Journalism" in *New York,* Wolfe returned to the subject, which he here described as a depth of information never before demanded in newspaper work. The New Journalist, he said, must stay with his subject for days and weeks at a stretch.

In Wolfe's *Esquire* piece saturation became the "Locker Room Genre" of intensive digging into the lives and personalities of one's subject, in contrast to the aloof and genteel tradition of the essayists and "The Literary Gentlemen in the Grandstand." For Talese, intensive reportage took the form of interior monologue to discover from his subjects what they were thinking, not, he said in a panel discussion reported in *Writer's Digest,* merely reporting what people did and said.

Wolfe identified the four main devices New Journalists borrowed from literary fiction:

- Telling the story using scenes rather than historical narrative as much as possible
- Dialogue in full (Conversational speech rather than quotations and statements)
- Point-of-view (present every scene through the eyes of a particular character)
- Recording everyday details such as behaviour, possessions, friends and family (which indicate the "status life" of the character)

Despite these elements, New Journalism is not fiction. It maintains elements of reporting including strict adherence to factual accuracy and the writer being the primary source. To get "inside the head" of a character, the journalist asks the subject what they were thinking or how they felt.

PRACTITIONERS

WRITERS

Which writer who are New Journalists is hard to define. In *The New Journalism: A Critical Perspective* Murphy writes, "A a literary genre, New Journalism [...] involves a more or less well defined group of writers [...].

Each is stylistically unique, but all sharing common formal elements." Among the most prominenet writers of New Journalism, Murphy lists: Jimmy Breslin, Truman Capote, Joan Didion, David Halberstam, Pete Hamill, Larry King, Norman Mailer, Joe McGinniss, Rex Reed, Mike Royko, John Sack, Dick Schaap, Terry Southern, Gail Sheehy, Gay Talese, Hunter S.

Thompson, Dan Wakefield, and Tom Wolfe. In *The New Journalism*, Johnson and Wolfe, also includes George Plimpton for his *Paper Lion, Life* writer James Mills, Robert Christgau and a few others. Christgau, however, stated in an 2001 interview that he did not see himself as a New Journalist.

CRITICISM

While many praised the New Journalist's style of writing, Wolfe et al., also received severe criticism from contemporary journalists and writers. Essentially two different charges were leveled against New Journalism: criticism against it as a *distinct genre* and criticism against it as a *new* form.

Robert Stein believed that "In the New Journalism the eye of the beholder is all—or almost all," and in 1971 Philip M. Howard, wrote that the new nonfiction writers rejected objectivity in favour of a more personal, subjective reportage. This parallels much of what Wakefield said in his 1966 *Atlantic* article.

The important and interesting and hopeful trend to me in the new journalism is its personal nature—not in the sense of personal attacks, but in the presence of the reporter himself and the significance of his own involvement.

This is sometimes felt to be egotistical, and the frank identification of the author, especially as the "I" instead of merely the impersonal "eye" is often frowned upon and taken as proof of "subjectivity," which is the opposite of the usual journalistic pretense.

And in spite of the fact that Capote believed in the objective accuracy of *In Cold Blood* and strove to keep himself totally out of the narrative, one reviewer founf in the book the "tendency among writers to resort to subjective sociology, on the other hand, or to super-creative reportage, on the other." Charles Self termed this characteristic of New Journalism as "admitted" subjectivity, whether first-person or third-person, and acknowledged the subjectivity inherent in his account.

Lester Markel polemically criticized New Journalism in the *Bulletin of the American Society of Newspaper Editors,* he rejected the claim to greater in-depth reporting and labelled the writers "factual fictionists" and "deep-see reporters." He feared they were performing as sociologists and psychoanalysts rather than as journalists.

More reasoned, though still essentially negative, Arlen in his 1972 "Notes on the New Journalism," put the New Journalism into a larger socio-historical perspective by tracing the techniques from earlier writers and from the constraints and opportunities of the current age.

But much of the more routine New Journalism "consists in exercises by writer... in gripping and controlling and confronting a subject within the journalist's own temperament. Presumably, " he wrote, "this is the 'novelistic technique.' " But he conceded that the best of this work had "considerably expanded the possibilities of journalism."

Much negative criticism of New Journalism were directed at individual writers For example, Cynthia Ozick asserted in *The New Republic,* that Capote in *In Cold Blood* was doing little more than trying to devise a form: "One more esthetic manipulation." Sheed offered, in "A Fun-House Mirror," a witty refutation of Wolfe's claim that he takes on the expression and the guise of whomever he is writing about. "The Truman Capotes may hold up a tolerably clear glass to nature," he wrote, "but Wolfe holds up a fun-house mirror, and I for one don't give a hoot whether he calls the reflection fact or fiction."

"PARAJOURNALISM" AND THE NEW YORKER AFFAIR

Among the hostile critics of the New Journalism were Dwight MacDonald, whose most vocal criticism compromised a chapter in what became known as "the *New Yorker* affair" of 1965. Wolfe had written a two-part semi-fictional parody in *New York* of the *New Yorker* and its editor, William Shawn.

Reaction notably from *New Yorker* writers, was loud and prolonged, but the most significant reaction came from MacDonald, who counterattacked in two articles in the *New York Review of Books* In the first, MacDonald termed Wolfe's approach "parajournalism" and applied it to all similar styles. "Parajournalism," MacDonald wrote... seems to be journalism—"the collection and dissemination of current news"—but the appearance is deceptive. It is a bastard form, having it both ways, exploiting the factual authority of journalism and the atmospheric license of fiction.

The *New Yorker* parody, he added, "... revealed the ugly side of Parajournalism when it tries to be serious."

In his second article, MacDonald addressed himself to the accuracy of Wolfe's report. He charged that Wolfe "takes a middle course, shifting gears between fact and fantasy, spoof and reportage, until nobody knows which end is, at the moment, up" *New Yorker* writers Renata Adler and Gerald Jonas joined the fray in the Winter 1966 issue of *Columbia Journalism Review*. Wolfe himself returned to the affair a full seven years later., devoting the second of his two February *New York* articles (1972) to his detractors but not to dispute their attack on his factual accuracy. He argued that most of the contentions arose because for traditional *literati* nonfiction should not succeed—which his nonfiction obviously had.

Gail Sheehy and "Redpants"

In *The New Journalism: A Critical Perspective* Murphy writes, "Partly because Wolfe took liberties with the facts in his *New Yorker* parody, New Journalism began to get a reputation for juggling the facts in the search for truth, fictionalizing some details to get a larger 'reality.'

"Widely criticized was the technique of the composite character, the most notorious example of which was "Redpants," a presumed prostitute whom Gail Sheehy wrote about in *New York* in a series on that city's sexual subculture.

When it later became known that the character was distilled from a number of prostitutes, there was an outcry against Sheehy's method and, by extension, to the credibility of all of New Journalism. In the *Wall Street Journal*, one critic wrote: It's all part of the New Journalism, or the Now Journalism, and it's practiced widely these days. Some editors and reporters vigorously defend it. Others just as vigorously attack it. No one has polled the reader, but whether he approves or disapproves, it's getting harder and harder for him to know what he can believe. *Newsweek* reported that critics felt Sheehy's energies were better suited to fiction than fact John Tebbel in an article in *Saturday Review*, although treating New Journalism in its more generic sense as new a trend, chided it for the fictional technique of narrative leads which the new nonfiction writers had introduced into journalism and deplored its use in newspapers.

CRITICISM AGAINST NEW JOURNALISM AS A DISTINCT GENRE

Newfield, in 1972, changed his attitude since his earlier, 1967, review of Wolfe. "New Journalism does not exist," the later article titled "Is there a 'new journalism'?" says. "It is a false category. There is only good writing and bad writing, smart ideas and dumb ideas, hard work and laziness." While the practice of journalism had improved during the past fifteen years, he argued, it was because of an influx of good writers notable for unique styles, not because they belonged to any school or movement.

Bibliography

Brundson, C. and Morley, D. (2000) Everyday Television: 'Nationwide'. London: British Film Institute.

Edwards, C. (2001) Interview with Hugo de Burgh, 25 June 2001.

Foot, P. (2002) Murder at the Farm: Who Killed Carl Bridgewater? London: Penguin.

Herman, E. and Chomsky, N. (2004) Manufacturing Consent. London: Vintage.

Knightley, P. (2000) Interview with Hugo de Burgh, 22 May 2001.

Langdon, J. (2002) High noon at the Holborn oasis. Guardian, 29 March 2004.

Milne, S. (2001) The Enemy Within: The Secret War Against the Miners. London: Pan.

Northmore, D. (2003) Lifting the Lid: A Guide to Investigative Research. London: Cassell.

Pilger, J. (2001) Interview with Hugo de Burgh, 29 June 2001.

Rusbridger, A. (2002) Interview with Hugo de Burgh, 25 May 2002.

Shoemaker, P. (2004) Mediating the Message. London: Longman.

Tuchman, G. (2001) Making news by doing work: routinizing the unexpected. American Journal of Sociology, 79.

Weir, D. (2002) How the Center for Investigative Journalism Gets a Story. Reading, MA: Addison-Wesley.

Weymouth, A. and Lamizet, B. (eds) (2004) Markets and Myths: Forces for Change in the European Media. London: Longman.

Index